GO AND
TELL
PHARAOH

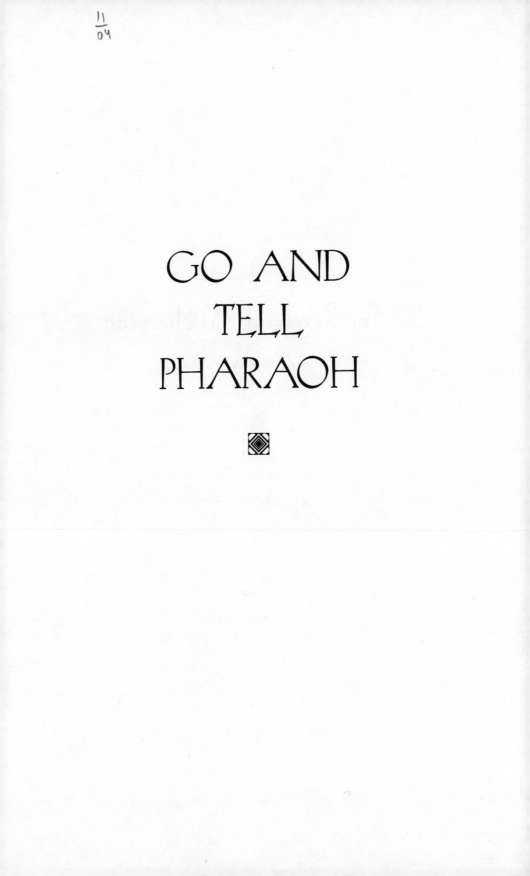

by

The Reverend Al Sharpton

and Anthony Walton

DOUBLEDAY
New York London Toronto Sydney Auckland

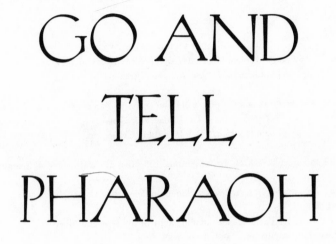

GO AND TELL PHARAOH

The Autobiography

of the Reverend Al Sharpton

PUBLISHED BY DOUBLEDAY
a division of Bantam Doubleday Dell Publishing Group, Inc.
1540 Broadway, New York, New York 10036

DOUBLEDAY and the portrayal of an anchor with a dolphin
are trademarks of Doubleday, a division of
Bantam Doubleday Dell Publishing Group, Inc.

All uncredited photographs courtesy of the personal collection of the Reverend Al Sharpton.

Library of Congress Cataloging-in-Publication Data
Sharpton, Al.
    Go and tell Pharaoh : the autobiography of the Reverend Al
Sharpton / Al Sharpton and Anthony Walton.
        p.   cm.
    1. Sharpton, Al.   2. Afro-Americans—Biography.   3. Afro-American
clergy—New York (N.Y.)—Biography.   4. Clergy—New York (N.Y.)—
Biography.   5. Politicians—New York (N.Y.)—Biography.   6. Afro-
American politicians—New York (N.Y.)—Biography.   7. New York
(N.Y.)—Biography.   I. Walton, Anthony, 1960–   .   II. Title.
E185.97.S54A3   1996
973.92′092—dc20
    [B]   95-43050
                                                                                              CIP

ISBN 0-385-47583-7

1   3   5   7   9   10   8   6   4   2

First Edition

to Ada, my mother

to Kathy, my companion

and to my daughters
Dominique and Ashley

*the four women who have
shaped my life*

Go down Moses

Down to Egyptland

Go and tell Pharaoh

Let my people go

—*spiritual*

GO AND
TELL
PHARAOH

PROLOGUE

T wo things happened to me in the early nineties, in a span of eighteen months, that I now
see as defining episodes of my life. On January
12, 1991, I was stabbed while leading a protest
march in the Brooklyn neighborhood of Bensonhurst. I
was hit two inches from my heart, and I realized, all of a
sudden, I could die doing the work I was doing. I began
to question how I wanted to be remembered. I was getting older. I was thirty-eight, not twenty-eight. I was a
husband and a father. My generation was assuming leadership in the community, and I realized I had to start
thinking about the generation that was coming along
after mine. What were the adults, and me in particular,
preparing for them? What would we leave? Black people,
in various ways, were moving ahead, falling back, and

standing still. Had I done anything, could I do anything, to change all of that for the better? What was I doing with my life?

The next year, in 1992, I ran as a candidate for the United States Senate in the New York Democratic primary. In many ways I risked my career to do so, because the media had painted me as a loudmouth, a walking sound bite, a con artist, a charlatan, and, worst of all, an imposter, with no real constituency and no true issues, a self-created media manipulator. One critic went so far as to call me "a practitioner of the big lie." What hurt most in all this— and feels patronizing—was that my vilifiers and critics never tried to look at me as a man and as a person. How could they know what I was talking about if they didn't know where I'd been? How could they know if the conditions I was complaining about and demanding redress for were actual if they didn't come look? I was speaking for people who didn't normally have a voice, I was speaking from neighborhoods that didn't normally gain attention. I had to be dramatic, I had to be loud.

In that primary election, I gained 15 percent of the vote, finishing third in a field of four, and established my credentials in the mainstream as a serious community activist. Since then my fortunes have continued to rise and I'm able to speak to more people in more places, but the fortunes of black people as a group remain complex and often dispiriting. The country as a whole is drifting and polarized. Things seem to be falling apart. And everyone is talking past each other. I've wanted to say something, at length and in depth, about my life, my community, and my country for some time. That is what I hope to do here. I want to speak up, speak out, and tell some stories. I hope to shed a little light.

From the age of four until the age of eighteen I operated mainly on instinct. Certain problems caught my attention and I simply responded in ways I thought or felt were right. I was preaching in black churches for most of my childhood, and when I became a teenager, I was more and more involved in social activism, both within my local neighborhood and in the larger civil rights movement. As we say in the church, I was "called": I believed my activities were driven by spiritual concerns.

From the time I graduated from high school until the day I was stabbed in Bensonhurst, I would say I was acting, consciously, out of my understanding of the depth and pervasiveness of racism in New York City and the nation. I acted out of emotion—primarily anger and rage at how a supposedly just society viewed and treated blacks and imposed a regime that greatly limited the life choices of most blacks. I saw how black people were shot down like dogs and demonized by the media and by politicians. I, and the people I was working with, worked at and were successful in putting race on the front burner: we put the value of black life out as an issue in New York State, and we showed the nation the ugly face of northern racism. I was outraged by Bernhard Goetz, Howard Beach, police brutality. But I was still in many ways just reacting. Something would happen and I'd run over there to deal with that incident, then the phone would ring and I'd head off someplace else, putting out fires.

After I was stabbed, I decided to try to begin acting out of resolve, out of an overall plan, to become proactive. That's why I entered electoral politics: I realized that running around from problem to problem, chasing phone call after phone call, would never move society. We have to change the broad socioeconomic conditions in this society, and will require changes in the body politic, the education of Americans of all ethnic groups and classes, and alliances with other groups who also hope for substantive change.

I still see all this, though, in the same way I saw it as a little boy: as a calling. Everything I've tried to do has been a Christian walk, an effort to live the gospel, to live the sermons I preached when I was young, to feed the hungry, shelter the homeless, comfort the afflicted. My social activism has stemmed from, and has deepened, my interior life as a Christian. The stabbing made me want to be clearer in saying that and in styling my activities in that way. In the past I have been guilty of letting ungodly things around me, of excusing hate and violent intent and imagery in my presence. After the stabbing I saw the gravity of what we were doing and realized that I had to choose sides, to decide who I was and what I stood for. I started taking myself, and my movement, a lot more seriously than I had; I started judging the means as well as the end. The episodes of my life when I flirted with darkness are really a testimony to how many kids just get caught up in worlds beyond their ability to get out of. I was able to break out of things I had gotten myself caught up in, but many can't, and these small tragedies happen every day in this country.

As my children grow older, I've become more and more sensitive to how they see me: I watch what I say, I want to be credible because my daughters are watching. I have fought my way out of the defensive mode, running around from case to case and defending myself against false allegations, tax cases, the FBI scandal. I have had to work to defend my credibility as a leader and activist; I've spent years trying to survive, ducking blows. I didn't have time in those years to explain the beliefs that fueled my actions, and, if the truth be told, few were asking: the media seemed to enjoy portraying me as a substanceless gadfly.

But now I think it is time that I explain myself, not because I feel the need to justify to anyone the things I've done, but because I believe that if people can see past the false caricature that has been made of me to the reasons for my actions, the deep injustices in our society that I have always fought against, then they will desire as I do to do something about these injustices. I'm happy finally to have the chance to clear up many of the issues about me and to offer my opinions and thoughts about what's going on in the country and the world, and where things are going.

I think many of the tragedies we are facing in this country right now are the direct result of Reaganomics. We spent a great deal of money we simply didn't have as a country under Reagan, and now the bill is coming due. Unemployment, and the resultant problems of family breakdown and social disorder, have to be someone's fault, so Reagan and Bush, to divert attention from their own policies, brought back the scapegoat of blacks. "Blame the black folks" is the oldest game in the Republic. Trickle-down economics didn't trickle, tax cuts for the rich, of course, helped only the rich, and rather than admit that it didn't work, Republican politicians claimed that affirmative action, welfare, and freeloaders were at fault. Blacks. We became the scapegoats of a failed national economic policy. It's no accident that all the violent conflicts, the Howard Beaches, the Bensonhursts, occur in blue-collar areas of white working-class people who have been deluded by their heroes, Ronald Reagan, George Bush, and Mario Cuomo. It is the old American way, all the way back to Reconstruction, that when nothing else works, blame the black folks. And that strategy has proven successful every time.

Those people, blacks, are my people. I set out to serve them when I started preaching at the age of four, and that is all that I've ever wanted to do. Those people, the lower class, the lower part of the middle-income class, trust me. I was their child prodigy; those working black folks, the maids and janitors, cooks and doormen, watched me grow up. They know me; I carry many of their aspirations. I was out in Long Beach, California, once when a lady came up to me and showed me a flyer she had kept from the time I'd preached there at the age of seven. Those people chart my progress and treat me like a grandson. They're there every Saturday at my rallies, every Sunday at the churches. That's why they give their money, which doesn't come easy, because they believe in me and the things I stand for. Even at the height of my unpopularity in the media, they never stopped giving their money, because they see very clearly how things are in this country: they have no illusions and have nothing to lose, and so are not fooled by media manipulation. I'm totally financed by the black community, by the very people that the white media have said don't trust or believe in me, not the foundations or universities or think tanks. My detractors have said that I had two hundred friends and followers. That means two hundred people voted for me 166,000 times in '92, and 178,000 times in '94. That's a busy two hundred people.

This is a time of decision in the United States, unparalleled by any, I think, since the Great Depression. Large segments of society, I think, are not functioning, plagued as they are by the domestic problems of crime, drugs, family discord, and unemployment, and on a larger, international scale by the new era of global competition and corporate downsizing, potential health and environmental catastrophes, and the way that the evolving world situation after the cold war is changing America's position in the world. Americans are going to have to decide to accept that we are, literally, all in this together, in the same boat, and that the boat will sink or sail depending on our decisions.

The bitter and divisive reaction to the O. J. Simpson verdict confirmed something I've been talking about for years: the sea of misunderstanding that exists between whites and blacks. I was talking about that in my first widely known protests, against subway shooter Bernhard Goetz, and I was talking about it in my two Senate campaigns, and everything in between. If people had paid closer attention to the issues, they wouldn't have been as surprised. Blacks have always seen the criminal justice system, and a lot of other things, differently. Whites and blacks in this country face an imperative to develop a language that will enable them to communicate openly and fairly about the problems facing all of us.

That coming together can't be achieved, however, without some internal healing. This country is like a bickering family, and until we resolve some of those differences and find some common ground we will not be able to work together in the ways that will make it possible for us to rebuild our towns and cities and reclaim the promise that has traditionally been the animating passion of our society. It is my hope that this book will shed at least a little light on one man's experience at the front lines of racial and ethnic conflict in our society, and in so doing contribute to the sort of understanding that will allow all of us to forgive each other what has happened here and begin the real work of providing a just and prosperous society for all our citizens, protecting the sick and the needy, and securing the as-of-now-uncertain future for our children and grandchildren and beyond. It is that serious, and I want to do my part in bringing it to pass.

I.

In many ways I grew up without a childhood. I never was a member of the Boy Scouts, I didn't play Little League, I was never on any kind of team. I was always a preacher. In kindergarten and first grade during playtime I would take my blocks and build a church. School was weird to me as well, because I wasn't scared of things early on like the other kids. How could I be? I'd been preaching to several hundred people a week.

I was the odd guy. Even on the block, when we'd play punchball and stickball and all, I was respected on that level. I was always husky and could take care of myself, but the kids were also always a little amused by me, because they knew I was the boy preacher. Here we are, six, seven, eight years old, and I'm their playmate, but I'm also the boy their parents went to hear preach on

Sunday. This must have been a mental adjustment for my friends.

I don't know if I've missed anything because of that, because of the distance between me and my peers. I never knew anything else, and I can't say that it made me consciously unhappy. It may have made me closer than I otherwise would have been with my sister Cheryl. We had our own little secret world where we'd eavesdrop on our parents to try to find out stuff we thought we weren't supposed to know, tell private jokes, and stay up all night and watch television when we weren't supposed to. And I watched television, *Leave It to Beaver, The Beverly Hillbillies, Amos 'n' Andy.* We especially liked to watch *Ed Sullivan* to see if there were any black folks on. So I did some of the normal kid things, but I was always in the public eye. I never had a private life. But I always knew how to attract attention; I grew up attracting the attention of the crowd. I grew up understanding the psychology of standing out. And I understood the emotions of the people.

I started preaching in public when I was four years old, but I remember coming home from church when I was even younger than that, about three, and taking all my sister's dolls and lining them up in my mother's bedroom and preaching to them, just as I'd seen our pastor, Bishop Frederick Douglass Washington, do at church that morning. Then I would go and put on my mother's wig and sing whatever the bishop's wife and our musical director, the great gospel singer Ernestine Washington, had sung at the service.

I did that for weeks. My father didn't like it, but I remember that my mother thought it was quite humorous. She had always thought I would be someone different. She thought that from the time she was pregnant with me. A lady had walked up to her one day while she was shopping and said, "God bless you and God bless the baby you're carrying. God's gonna bless that baby." My mother would often tell me about this when I was a kid.

I started out in the church as one of the junior ushers. There were several of us—my sister Cheryl, Ronnie Dyson (he later became a famous singer), and some others—and our adviser was a nice older lady named Hazel Griffin. We would stand in the foyer of the church before services, greet people as they arrived, pass out the weekly bulletin, and escort newcomers to their seats. It was a lot of fun, and a way of feeling responsible.

The junior usher board met one day up in the balcony after church, and Mrs. Griffin told us that the church was planning a special anniversary service July 9 of that year, 1959—I'll never forget it—and that each one of us was supposed to do something special for the program. Ronnie said he wanted to do a reading from the Bible, and Cheryl or somebody said they wanted to do a song, and then Mrs. Griffin looked at me and said, "Well, Alfred Sharpton, what do you want to do?" and I blurted out, "I want to preach." Everybody laughed. But I had been preaching at home, to the dolls, so I thought I could do it. Then Mrs. Griffin looked very sternly at the other kids and said, "Don't laugh, Bishop Washington started when *he* was four."

So she talked to the bishop, and they agreed that I would do the sermon for the anniversary service. My older half sister, Ernestine, whom we called Tina, helped me get ready for the sermon. She helped me think up just the right words to use and to type out a little manuscript. You have to remember, I had not yet gone to school. I was a year out of kindergarten. But I'm not only going to preach, I'm going to read the sermon. And I did, in front of about nine hundred people on a Sunday afternoon.

I preached from the Gospel of John, the fourteenth chapter: "Let not your heart be troubled: ye believe in God, believe also in me." I remember being nervous. They had to put me on a box because I was too small for the pulpit and no one could see me. I hoped I didn't look silly. I stood on that box on the steps in the front of the church and started reading. I was a little scared, too, but after I got going and fell into the rhythm of my speaking, the audience started responding with "amens" and I was fine. In fact, I felt right at home.

I have often wondered about what was driving me to get up there that day, and while I've never truly decided, I think it had to come from the Spirit, the Spirit of the Lord. If I had just wanted to be up in front of the crowd, I could have read a passage from scripture like Ronnie did, or sung. But I wanted to preach, and I had already been doing so with the dolls for several months. I felt a real spiritual compulsion, and it felt very comfortable, natural.

Then Bishop Washington, who had been tremendously kind and encouraging to me while I was getting ready, said I couldn't just preach one day if I was going to be a true preacher, and so once a month after that they let me give another sermon and I got better and better, and by the time I was seven I had become known in black Holiness circles as "the Wonderboy." By the time I was nine I was traveling all over the country and preaching with the bishop, who was one of the two or three most prominent black Pentecostals in the country. I was well received all over.

A lot of people I met didn't know what to make of me: some were amused, some thought I was cute, some thought that I was too young and was being corrupted, some took it very, very seriously, very, very spiritually, reasoning that if I was so young I *must* be anointed, there must be something very special happening. Among the kids my age, half thought I was an oddball, half looked up to me. The ones who didn't like me thought I was strange because I didn't play with them after church, I didn't rip and run up and down the halls, didn't try to sneak extra cake and punch at church socials. I would sit instead up in Bishop Washington's office with him—he'd be in there all the time, reading books, writing—he was a very studious person. He was the first person I ever saw that would just sit there reading books and underlining things. So *I* would have a book and I would underline just like him and I might not even understand what I was underlining! But my mother would always make sure to get me books and magazines, and I would carry them around and have them with me.

A year or two after I started preaching I started school, and the teacher had to send for my mother because I wasn't conforming to what the teacher's view of a correct heading for our schoolwork was. I would always write—and mind you, I'm in the first grade here—P.S. 134, year, Classroom One, whatever, and then your name over here, and I would write, "Reverend Alfred Sharpton" or "Minister Alfred Sharpton." The teacher would send for my mother and say, "What is this?" And my mother would say, "He's a minister," and the teacher would say, "Not in school, he's not," and I would refuse to sign anything but "Reverend Alfred Sharpton" on my schoolwork.

My father, who had been adamantly opposed to letting me be a boy preacher, overnight became proud of it. He would drive me to my sermons, out on Long Island, up to Yonkers and Peekskill, as far as Trenton, Rochester and Buffalo, and I remember he would always say you can't preach if you eat first. One time we went out to Amityville, on Long Island, and we stopped on the way to eat. My father said, "Junior"—he used to call me Junior—"you can't have anything because you can't preach right if you got all that food inside." And I started crying—I must have been six or seven—and protesting, and finally my mother said, "It's not fair, the boy has to eat, everybody else is eating." And I got my way. And when I got up to speak, it felt like the food was sitting right there in my chest. It was the worst sermon I've ever preached. And to this day, I can't eat before a sermon. My kids hate it if I do two or three sermons in one day as I sometimes do, because they know there won't be any dinner until after that last church.

•   •   •

My earliest memory is of the house my family lived in at 542 Logan Street, in the East New York section of Brooklyn. It was a very quiet, very tidy neighborhood. Working-class people. This was long before anybody in the neighborhood had heard of drugs. The house was one of your regular brick row houses, with a little stoop on the front, and when you came in, there was a small vestibule. The front apartment on the ground floor was to your left, and to get to the rear apartment you had to go down the hall. I still remember how the stairs dominated the hall. I remember going up those steps, and at the top of the landing was the upstairs back apartment. If you turned left from the top of the stairs, around a little banister, you saw a yellow door, and that was our apartment.

All of the people in that house—a four-family house, owned by my mother and father—were black, but our neighbors were mostly Italian. My father owned a little grocery store and newsstand right around the corner, and the first things I remember involve playing in that upstairs apartment, or walking down the street and around the corner to Mommy and Daddy's newsstand, and my sister Cheryl and I would play there.

Those were happy times. I don't remember any sadness until much later. The only negative I can think of is sort of humorous now. My father had a serious penchant for courtesy, and it caused me a problem almost every morning. The way our apartment was, you had to go through my parents' bedroom to get to the bathroom. And if I would get up in the morning and walk through their room on my way to the toilet, I was expected to say good morning to them, even if it looked like they were asleep. If I didn't do this, my father would make me go back and forth what seemed like fifty times and say good morning. This happened almost every morning, because I'd be half-asleep and running for the bathroom, and would forget, or sometimes I would look and assume he was asleep. And as soon as I came back out, he'd sit up and say, "Give me fifty good mornings." I never figured out why this meant so much to him, except that maybe he thought good manners were crucial for a black man with ambition—they've certainly served me well—but I remember it as clear as the day.

My father's name is Alfred Charles Sharpton, Sr. He was born May 3, 1925, in Wabasso, Florida, which is a little town on the east coast near Vero Beach. He was one of seventeen children, and I vividly remember our trips down to Florida to see his family. My grandfather's name was Coleman Sharpton, and my grandmother was named Mamie. We called her Big Mama. She was extraordinarily religious. We used to say, "Big Mama lives in the church." My grandparents owned a country store in Wabasso, which was rare for blacks in that time, and was how they supported all those children. My father was the eleventh or twelfth.

My father was twenty-nine years old when I was born. He was a good-looking man, 5'8" or 5'9", dark-skinned and very muscular. He had been a boxer when he was younger and claimed to have sparred with Sugar Ray Robinson. I never learned whether or not that was true. He wore his hair like I wear mine; they called it a conk in those days. He loved good things, he liked fun, he liked women. He loved to go to the Apollo Theater in Harlem, and would take me, my mother, and my sister Cheryl to see James Brown and Jackie Wilson. There would always be long lines outside the theater when James Brown was there, and my father would give somebody a couple of dollars to move us up on the line. That was about all he would do outside of church: go see James Brown, his favorite, whenever he came to town, and Jackie Wilson, because my mother liked him.

My father wasn't nearly as religious as my mother, but he tried to act like he was. I remember once we were in Florida, and we went to my grandmother's church, and my mother had gotten us ready before he had finished his hair and pulled himself together. At those black Holiness churches they have something that they call the testimony service before the beginning of the worship, where the parishioners stand up and talk about some good fortune they've experienced recently and attribute to the Lord's good grace, or some personal or job problem that they'd like the church to support them in prayer with, things like that.

I'll never forget my grandmother getting up and saying during testimony hour that day how she was so proud that her daughter-in-law and grandchildren were there from New York, and that I, the Wonderboy, was going to preach for them. Then she said that she wanted everybody in the church to pray for my father, her son, because he wasn't saved and he wasn't in the way of the Lord, though he had a good heart. My father came to church about twenty minutes later, still during testimony, not knowing his mother had stood up and said that. He got up and said very enthusiastically, "I want to thank God for my being here. I'm saved and sanctified and filled with holiness!" Everybody in the church, of course, started laughing, because his mother had already told on him. He wasn't very happy about that.

But he insisted we have religious training. Which was a little bit strange, because we were Pentecostal and going to Sunday School and services three and four nights a week. He would have the Jehovah's Witnesses come and do a Bible lesson with me and my sisters two nights a week. He bought a piano and made my sister Cheryl take lessons. He was very ambitious for us. He said he wanted us to be smart, as he put it, and he was always talking about him and us owning and operating businesses and equipment and having expertise. He always wanted us to have more than whatever it was we had, and firmly believed that we would.

That was why, in 1960, we moved to Queens. He was so industrious. He was a slumlord, to be honest. He figured out that if he could get one building in his name, it would pay for itself, and he could then leverage it into several more. He wanted to rise in society and didn't mind doing so on the backs of those he saw as having less initiative. He used all these buildings he had managed to own in poor neighborhoods in Brooklyn as collateral to borrow money, and as his contracting business, pouring concrete and doing repairs and renovations, started doing well, he closed down the newsstand and bought a big house in Queens. It had a finished basement, a raised lawn all the way around the corner of the house, and a small apartment upstairs, which we rented out. The address was 100-50 199th Street, Hollis, Queens. Black middle class. I think another reason we moved was that my parents wanted me and my sisters to go to school in Queens instead of Brooklyn. At one point my father was doing so well he bought two Cadillacs every year, one for my mother, one for him.

He was very soft-spoken but firm. He ruled the house with an iron hand. I remember that I thought he was invincible because he was so strong-looking. We were driving down South one day on one of our many trips to see his mother in Florida, and we stopped somewhere in North Carolina to get hamburgers, and they told him that they didn't serve niggers. He stood there and took that, I couldn't believe it. He went and got back into the car. And I said, "Why'd they do that?" He kind of tried to explain it to me, but didn't want to talk. More than the racism, what affected me was to see my father mistreated, because until then I'd thought that nobody could tell my father no. It was really traumatic for me. I now realize that there was more going on than I could recognize, that he was in a strange place in the South with his wife and children and he had to think about protecting them and getting out of there rather than starting something, but it was a signal event.

My father was not one to stay in a black man's place: he always wanted more, and at that time he was unusually independent for who society expected him to be. I think it hurt him eventually, broke him, even, because later, after he and my mother separated and he lost his properties, he couldn't accept not being successful. He would never accept being a regular black man in what society considered to be a black man's place in life. It was always, "I'm gonna buy a building, I'm gonna get a contracting job, I'm buying a new Cadillac." He never accepted just going along with the status quo.

My mother, Ada Richards Sharpton, was born on September 28, 1925, in Dothan, Alabama. Her parents, Emmett and Mattie Richards, lived in the town of Eufaula, Alabama, right on the Chattahoochee River, just south of Columbus and Fort Benning, Georgia. Deep South. My mother also had a sister, Redell, who lived on Vernon Avenue in Brooklyn all her life and was very close to us, very important in our lives until she died in 1975.

My mother is fair-skinned, and when she was younger, was very slender and well shaped. People used to say she looked like Eartha Kitt. She is a very dignified person, with an almost regal bearing. She had done other things in her life before becoming a wife and mother, including working as a seamstress, but for most of my young childhood she was a housewife. While my father was more flamboyant and more overtly ambitious, my mother was more industrious in a down-to-earth way. She was the one who would save money, she was more frugal with the daily management of the household, more self-effacing, and she was deeply, seriously, sincerely religious.

There was a legend in my mother's family that my great-grandmother Minnie was a slave child of General Robert E. Lee. We grew up believing we had this Confederate general's blood in us. I've sometimes thought that might account for the extremely light skin color of some of my mother's people. If this business about Robert E. Lee wasn't true, it was an untruth the family always believed. The family owned all kinds of land, which was extremely rare for black folks. The old folks claimed General Lee had given this acreage to Minnie's mother, who had been his slave. They still own that land, it's still in the family.

My mother's great belief in life outside of the Pentecostal Church was education. She felt that was something she had been denied, and she was determined that her children have it. She pushed us in everything, in school, homework, and my sermons. She wanted us to be something she considered respectable. She didn't care what it was, a doctor, a dentist, a lawyer; if, for me, it was a preacher, then she was determined that she would help me become that. And I never doubted that I could do any of those things, or anything else, largely because of my mother. I was never told, "No, you can't do that." Never. I never knew doubt until I was a grown man. When I was ten years old, they asked Washington Temple to do a religious service at the World's Fair. The pavilion held thousands, and I preached. Over ten thousand people were there. But I never flinched, never even thought about it, because my mother had told me that I could do it.

And it wasn't just me. My sister Cheryl was an artist, had a great talent for drawing. My mother got her lessons, and later, enrolled her in art school in Manhattan. I can be sad when I think about it, actually, because there are times when I feel that my mother at some point gave up on herself and lived her victories through us. She seemed like the strongest, most determined woman I have ever known, but only for us, with almost no ambition for herself. At some point in her life she just decided she wanted us to have everything and she didn't worry about herself.

When I think about my parents, what comes to me is how they both wanted more than they had, more than what life promised for uneducated black people. They were born in the early twenties in the South, so we're talking deep segregation, virtual invisibility for blacks in society. And in my father's case, being one of so many kids, there was a lot of competition just to eat. His parents had owned that little grocery store, and knowing Daddy, he came to New York—just like all the other black folks—looking for the Promised Land. He'd gone to Baltimore first and been married to a different woman there, but I don't know what became of that family. I have never really sat down and talked to him about his life, because he was gone by the time I was ten, which is when I would have begun to get interested. So I don't know as much as I might.

I never got to know my father well enough to understand the motive behind his drive, but he never seemed to relax; he always seemed to be on his way somewhere, with something in mind. It makes me sad to think about it, because it makes me wonder what might we have done if he'd had more stability in his life and opportunity in his education. By the time that he was thirty-two, he owned more than twenty buildings in Brooklyn, and through some weaknesses of his own, women, and the manipulation of his lawyers, lost everything. When I think about, in retrospect, what he might have become, it's awesome.

This business of frustrated ambition—they can see it all but they can't have it all—is one of the tragic threads I've seen in powerful black men I've known, from my father to my first hero, Adam Clayton Powell, to James Brown, who became like my father, to Jesse Jackson, who was my second hero, to Don King. They seem to hit a ceiling. And I think, and I don't mean to be psychoanalyzing myself, that in many ways the rage and determination in me was that I saw black men who I thought were great men succeed—but that their greatest successes always seemed to end up in more humiliation than other people's failures, because even though they went further than other blacks, they could never get to where they might otherwise have gone. The first black man I saw this happen to was my father. It is as if somebody else has always determined how far a black man could go.

My mother also had her dreams. She dropped out of school very young, was, like my father, married once before while very young, but her first husband was much older and the marriage didn't survive. She then ran away from home and came to New York City. She became a seamstress, and her sister came here, and they lived together and worked and sent money home. Then she met my father and they married and Cheryl and I were born and the rest is what it is.

Bishop Washington, the founder and pastor of the Washington Temple Church of God in Christ in Brooklyn, had an indescribable effect on my life; he was my first mentor, always believed in me, and was always incredibly kind to me. He saw possibilities in me as a leader when I was the youngest of children, and always set a perfect example of conduct and deportment. He didn't say a lot, but I could look at him and watch how he did things and know how to proceed. And he included me in everything he did.

I think in some ways my father resented Bishop Washington's influence on me. I think he may have felt I loved the bishop more than I loved him. There was always a tension there. All I knew was that I wanted to be like Bishop Washington, and though I loved my father, I never really wanted to be like him. I never wanted to be rich, I never shared my father's preoccupation with money, real estate, and all that. Maybe that was because of my father and the way he made the first ten years of my life fairly comfortable.

What I was interested in was crowds of people. So Bishop Washington's stature with adults was always more interesting to me than buying houses and collecting rent. Sometimes, after we moved to Queens, my father would take me on his rounds, and we'd ride around all day on Saturday, going here and there, doing this and that, and I couldn't wait to get back home to preach to my dolls, to conduct a service in the little church I'd built, with benches and everything, in the basement.

Bishop Washington was a truly great man, one of the kind of leaders of the self-contained black community that we rarely see anymore. He was a phenomenal preacher in the southern "whoop-ing" tradition, that singsong way of preaching that can just transport a congregation when it's done correctly. But at the same time he was an intellectual, he'd read and studied, he'd thought about things. He was probably the first preacher that a lot of us black folks were exposed to who had the ability to preach from a sound theo-logical basis—from proper homiletics. At the same time, he could then swing into that down-home climax that everybody loved. So people got that emotional uplift from the old ways, but they also felt that they had learned something, and so they didn't feel like they were just country. They were in New York City. This was brilliant. Down-home with dignity.

Bishop Washington's wife, Ernestine, was a major gospel singer, and she also had a large part in building the temple. She was a recording artist and had toured extensively with the gospel greats of that time. Mahalia Jackson often came to the church, Sister Rosetta Tharpe, the Mighty Clouds of Joy, the Five Blind Boys, James Cleveland. Washington Temple became a regular stop for all of them. They would do concerts. So the temple became *the* place for a certain segment of black Brooklyn. And you have to remember, at that time there were giants in the ministry in Brooklyn: Dr. Gar-diner Taylor, who pastored Concord Baptist, probably the largest black church at the time, and the Reverend Sandy Ray, who pas-tored Cornerstone. Adam Powell was over in Harlem. So Bishop Washington held his own and prevailed against some stiff competi-tion. And that's how it was: a preacher had to meet the needs of the people or the people wouldn't come. That's how my parents found themselves leaving the Baptist Church to become Pentecostals at Washington Temple.

I remember the night I joined, thinking the pulpit was *so* big. And Madam Emily Brown, as we used to call her, "opened the doors of the church," inviting new members to come down front and be received into the life of Christ. My mother took my hand—I was three—and my sister Cheryl's hand and marched us down there in front of the church, in front of two thousand people, and the next thing I know we're becoming members of the Washington Temple. We were baptized a couple of weeks after that.

I'd never seen such a large and vibrant crowd. To be in that theater, to be among fifteen hundred to two thousand black people singing and clapping and joyously energized, that was a totally new experience for me. I had been accustomed to the cloisters of my working-class environment on Logan Street, being in the house or walking around the corner to hang out at my parents' store—but there I was in the midst of all these people, praying, singing, clapping. It intrigued me, even as I walked down the aisle with my mother that night. I was three years old, and it didn't scare me, it intrigued me, because it seemed like the crowd had a life all its own.

Looking back on it now, I can see how we black folks had created our own world, our own meeting place. Washington Temple, and the places like it, were *safe*, and in retrospect, I now see that it was the only place that black people of that generation could be somebody. Think of all those butlers and bellhops and janitors and domestic workers and delivery boys, they had to bow down all week long. But on Sunday morning at Washington Temple they were chairman of the Deacon Board, they were trustees, they ran the Building Fund, they were Madam Chairwoman of the Mother's Board, they were the choir director. People that everybody ignored all week could stand up and speak their thoughts or perform before thousands of their peers. They would make decisions on what property to buy or sell, they'd decide what went to the bank and what went somewhere else. A black person who was "Willie" or "Ruthie" all week could be, on Sunday, "Mr. Manigault" or "Mrs. Bolton." The church was the place where you could be more than a boy.

Even the physical nature of the building—and this is where Bishop Washington was a genius, he always thought big—reinforced this. It takes up a whole block, from Bedford, from Bergen, almost to Dean on one side, then half the block on the other side. Bishop Washington had built a huge cross out front, that lit up with neon lights. You felt you were special just to be walking in.

Inside the church was a huge vestibule (the building was once a movie theater) and then, through some more doors, the sanctuary. As you walk into the sanctuary, there were chest-high walls setting off the seating, and past those walls, like crossing a threshold, there were three sections of seats, about 2,500 downstairs, and then the balcony with another thousand. In the front, a raised pulpit, and over the pulpit, the choir. For black folks living in the tenements of central Brooklyn, to be able to feel ownership in such an edifice was transformative.

I think that growing up in the environment of the Washington Temple had a great deal to do with my self-assurance, with the confidence that guided my actions in the wider society as I grew older. I was taught as a boy that black people were the masters of their own destiny, that they could do things on their own without the validation of whites. We didn't need permission. At Washington Temple all the finances came from black folks. Bishop Washington made all the decisions. White folks just didn't make any decisions for us. They had, in fact, nothing to do with us. And these people weren't Garveyites or communists or anything. Far from it. Black Pentecostals are by definition apolitical and unworldly. They see the everyday world of business and commerce and government as Babylon, ungodly, and don't want anything to do with it. They are among the most personally conservative people in America. But they do value independence and self-sufficiency, and will choose to be mistreated domestics for whites over welfare, dependency, and dishonor.

In retrospect, I see these circumstances as extraordinarily important factors in my development: the first authority figures I saw, the men and women I most admired when young, were black people in the church. I didn't really know then who or what white people *were,*

I didn't know how they were defined against me in the larger society, as an abstraction or as an enemy. We lived around whites in our
neighborhood, but they didn't really affect us in any way; it was
almost as if they existed in a parallel world. I never saw white
people giving orders or being in charge.

My idea of who was in charge was Bishop Washington and the
deacons and trustees of the temple. The power in Daddy's store was
Daddy. And he and Mommy were the landlords at home. So unlike
my parents, and other southern blacks who came out of a tradition
in which blacks were forced to go to the back of the bus, and drink
from separate water fountains and such, I had no firsthand experience with whites, negative or positive. I had no imagery of their
power.

I learned an awful lot from Bishop Washington. I learned how to
preach, I learned to love and respect books, I learned how to dress, I
learned the persona of the black preacher, who is part religious
leader, part social leader, part social worker, part entertainer.
Through imitating people you admire, you learn things you don't
come to understand until much later; you just do it. You act in
certain ways and only later come to understand the value and meaning of those actions. I learned more than I could have appreciated at
the time from the bishop, and I was only doing it because he did it. I
was extraordinarily lucky that my first mentor was a great and good
man and that he took a sincere interest in me. From the time I was
born until I was ten years old, no one other than my mother had as
big an influence on me.

II.

When I was nine and a half, my family's life changed. Our world fell apart. We had been living very comfortably, in a middle-class situation, and it looked like things could only get better—but there began to be rumors floating around the family that there was some relationship between my father and my half sister, Tina, my mother's daughter from her previous marriage. For a long period of time, six or seven months, my mother did her best to resist and ignore the speculation. Then, suddenly, Tina admitted that the gossip was true; she moved out of the house and began living back in Brooklyn in a place that was owned by my father.

Eventually, Tina had a child, Kenneth, my father's son. That was a great personal trauma for me, and continues to be, because it not only meant losing my father, dealing with the abandonment and with his choosing to walk away from us; it also meant learning to handle what the situation led to, which was real poverty for the family. And I had to face the pain of knowing that I had a younger brother, or nephew, who looked just like me, but from whom circumstances forced me to be estranged.

I had to watch my mother, whom I loved more than anyone, live with the fact that her daughter had stolen her husband, and that the two of them had given life to a child, out of wedlock. To this day I don't know how she lived with the humiliation. I was too young to interpret what was happening, and my understanding of her suffering only grows as I get older.

When my mother could no longer afford the house in Hollis, Queens, we were forced to move back to Brooklyn. She had to look for work, and while she did, we were on welfare. In the meantime, my father was in court trying to stop me from preaching. I don't know whether he did this for spite, or power, or my best interests, but he was further harming our family. My mother filed for child support in Kings County, and part of my father's defense as to why he didn't have to pay was that I was making money as a boy preacher. And of course there was some truth to it, but I might get a hundred dollars one weekend, I might get ten. It all depended on where I preached and how it went.

But we went to family court in Brooklyn, and my father had all kinds of excuses for the judge. He couldn't make any money, his business had gone sour, his buildings were being foreclosed on. The judge, of course, was outraged when he found out about the relationship with the stepdaughter, but he was also concerned about the charges of my being sent out as a child to preach and make money. He was, obviously, an older white man who had no understanding of our culture, who had never heard of a boy preacher.

The judge asked me into his chambers—and to this day I don't know if he was testing me or not—but he pointed his finger directly at me and says, "I order you not to preach anymore. Do you understand?" I was ten years old, and I said yes. He said, "Do you understand what a judge can do?" I nodded. And he said again, "You're ordered not to preach anymore."

That Friday night I was to preach at Washington Temple as I did every week. I came in and I sat behind the pulpit where no one could see me. As they were conducting the traditional opening of the service I kept peeking around the lectern to see if any police, any court officers, were coming down the aisle looking for me. I actually thought they might be. I was afraid, scared, even, but when it came time to preach, I went out and did it. That was the first time in my career that I defied a judge.

I didn't get paid for preaching on Friday nights, as that was part of my ministerial duty at Washington Temple, but I did get a free-will offering on Sundays when I gave my sermon. Two weeks later we went back to court, and the judge called me up in front of the bench. And he said, "Alfred, have you preached since you were here?" And I said, "Yes, sir." He was surprised. "You did? Didn't you understand me telling you not to preach?" I said yes. He said, "Did your mother make you do it?" I said, "No, sir. In fact, my mother told me not to do it." "Then why did you?" "Because I believe in what I'm doing." And he turned to my father and said, "Leave this kid alone."

The pain of my father's leaving was a shadow over all my growing up. But she kept pushing for me and my sister Cheryl and never gave up. She took whatever kind of job she had to, domestic, laundry, sewing, to keep us going, and that gave me even more of a drive to want to be something she could be proud of. Tina and my mother later reconciled after many years, but I don't think I ever got over it. And it has a lot to do with how I think of my father, why I don't get along with him. We never talked about it, but I'm sure he has to have a sense of guilt. No matter what he tells himself about what happened, he must know, at bottom, that he divided and harmed our family. That was his fault.

It's very strange, now, when I think about him. I haven't seen him in fifteen or sixteen years, but he seems to be very aware of me, and keeping track. I was at National Airport in Washington one night, and I bumped into a White House official whom I knew from the '92 Clinton campaign, and he said, "Reverend, I just got back from Orlando and I met your dad!" I was stunned. He said, "I got off the plane in Orlando and the limousine that picked me up, the guy had your picture all over the dashboard. He kept saying, 'That's my son, that's my son. You know my son?' I told him, 'Sure, everybody knows your son.' He said he was your father, and he has pictures of you from all the papers and pictures of you with him when you were a little kid."

I don't know whether to reconcile. I don't know that I'd want to. It's hard for someone who learned at a very early age how to be self-sufficient to break that, to give someone you don't really know or understand the position, respect, and power that is earned from an ordinary parent-child relationship. I remember something Mike Tyson told me, "You're out there throwing rocks against the wall all your life," and that's kind of how I feel about the thing with my father. At this point I can be cool with him, even cordial. But I've had to survive off my own instinct so long, have gone through so much, that it would be hard for me to have a father-son relationship with him. I've gotten over needing that, plus I've had surrogate fathers, like Jesse Jackson and James Brown. What would that reconciliation be? I'm forty years old and have fought more wars than Douglas MacArthur, so it would be hard for me to figure out how a relationship with him would go.

I think that emotion is true of a lot of children who grew up in broken homes. You get used to making it on your own, by yourself.

There's a parable in the Bible—I've preached this sermon a hundred times—where Paul talks about a ship sailing one night, and it was shipwrecked, and the people had to respond to the shipwreck in different ways. Some swam, some floated, some made it on broken pieces. And I always talk about how I'm one of the kids that made it on broken pieces. But when you've learned how to make those broken pieces work, it's kind of hard to rearrange the pattern, because you've made the broken ones do. And maybe, somewhere in your heart, you don't know if there *are* any other pieces, you've held on to the broken pieces for so long.

I was ordained and licensed as a minister in the Pentecostal Church when I was ten, shortly after my parents broke up. It didn't make a real difference in my routine or income, but I was officially a "reverend." I didn't really understand the significance of the title. I believed more in the spiritual depth of preaching, that the responsibility was basically being called to preach. It wasn't until I got older that I understood it empowered you to marry people and bury people and all of that. At ten years old, it was just a certificate to me. I was glad to have it, but I didn't understand it.

Bishop Washington named me junior pastor—quite a move up from junior usher!—of the church, and I was, by then, preaching all over the country and in the Caribbean, touring with Mahalia Jackson and Roberta Martin. I was the Wonderboy, and I was conscious that not all ten-year-olds were preaching.

That was a difficult time of life at home—I am speaking of when we were still in the big house in Queens. There was a lot of adult fighting and arguing going on around me and my sister Cheryl. The situation was particularly hard on my mother, of course, and she relied even more on her religion, using her convictions to sustain her. We had continued going to Washington Temple all along, and there was a church on Hollis Avenue, about two blocks from where we lived, called the Holiness Church of Jesus Christ, where my mother started going almost every night.

There was another rock for us at that time, a woman I'll never forget, Lula McBride, whom we called Sister McBride. She was a missionary, out of the South, maybe in her early thirties. She was illiterate, couldn't read or write. But she was very devout, and she would come over and watch me and Cheryl while my mother did whatever she could to make a living and keep the house. One night I got home from school at P.S. 134 in Hollis, and Sister McBride was there, and she took me to her house because my mother had been put in the hospital. Her nerves had gone bad. The separation, the pressures of keeping our heads above water, had just become too much for her. Sister McBride took me over to Queens General to see her, but they wouldn't let me in because I was too young. Instead I waved up to her window from the outside.

When my mother got out of the hospital, the three of us— Cheryl, my mother, and I—continued to live in the house in Queens. After a couple of months, the car was repossessed. After that, we were on welfare, but still living in the house. Then we couldn't pay the utility bills. The gas company cut us off, then the lights were turned off. We lived in the house another six months without light or gas. In fact, when the first big New York City blackout came in 1965, we were already blacked out. All the kids on the block used to laugh at me because I did my homework by candlelight, but the night of the blackout they all came to our house to borrow candles. And we couldn't watch television. That's probably why I hardly watch TV now, and love to read.

Finally, my mother had to give up and admit that we were not going to be able to sustain our former lifestyle, and we moved back to Brooklyn, this time to the projects. My mother had a friend from Washington Temple, Eleanora Martin, and we moved in with her and her children. I still went to school in Queens, though. I didn't want to go to school in Brooklyn. I wanted to finish school with my classmates. I would get up at six every morning and ride the long L-train that would connect at Broadway Junction out to Jamaica, Queens.

I had a teacher at that time, Mrs. Greenberg. Her husband was the assistant principal or the principal of our school, and the two of them were very good to me, counseling and cheering me up almost every day. I could have gotten into a lot of trouble then. I didn't want to sit in class, I would leave the room, walk the halls. I was upset all the time, concerned about my mother being ill, about my father being gone. Those two teachers really helped me through that period of my life.

About that time I was browsing through a bookstore—I used to like to do that for recreation—when I saw a book that had a picture on it of what looked like a white man in a clergyman's collar. Being that I was a preacher, I was interested, and I picked it up, excited that someone had written a book about a minister. Then I found out that the man on the cover of the book was black, and that as well as being a reverend, he was a politician, a very famous politician. The man was Adam Clayton Powell, Jr.

I saved up enough of my little money to buy the book—it was ninety-nine cents, I think—and that is what really first got me started in thinking about politics and social ministry. So I used to sit by myself on the L-train every morning, every evening, eleven years old, reading about Adam Clayton Powell. In that book I read that Adam's hero was Marcus Garvey. That got me started reading books about Garvey. And so I began delving into Black Consciousness.

Though I had seen Martin Luther King and others at Washington Temple when I was younger, I hadn't really taken them seriously. But I think I must have been looking for something coming out of my parents' divorce. At that same time Bishop Washington started taking even more of an interest in me, taking me around with him even more, talking to me more and in more detail, and going into his thinking and reasoning on various matters much more thoroughly with me. He wanted me to understand not just the how, but the *why* of things. And since my mother couldn't afford to buy things for me, Bishop Washington would buy me suits to preach in.

There was another minister at Washington Temple who was crucial to my development, Rev. Walter Banks. Reverend Banks would come by and pick me up every weekend and take me to Manhattan, because he had made it his mission to ensure that I would know about church life, preaching, and being a clergyman outside of the vernacular and ghetto traditions I grew up in. He was not an educated man, but he had been in the army and exposed to a few things, and he would take me to Saint Patrick's Cathedral, to the Anglican Church, the Marble Collegiate, and then we would go to Kroch's and Brentano's on Fifth Avenue, where I would pick out books, books he'd buy me. Later, he would quiz and question me to make sure I was reading them. If I have to give credit to anyone for my reading appetite—and it is quite extensive—it would have to go to Reverend Banks, who was really just a guy at Washington Temple, but one who took a serious and sincere interest in me. He wanted me to go farther than he had, and the older I get, and the more I understand, the more I'm stunned by the depth of his simple kindness and generosity.

When I was ten, Bishop Washington took me with him on a Caribbean tour. There were about twelve of us from the church who went. I did most of the preaching. We went to Haiti, Jamaica, Barbados, Trinidad, Puerto Rico. We flew all over the islands. I used to wander off by myself or with the bishop's daughter, Frederica, who was a year older than me, to try and see what was going on in those places. We generally didn't get very far.

When we were in Jamaica, I remembered the book I had read about Marcus Garvey and remembered that he was from there, and I decided to find his family. They were listed in the phone book! I called Mrs. Garvey and said that I was Rev. Alfred Sharpton, Jr., from New York City in the United States and that I'd read a lot about her husband. She invited me over.

I preached that night, and the next morning I got up, got a cab—I was ten years old, but the driver took me—and I went over to her house. 12 Mona Road. I knocked on the door, she looked out—she couldn't see me because I was too short and she came to the door three times before opening it—and she looked down and began laughing hysterically because she couldn't believe this little kid was the preacher who had called.

She sat with me all day, serving tea and talking, while I asked all kinds of questions about Garvey. I remember her saying to me, "You're going to be like Garvey because you got a big head like Garvey, Garvey had a very big head." And she kept rubbing my head and laughing. After I left Jamaica, I used to write her, and I still have letters that Mrs. Garvey sent me when I was eleven, twelve years old. She died not too long after that, but for a few years we would write each other two or three times a year.

After we'd lived in the Albany Gardens Housing Project for six or seven months, my mother found an apartment for us on Lincoln Place in Crown Heights. The projects had been quite an experience for me, because the entire environment was different. I went from an upstairs apartment in a building my parents owned in a stable section of Brooklyn to a pretty good-sized house out in Queens, which was then considered a suburb, to a large urban housing project. This was the first place that we had lived in my experience that we didn't own. We didn't have a yard, and my parents weren't collecting the rent. Environmentally, it was extraordinarily imposing and intimidating to me. Everybody was stacked up on top of one another. And the only backyard was the basketball court, which was always full of kids.

I was lucky I never got into any real altercations because Aunt Eleanora Martin, as we called her, our "sponsor" in the project, had two kids who were older than me. They protected me, made the others leave me alone. Also, everybody knew I was the boy preacher, so they didn't expect me to gangbang. In those days, kids respected church kids. They would see me, of course, and tease, they would yell, "There's the preacher!" They would laugh and there would be a sense of ridicule, but the mockery was actually tame, and within it was an unspoken but large measure of respect.

Back then was like another ecology in the neighborhood. It wasn't all predators. It was pre-drugs, so there wasn't all the crime that is related to that trade. There were some youth gangs, but there were limits, demarcations. Those who were doing something with their lives, with their time, were left alone.

What bothered me about moving to the ghetto wasn't that I was going to an all-black situation; I'd known that in the church and enjoyed and respected it. The troubling thing was that I knew from living in Hollis, Queens, what it was like living in a community where the garbage was picked up on time, where the police would come when you called, where the hospitals took care of you in the emergency room. And I couldn't believe the conditions that black people not only lived in but accepted as inevitable in the projects. I knew better.

I think that this is why Marcus Garvey and Adam Clayton Powell and later Martin Luther King captivated me so. I really, actually, knew how unfair things were, at a very young age. I had lived on the other side of the tracks, at least the other side of the black tracks. And I knew that what we were getting in the projects and on Lincoln Place meant we were getting, quite frankly, shafted, because I'd seen better, with my own eyes. I hadn't heard about better, I hadn't read about better; I'd *lived* better. So I knew that white folks were beating us, badly.

So many black people accepted this situation, these conditions, because they didn't think they could do anything about it. Most of them didn't know any better. The system has a way of breaking your self-esteem. And once you feel like you don't deserve anything, you won't fight to have anything. That's why my family's journey was so crucial to my development. I've always felt that I deserved better than what was proffered because I had known a more fulfilling, more satisfying, more rewarding life. I knew it was there. Even when I couldn't do anything about it, I didn't have to accept it.

While we lived on Lincoln Place, I stayed in public school in Hollis, taking that long subway ride to P.S. 134, then to 109 for junior high school. I think it was my mother's desire, and mine as well, to not entirely give up that Queens middle-class life that kept me going that hour and a half out there and an hour and a half back every day, by myself. By the time I got home from school it was five o'clock. By the time I did my homework it was time to go to bed and get up at 5:30 so I could get back on the train. That was all I did, except for church Friday night, often Saturday night, and all day Sunday. That was my life on Lincoln Place. I was eleven years old.

Ever since I'd read that book about Adam Clayton Powell I'd wanted to meet him. I thought about him constantly. He was on television most days, always in the news. He had a way about him that was provocative and exciting, as well as being particularly irritating to whites. Yet he was so deft in his maneuvering that he was one of the most effective legislators in Congress.

He and Malcolm X were the first northern black leaders dominate the mass, electronic, media. The media age was just coming into being at that time, moving from print and radio to television, and Adam had the style and sense of drama to know how to stick out. I was captivated, and constantly told my mother that I wanted to meet him.

Finally one day I convinced her to let me go to his church, the great Abyssinian Baptist up in Harlem. I had a feeling he was going to be there to preach that Sunday. My mother agreed to let Cheryl take me on the subway. In those days, people in Brooklyn considered Harlem dangerous, and vice versa, and she almost didn't let us go. We got on the L-train and rode all the way to Harlem, to 135th Street, and from there we walked to this huge church that was very different from our Pentecostal Washington Temple because the service was so quiet and refined. You didn't hear a lot of "amens," you didn't hear any real *gospel* singing; they sang anthems. Now I would call it bourgeois. The people there were much more proper than in the churches I was used to preaching in.

Powell didn't show up that day, but through steady requests I convinced my mother about two weeks later to let me try again. There we were, sitting quietly and listening to the choir sing their anthems, when suddenly the side door opened and Adam Clayton Powell walked out. I was never so enthused at seeing anyone in my life as I was that morning. It was like he was God. He was very tall, he was so striking, he was charismatic, all of that. And he strutted into the pulpit—Adam had a way of not walking, but strutting, like a peacock. He preached that morning on "God is love." And while he was preaching, this refined audience came alive, with "amens" and clapping and everything. It seemed like he was the only one in that church allowed to get emotional, and then they went with him. Because I've been in that church a thousand times since then, but only with Adam did I see that kind of reaction.

After the service I found my way to the pastor's office (when you'd been in as many churches as I had, you knew how to do that). In those days they had offices with doors where the top would swing open while the bottom stayed closed, and I can still see the church secretary leaning over the top and looking down at me, laughing and wondering what this little kid wanted. I said, "I'd like to meet Congressman Powell." She smirked and said, "Who should I say is calling?" "The Reverend Alfred Sharpton," I said. She said, "*Reverend* Alfred Sharpton?" I said yes. And she looked at me superciliously and walked away and didn't come back.

After ten minutes I knocked and asked again. She hadn't delivered the message and obviously didn't want to be bothered. Who was this kid? But I convinced her to at least ask if I could meet him, so she disappeared into his office and immediately came back out with a confused and sheepish look on her face. She waved to me and said, "Follow me."

When I went in behind her, we walked behind a Plexiglas wall and there was Adam Clayton Powell standing in the middle of the floor with his pants on, no shirt, no T-shirt, bare-chested, and his arm was around two or three older women—they looked like they were in their seventies or eighties. And he looked at me and said very dramatically, "Here's the wonderboy preacher from my good friend F. D. Washington's church, Alfred Sharpton!" I was in heaven. Adam Clayton Powell knew who I was. I said, "You know me?" And he said, "Of course. I listen to Bishop Washington's broadcast when I'm in town. Everybody knows you." Then he gestured. "Have a seat."

I was totally mesmerized. I would have killed for him. I sat down and watched him talking to the ladies, talking to the deacons. He put his shirt and tie on, and his jacket, then he looked at me and said, "Come on, Reverend, let's go have a drink at the Red Rooster."

A drink? I said, "I don't drink, I'm ten years old." He said, "A soda, then." So we walked over to the bar, and I sat there with Adam as he drank Scotch and held court. It was the most incredible exhibition of power that I've ever seen, with people from every walk of life, including the top business and show and sports people that you'd see in the *Amsterdam News* and on TV, coming up to him one by one seeking favors or just to pay their respects, having little meetings and huddles with him all afternoon. I knew then what I wanted to be, that's when the other shoe dropped. After that, every time he came to town I would try to attach myself to his entourage, and I was usually successful, hanging around with him after church or riding around the city in his car. He liked me, and I think he knew that all I wanted from him was to be around him—and since everyone else always had a request for something specific, that was easy for him, and even relaxing, because I would let him talk and blow off steam and was happy simply to listen.

Adam just had his own style, his own way of doing things. I'll never forget the night he was on *The David Frost Show*. He was wearing a black turtleneck sweater and he had on this gold medallion and Coptic gold cross that Haile Selassie had given him. Frost's first question was, "Congressman, you know what's said about you, that you're arrogant, but how would Adam Powell describe Adam Powell?" And Adam said, "I'm the only man in America that doesn't give a damn." I think that's why I liked him so much. He *didn't* give a damn, he couldn't be intimidated, not in Congress, not in New York, not on the street, not anywhere.

There was this picture of Adam sitting in front of the Capitol with his Jaguar, and at about the same time he toured Europe with a white woman and a black woman, both of them beauty contest winners—all of this at a time when black men were regularly being lynched for walking down the street with or looking at white women. One way of looking at Adam's flamboyance is that he was raising consciousness. He defied the taboos, he defied the limitations of black men.

I've always thought that Adam, because he represented to blacks the assumption of real power—you have to remember that for a long time he was the only black congressman—affected the body politic in a way that no other black leader did. He threatened the domestic picture of this country. I think that's why the media never really understood him, other than their predigested vision of him as a troublemaker. The establishment didn't want blacks to emulate that independence, that self-assurance, that arrogance. The media and the establishment could tolerate Martin Luther King, because he was "thoughtful" and "philosophical," and after they got through with him they made him almost harmless, in their distortions. He certainly *wasn't* harmless, but he could appear to be. Adam Powell, there was no way to soften him, you couldn't make him palatable. When Newt Gingrich talks now about erasing the legacy of the Great Society, what he's really saying is that he wants to erase what Adam did for this country. Adam created much of that poverty legislation.

Most young Americans, particularly whites, do not understand Powell's significance. Most of what the SCLC, SNCC, MFDP, CORE, NAACP, and the Freedom Riders did in the Civil Rights Movement, Powell did years before—boycotts, marches, sit-ins and the like. I think that the media and scholars have overplayed his flamboyance and excesses and underplayed his substance and real contribution. Some of it was Adam's fault—he was a preacher, and preachers have a natural tendency for showmanship—but beyond that, I think he had a very deep resentment of whites because of how his family was treated, particularly his mother, by white relatives who denied their tie to the black side of the family. Also there was a time when he was going to college and passing for white, but then he was found out and dismissed for being black. So I think his outrageousness was a deeply personal way of mocking the system that had caused him such pain. And perhaps, at times, he carried it too far, masking his own achievement. He didn't take himself as seriously as he should have. And even though his mockery at the system was justified, it robbed him of his legacy.

Whenever you are going to study a political leader, Mao or Castro or Churchill, you have to study them in the context of their environment and their times. Northern black politicians and activists should study Powell, because Martin Luther King is not really a model for them. King didn't operate in the northern urban context, King didn't have to deal with Caribbean blacks, West Africans, Latinos, twenty different white ethnic groups, all at each other's throats and all of them against African Americans. In the South it was black and white. The North is much more complex. To study and master the King movement is informative and worthwhile, but it doesn't give you everything you need to operate in New York, Chicago, Detroit, or Los Angeles. I could take some of the tactics and techniques of Cicero to Howard Beach, but to negotiate with the Cuomos and D'Amatos of this world I had to study Powell. Mayor Daley gave Dr. King fits. But Adam Powell handled Eisenhower and Adlai Stevenson, he wrestled John Kennedy and Lyndon Johnson. It just makes good strategic sense to understand him.

I've tried to learn from Powell's strengths and weaknesses in my own life journey. Something Jesse Jackson always pounded into me was to remember my dignity. During the Brawley case, when I had an especially high profile, I foolishly allowed a photograph to be taken of me while I was under the dryer having my hair done at the salon. The picture was on the front page of the *New York Post.* Jesse went nuts. In my mind, I was mocking white folks, a la Adam, but Jesse said, "Do you want to be remembered for hot curlers?" I realized then that was not what I wanted to be remembered for, and it has taken me many years to erase the caricatured image of me that the media built up.

I don't think Adam ever fought to protect his image, because I don't think he ever really wanted to. He was telling the truth, he *didn't* give a damn. Ultimately, he didn't care what white people, or black people, for that matter, thought about him. No one was a thorn in the side of the power structure of society for as long as him. And on one level, that type of defiance is good—it makes you do things—but on another level it causes you to trap yourself in an image that may be counterproductive. But, when all is said, he was a great man, one of the two or three greatest men in public life I have ever known, and he was exceedingly kind to a young boy in need of a hero.

When I was twelve, we moved from Lincoln Place in Crown Heights to Lenox Road in East Flatbush. A friend of my mother's had found an apartment for us with five rooms, which meant that me and my sister could each have our own room. The neighborhood was at that time half Jewish and half black, and my mother's friend, Rose Williams, helped us get into the building even though we were on welfare.

An organization was forming in Brooklyn then under the auspices of Dr. King's Southern Christian Leadership Conference (SCLC) called Operation Breadbasket. Their strategy was to boycott corporations, picket places of business, things like that, with the goal of improving economic conditions for blacks. The leader in New York City was a minister named William Augustus Jones, of Bethany Baptist, and he became another of my mentors. Reverend Jones was tall, thin, had a big bushy Afro and a baritone voice that could break windows. I met Reverend Jones, went to Breadbasket meetings for a few weeks, even tried to get other kids to go, but grew tired of it. There was a lot going on. This was the time of the Ocean Hill–Brownsville fight over local control of the schools, there were boycotts and marches and demonstrations. To be truthful, Breadbasket seemed a little tame.

When we moved to Lenox Road, I changed to a Brooklyn public school, Somers Junior High, P.S. 252. My mother became a domestic worker, a maid in Greenwich Village, and every morning I would walk her to the subway. Even then, after the huge reversal we had suffered, she would constantly lecture me about how I could still achieve anything I wanted, saying it didn't matter where you were from but where you were going.

We lived on the corner of Lenox Road and East 96th Street, in a forty-family building. The junior high was close, up the block and across the street. I remember that as a very active time. I was involved in a lot of activities, the Oratorical Society and the Social Action Club, and I had a lot of friends. The school was integrated. I had a friend named Shelly Gannon, a Jewish girl. We were very close. That was the closest I ever came to dating someone white, but it never got that far. I had another friend, Stephen Zuckerman. I used to go to his house, he would come to mine, I called him Zucky.

My two best friends were a white kid named Richard Farkas and a black kid named Dennis Neal. All three of us were very political, and we used to have nicknames: Dennis was "Stokely Carmichael," because he was into black power and against nonviolence, I was "Adam" because of Congressman Powell and my love for him, and Richard was "Bobby Kennedy," because RFK was his hero.

Then Dr. King was killed. We were watching television that Thursday night when it came across the screen that he had been shot in Memphis. My mother started crying. I didn't understand why she was so upset, crying like he was a member of our family. I'd met Dr. King and admired him, but I didn't feel the personal connection. I asked my mother why she was taking it so hard, and she said that I would have had to grow up in Alabama, have had to spend my life going to the back of the bus, have had to travel miles holding my water when I needed a rest room while passing facilities I was forbidden to use, if I wanted to understand the meaning and importance of Martin Luther King. That has always stayed with me.

A few days later we had a memorial for Dr. King at school, and I was chosen to read the "I Have a Dream" speech. This led to a conflict with one of my teachers, Miss Barber, who wanted me to read it very straight and plain, what I would call "white" style, while I was trying to put some spin on it, do it "preacher" style, because I thought I understood it and knew what I was doing. The other kids agreed with me. It was a huge dispute. I gave in and rehearsed it the way she wanted, but when the day came, I got up, left the text on my chair, and recited it from memory, my way. I knew she was going to be furious. When I finished the last lines, I looked over in the wings where she was, and she was standing there with tears running down her face. Everybody was crying. Later, she hugged me.

Most of my social life in junior high was in the church. I was starting to get interested in girls, but most of the girls I got to know well were church girls. That's where I spent my time. Shelly and I were close, and there were some other girls in school that I knew and liked, but the girls I would call "girlfriends" were at Washington Temple. In fact, I dated Bishop Washington's daughter, Frederica, for a while, and I had another girlfriend, Marsha Tinsley, whom I saw for a while when I was a teenager. She became a gifted recording artist (signed to RCA), and we were later married very briefly, a marriage that didn't last, I think, because I was not ready for the responsibilities of being a husband.

III.

About six months after Martin Luther King's death, a film came out called *King: A Filmed Record . . . Montgomery to Memphis*. There was a song on the sound track by Nina Simone, the refrain of which was "What are you gonna do now that the king of love is dead?" I began to hear that song as a challenge. I felt guilty, like I had let Dr. King down, that I wasn't doing my part. So I went back to Operation Breadbasket, and I asked Reverend Jones if I could organize a youth division, and he said he'd been hoping I would want to do that. He made me youth director, in early 1969.

A couple of months later, the national director of Breadbasket came to New York and we had a rally at Friendship Baptist before cutting the ribbon on our new office on Fulton Street. I had read about the national director in magazines and seen him on television, and I liked his style. He was young, brash, had a huge Afro, and wore a medallion. I started wearing a medallion to emulate him. His name was Jesse Jackson.

I met him in the back office of Friendship, where he was talking with all the New York leaders of Breadbasket. Reverend Jones brought me in and said, "Reverend Jesse"—no one called him Reverend Jackson in those days—"this is Alfred Sharpton. He is going to be the youth director, and we'd like you to give him some advice."

Jesse didn't really look at me, he actually kind of looked past me, but he said, "All you got to do is choose your targets and kick ass." That's the first thing he said to me. And we had the rally and cut the ribbon, and in the middle of all of it, Mahalia Jackson came and joined the festivities, and when she saw me she grinned, pointed at me, and said very warmly, "There's my little boy preacher," and as a result of that they let me speak. She knew Jesse from Chicago, and that kind of broke the ice between us.

From that night Jesse and I became tight. Jesse started telling me, "Don't let these old guys use you, stay in school, don't be nobody's parrot." He was very hard on me about that. Bishop Washington was concerned about me at this time—I think he saw me getting involved in "the world," and there were a lot of things in the air at the time, the Black Panthers, student protest, drugs—and I think he was worried about me falling in with the wrong crowd. I think he was encouraging people to bring me into Breadbasket because at least those ministers were serious and working on civil rights, and would look out for me as he had. The Pentecostals stayed out of politics; I think they felt it was better to help black people on a personal, spiritual-strength basis. I think their comfort zone was in their faith and religious practice. Civil rights activists tend not to come out of that zone. And I think they doubted as to whether they could handle the political powers-that-be of that time.

Washington Temple was, by this time, one of the largest churches in Brooklyn, but the Methodists and Baptists looked down on Pentecostals. As ministers, we were considered to be "jacklegs"—improvisers—while they were elite seminarians. But I was mesmerized by Reverend Jones. He was so well educated, and he could just fling around these polysyllabic words, but he would also take seriously and talk with a street kid who couldn't spell.

One of the first times I heard him speak, he said America was suffering from "a faulty theology emanating from a sick sociology based in a false anthropology." I said, "This guy's it." The only other person I had ever heard with that command of the English language was Dr. King. I also began to learn about academic theology from Reverend Jones. Liberation theology, Karl Barth, Paolo Freire, Walter Rauschenbusch. I'm fourteen and I'm reading this stuff because I'm around these big Baptist preachers. And I knew from reading and talking with Reverend Jones that Dr. King had been strongly influenced by, for example, Rauschenbusch and the Social Gospel, so that gave me even more incentive to get involved in the movement.

By then, it was known that I—though a teenager—could reach people and get out the youth. When we did a protest, the adult leaders never had to worry about the picket line. I'd have hundreds of kids at the site, marching. I knew how to talk to them, get them to come out. If Bill Jones said we're hitting A&P, I'd say "What time?" and have the people there.

The first battle we had was Robert Hall. It was a clothing store that sold principally to blacks, but there were no blacks on the board and no blacks got service contracts. We called a boycott. We wanted the contracts, we wanted summer jobs for inner-city kids, we wanted training programs. We won, because we were able to hurt their business. They had to begin taking black customers seriously. It set the stage for some incredible things.

In 1968, as I was entering my freshman year in high school, black community leaders in Brooklyn called a school strike. This was the famous Ocean Hill–Brownsville dispute, when black parents and teachers fought the United Federation of Teachers over ultimate control of neighborhood schools. The word being thrown around at the time was "decentralization," meaning that local school boards would run things. The UFT didn't want their teachers to have to submit to that regimen, and the conflict took on racial overtones, because most of the UFT teachers were white and Jewish, and the local people were black. The UFT, led by Albert Shanker, made insinuations that the blacks were anti-Semitic (a very early instance of that charge), while the blacks wondered if the Jewish teachers thought they were too good to be under black authority. I marched in the picket lines for community control along with many of my friends.

When school finally started, I joined the debating team, the Afro-American Club, and I was the co-editor of a school newspaper we called *Gadfly*. I also joined a group of students called the Panel of Americans—all the different ethnic groups were represented, Jews, blacks, Latinos, Asians—that went around to different schools encouraging racial harmony. This was the first time I'd experienced so many kinds of people. We went to all the neighborhoods, all-white schools, all-Hispanic schools, all-Asian schools, all over the city. I was very busy at this time, because I was working at Breadbasket a lot, and I was still preaching every weekend. And I had a lot of girlfriends.

The school control strike had galvanized us, the students, to an extraordinary degree. You'd probably say it radicalized us, but that was the mood of much of the country then. If we went down to the cafeteria at Tilden and we didn't like the food that day, we'd call a strike and close down the whole school. We hated the dress code—you couldn't wear jeans, you had to wear a shirt with a collar. We wanted to wear shorts, jeans, dashikis, kufis. We had strikes and demonstrations and we won.

I was one of the ringleaders, and it got so bad that the principal, Joseph Shapiro, would call my mother before school and ask, "How's Alfred doing this morning? I need to know how many problems we're going to have at school today." I was learning how to confront the system.

There were a couple of teachers who really helped me at Tilden. Gertrude Cromwell was one of two black teachers at the school, a home economics instructor, and she was like a second mother to half the kids there, and she would always say to me, "Alfred, you've got to spend *some* time studying and doing homework." She was looking out for me, but what she didn't know was that I was studying very hard, thanks to another teacher, Elliot Salow, a white teacher who ended up being in charge of social studies for the entire Board of Education. He spent a lot of time with me, he gave me books, and I'd study Marxism, Socialism, Mao Tse-tung, things like that. I even went through a little Mao phase, wearing a red button and carrying the Little Red Book around with me. I learned everything there was to learn about leftist politics from Mr. Salow.

One other thing that really sticks out in my mind about Tilden is the policeman who used to stand in front, guarding the door. He was Italian, his name was Ralph, and he was the nicest guy in the world. He always spoke to us, talked to us, he'd advise us about our girlfriends and other things, he really cared about the kids in that school. I've never forgotten him, or his kindness at that very difficult time. He always looked at each individual person and tried to treat him or her as a human being, which few people did, then and now, and at a time of significant racial tension in the neighborhoods, this contributed mightily to smoothing day-to-day life at school.

During the sixties New York City didn't suffer any of the riots that ravaged Los Angeles, Newark, Chicago, Detroit, and other places, but the institutional racism in New York was as bad as or worse than anywhere else in the country. The Ocean Hill–Brownsville fight, the viciousness of it and the way it got personal, was an indication of that. Blacks in New York City had only one leader with any political power or vision, Adam Clayton Powell, and we had *no* economic power or stability. We had to be careful, and fearful. There were entire areas of the city you didn't go to if you were black: Canarsie, Howard Beach, Bensonhurst.

In response to these historical realities, many of the young blacks in the city moved toward black nationalist politics and black power views and conceptions of the United States and the world. During this time was the first phase of the Afrocentric movement, in clothes and hairstyles, as blacks were beginning to try defining themselves and their images, and trying, as well, to relate to being black and the fact of blackness in more positive fashion. For centuries blacks had been caught in various negative self-images and media portrayals: Buckwheat, Stepin Fetchit, and Amos 'n' Andy and the like. The generation that came of age after World War II was better educated and thus more aware of how these things worked. Afrocentricity, Pan-Africanism, and the Black Arts Movement were all responses to this new consciousness.

Nationwide, blacks were starting to move toward power. Carl Stokes had been elected mayor of Cleveland, and Richard Hatcher took over in Gary, Indiana. In Chicago, Jesse Jackson was building Operation PUSH, one of the organizations that helped create the climate that led to the election of Harold Washington. But there was nothing comparable happening in New York, no one was able to build an identifiable presence through the civil rights model. Rallies and marches didn't really work there because the city was so

My parents, Alfred Charles
Sharpton, Sr., and Ada Richards.
(Photo courtesy of Pope Studio)

With my sister
Cheryl—I'm four
years old.
*(Photo courtesy of Pope
Studio)*

Eight years old and preaching at Washington Temple in Brooklyn.
(Photo courtesy of Bert Smith)

One of my first attempts at grassroots organizing—here I am with members of the
National Youth Movement. *(Photo courtesy of Darrell Ellis Fleming)*

What a hippie—sixteen years old and reading Allen Ginsberg.
(Photo courtesy of Chris Ross, The News)

Kathy and I at Caesars Palace in Las Vegas, 1980.

In honor of Martin Luther King, Jr.'s, birthday, James Brown and I are invited to the White House, 1981. *(Photo courtesy of the White House)*

Michael Jackson gives something back to the community—the Pride Patrol, part of his 1984 Victory tour. *(Photo courtesy of Lawrence Harvey)*

Some members of the
National Youth
Movement Choir, 1985.
*(Photo courtesy of Lawrence
Harvey)*

With Kathy in a
prayer vigil against
police brutality,
Newark, 1986. *(Photo
courtesy of Lawrence
Harvey)*

With no blacks serving
on the board of the
Metropolitan Transit
Authority, I started to
lead protests by sitting
down on the tracks at
Grand Central during
morning rush hour, 1986.
*(Photo courtesy of Mike
Lima, the* New York
Tribune*)*

Responding to our protests, Governor Cuomo did appoint a black to the board of the MTA. Here we are at the press conference, 1986. *(Photo courtesy of Anthony Charles)*

With Tawana Brawley's family, 1986. The family took sanctuary in Bethany Baptist Church in order to avoid a subpoena to appear before what we felt was a rigged grand jury. *(Photo courtesy of Anthony Charles)*

Football great Earl Campbell, James Brown, and I, 1988.

Arrested in 1990—a very familiar pose for me. *(Photo courtesy of Anthony Charles)*

Very scary—a friend of mine happened to be snapping pictures during my stabbing in 1991. *(Photo courtesy of Anthony Charles)*

big and the media were so mammoth. You could have a march, or an ongoing protest, out in Jamaica, Queens, and the people in East New York, Brooklyn, would never hear of you.

I sometimes speculate that part of the media game *was* to keep it spread out, to keep people out of the media, because that kept blacks from organizing a mass movement that might have eventually totaled 6 to 8 million people and been unstoppably effective. Added to all this was that black people in New York City were frustrated and angry because they knew they were disconnected and disorganized. They'd see what was happening in Alabama and Mississippi, all the civil rights activity and social change, and wonder why progress couldn't happen in New York.

The Civil Rights Movement never came to New York. The closest we had to a movement was one man, Powell, and then the school board activity of the late sixties, but there was never a real, true confrontation with the status quo in New York. White liberals got away with donating to the southern movement, sending money and food and clothes and reporters, but at the same time they were reinforcing their own racial double standards in New York. These people, the powers-that-be in New York, needed to be challenged for giving $50,000 to the NAACP or $10,000 to Martin Luther King and portraying and celebrating each other as progressives and humanitarians, while they themselves lived in ruthlessly segregated neighborhoods, their children went to segregated schools and universities, and they ran segregated school systems. In short, their lives were monuments to institutional racism. And this was the liberal, northern establishment.

New York is perhaps the most racist city in the country. This is important because the people holding power there, that northern liberal establishment, are the most powerful whites in the world. New York City is Wall Street, it's the TV networks, it's Broadway and all the other entertainment industries. This is the center of the world. We're not talking about some redneck whites down in Mississippi or Louisiana; the New York power structure shapes public opinion the world over. The *New York Times, Time, Newsweek,* CBS, NBC, ABC. I think that's why I became such a pariah for a while. At Howard Beach, in Bensonhurst, in the Days of Rage, all over, I was ripping the veil of progressiveness off New York and exposing all this evil in these powerful people's backyard. It's one thing to fly down to Mississippi and ride around and say, "Look at all this white trash mistreating black people." It's another for me to stand on Fifth Avenue in front of some rich man's house and for him to have the police and security roust me while he's thinking "Nigger, go home." New York has never, to this day, been exposed for what it is.

What really surprised me as I moved forward in my life was that there was as much, if not more, racism among the liberal Left as with conservatives or moderates. The left-wing whites demand the right to choose who the black heroes will be. Think of how so-called revolutionaries are created. Whites make these people poster heroes, not blacks. They don't speak for blacks, because black folks were never with them. *The Village Voice* is as paternalistic as the *New York Times.* They both have their visions of what black leadership should be, try to build it up, and none of it emanates from the black community.

The reason I never fell into any of this is simple: I preached, and still preach, to hundreds, sometimes thousands, of black people each and every week. I have always known the difference between the media polls and what black people were really thinking and talking about. So while my high school and college friends were running off and joining ideological groups that weren't going any-where, I was preaching to a thousand people at Washington Tem-ple, another thousand at Bethany, or spending a Sunday going from storefront to storefront in Harlem or on Long Island. Some of these friends called me a counterrevolutionary because I disagreed with some of their more outlandish plots and schemes, but I couldn't be fooled as to what everyday black folks would go for and what they were thinking, because I was out there talking to them. I know what they respond to. When I'm giving my sermon, that's my job.

I never lost that. That's why I never stopped my weekly rally. Meeting with three or four hundred average, working black folks—secretaries, teachers, postal workers, janitors, truck drivers—gives you a reality check. Those people don't want to hear "pie in the sky, by and by." And the unsaid thing about many of those black so-called revolutionaries is that they were as addicted to pie in the sky as the loudest holy roller at Washington Temple. They're all waiting for someone to come and do something for them. The holy rollers are waiting on the Lord, the revolutionaries on the revolution. For both it's an excuse to not do anything themselves. I realized at a young age that *we* are supposed to enact the Messiah's wishes, *we* are supposed to make the revolution, the New Jerusalem. I received a lot of guidance in this from Dwight McKee, the youth director of Operation Breadbasket in Chicago, and the best civil rights strategist I've known. That's why I was successful later, and why whites couldn't comprehend my success: I was closer to the *black* mainstream, that person riding the bus or the subway.

That's why I always had the upper hand on the white media. I knew the people, and the people knew me. It took until the early nineties before anyone white would admit I had a following, but one of the things that kept me going during the Brawley case was that I knew that a lot of black people were behind me, that I was saying what they wanted said. They may not have had the nerve to say it themselves—they had to be concerned for their jobs and families—but they wanted it said. The reason I knew this was that they would say it to me.

When I was working with Operation Breadbasket as a teenager, the biggest confrontation we had was with the grocery chain A&P. The largest company we targeted, they had stores ev-

erywhere in the metropolitan area. They had unfair hiring practices—we wanted more people from the neighborhoods where the
stores were located—and were shortchanging the inner-city stores
on cleanliness and quality. I remember one day we were picketing
the A&P in White Plains, yelling "Boycott A&P!" "Unfair practices!"
and things like that when I looked over toward the parking lot and
this white lady was coming toward me with a shopping cart. She
leaned into the cart and shoved it straight into my stomach. I can't
describe how much it hurt.

But that was pretty much the reaction to what we were trying to
do. We couldn't get anywhere. William J. Kane, who was the president of A&P at that time, refused to meet with the ministers who
were the local leaders of Operation Breadbasket. Jesse Jackson came
in, then Ralph Abernathy of the Southern Christian Leadership
Conference, and Kane refused to meet with *them*. Reverend Jones
and the others decided they had to turn up the heat, escalate the
attack. We went to 420 Lexington Avenue, A&P national corporate
headquarters, at closing time, and walked right past a receptionist
into William Kane's office and said we weren't leaving until we had a
meeting. A&P called security, and then the police, but we just sat
there singing "We Shall Overcome" and "Come by Here, Lord," and
all the other freedom songs. Six o'clock came and went with no
meeting, or even the promise of one, then seven, eight, and finally
it's nine o'clock. We figure out that they're not going to have us
arrested, but they're not going to meet either. They're going to wait
us out. So all the ministers start taking off their jackets and loosen-
ing their ties, preparing to spend the night right there in the executive office of A&P.

We knew that Kane lived in New Jersey, so I called directory
assistance for the town he lived in. He was listed! I got his home
phone number and called him. I said, "Mr. Kane?" and he said, "Yes?"
and I said, "My name is Rev. Alfred Sharpton, and I'm a young

minister, and right this minute I'm sitting at your desk. I want to know why you won't meet with Reverend Jones and Operation Breadbasket and the other leaders of our community." He went off. "The nerve of you!" he screamed. "You call yourselves ministers!" He lectured me about destroying other people's property, how we should be ashamed of ourselves, etc., and I just kept responding with the entire SCLC line about equity and opportunity and progress through shared business and how you have to give something back, and he finally just hung up. And I see Jones and them laughing, they say, "That Sharpton has too much nerve for his own good." And they didn't believe that I called him. They thought he had called us.

So we spent the night. We had a time, singing and talking, and something happened that I'll never forget. Sometimes when I hear people talking about white folks and hate, I remember this. A white guard, part of A&P's security force, came over to me about midnight and said, "Aren't you gonna go home, kid?" And I said, "No, I'm going to stick it out." He said, "Have you had anything to eat?" I said I hadn't. He said, "Don't you want something?" I said, "I can't leave the ministers." He said, "No, I'll go get you something. I respect you men and what you're doing." He ran out and got me a couple of hamburgers. He was about sixty years old, and when he handed them to me, he said, "I hope my grandchildren believe in something like you do one day."

The next day the press started coming. About three o'clock that afternoon A&P decided that they'd had enough, and asked the police to arrest us. Reverend Jones and everybody got up off the floor and assembled around the reception desk to wait for the police to decide what they were going to do, and I saw the white guard from the night before ask the police not to arrest "the kid"—me. Then Reverend Jones's brother, who was a lawyer, came and said there was a danger of Reverend Jones being charged with contributing to the delinquency of a minor if I was taken into custody. So they decided I wouldn't be arrested and the white guard pulled me over and had me stand by him.

They put all thirty-two preachers in jail, where they had to spend the night, and though I wasn't "in jail," I wanted to stay there with them. So I called my mother and told her where I was, and lay down on the floor and went to sleep. The secretary of Breadbasket had come to the jail to help out, and about two o'clock in the morning the phone rings and the secretary comes in to the holding cell and says, "Reverend Sharpton, someone wants to talk to you." I got up and answered the phone, and a voice said, "Young buck, give me a report, tell me what happened." I said, "Who is this?" He said, "This is Reverend Jackson." I jumped for joy. I said, "Jesse?" This was the first time he had called me, I couldn't believe Jesse Jackson wanted to talk to *me*. I felt like I had arrived. I told him what had happened, and he said, "Can you get the youth together for tomorrow, and some of the preachers?" I said I thought I could. He said, "I'm flying in tomorrow, and we're going back to A&P."

This is when I began to understand that Jesse was a very sharp strategist. With Reverend Jones and the others in jail he felt it was imperative that we send a second wave, and that he get arrested. We went back to 420 Lexington and got in the elevators to go up to A&P, but they didn't work. A&P had cut them off. Jesse pulled us all off the elevators and down one of the corridors. He told me to call a "meeting," a press conference, and, sure enough, camera crews started coming. Jesse took us back to the elevators, we sat down inside them, and after a while the police started arresting everyone, including Jesse (the police told the teenagers to step aside and refused to arrest us). His plan had worked. It went out over all the wires, all the news, that Jesse Jackson had been arrested. That finally got A&P to negotiate.

Right after that, Ralph Abernathy came to town. He led a march on Wall Street, and we combined it with the A&P conflict, talking about corporate greed, irresponsibility, and how the blood of poor people was being sucked dry by the powers-that-be. Except for some hard hats throwing bricks down on us from a high-rise they were building—the World Trade Center—the march went off well, but that night at a meeting I saw for the first time some of the personal tensions that would eventually undermine the Civil Rights Movement. Reverend Abernathy was there, along with Hosea Williams, and Williams says that he wants to know why the New York ministers aren't working with their "white allies" in the Village. Hosea had disrupted mass at Saint Patrick's Cathedral the week before, and all the Catholic priests who had been coming to Breadbasket stopped. Another minister accused Hosea of disrupting the movement, and they actually came to blows. This was the nonviolent SCLC, Martin Luther King's organization.

The real conflict was between Abernathy and Jesse. People were accusing Jesse of insubordination, and it slowly became clear there was going to be a split. If there was a division, I knew which side I was on. When the breakup came and Jesse formed PUSH, I left as well and formed the National Youth Movement. With Jesse's departure from SCLC and Operation Breadbasket, they lost a lot of energy and youth appeal and that killed the organization.

Twenty-five years later, Jesse Jackson is the only one of those men still on the stage, so I guess it was the right move. He went on to bigger and better things. Jesse took a lot from those people, they were trying to break him. Abernathy was jealous of Jesse's star power and didn't want him around. They suspended him from SCLC for no reason. They worked at openly humiliating him. There's a lot of human drama that goes on behind closed doors in the ministry. Ego, envy, somebody's wife telling him, "Don't take that," or his children saying, "Why is he on the cover of *Jet* and not you, Daddy?" Abernathy and the others knew they didn't have the people with them, and Jesse did. You can't have ten chiefs, there has to be only one chief to lead the tribe. Abernathy was only there because he was Martin's friend, he never caught on with black people. Abernathy was well regarded by fellow clergymen, he could lead ministers, but the vast majority of ordinary black America never saw him as their leader. History has proven how they saw Jesse.

The idea behind my organization, the National Youth Movement, was that we were going to do a youth version of what Operation Breadbasket was trying to do. We were going to go after major corporations with young people and get economic concessions. We were going to go after thousands of new voters, particularly young people, since they'd just given eighteen-year-olds the vote. I went to Bayard Rustin and told him what I wanted to do, and he donated the first five hundred dollars toward our organizing. I went and got all these black establishment types, including David Dinkins and Percy Sutton, to help us put it together and be on the board. Dinkins was the lawyer who drew up the charter. It's ironic in retrospect. We young people thought of ourselves as so radical, but there we were working with those guys, as button-down and establishment as they come.

We marched on corporations and hospitals, trying to get them to be more socially aware and concerned. One of our biggest early activities involved the killing of Claude Reese, a nineteen-year-old from Brooklyn. The police shot him in the back. We had many demonstrations behind that. I also at that time began to understand that the black nationalist movement suffered from the same sorts of divisions and jealousies that the civil rights groups did. When Amiri Baraka came over from New Jersey to support us in the Reese case, the Brooklyn black nationalists got angry and said, "This is our territory." I didn't see what any of that had to do with Claude Reese.

The National Youth Movement has received a lot of criticism

over the years, including the charge that we were used by Percy Sutton and others to help their business activities or that we didn't sustain anything of permanence. I never had a problem with people "using" me, only with them misusing me. I think that the older black businessmen did gain some advantages—we helped them leverage contracts and such—and I think that some of them were cynical in that use. But my goal was to be used, to help expand black business, and that is what we did. I wanted to help make black business powerful. So if we went to Macy's and picketed and got some contracts, or helped establish Inner City Broadcasting, well, that's what we set out to do. Where I would criticize those older men is that they might have then done more to help young people. The exception to this was and is Percy Sutton, who, simply put, has been there to help every time I've asked, since I was a teenager.

The National Youth Movement provided a lot of troops to several important causes, but we all got older and went on to other things. We need to institutionalize these organizations, build structures that allow the movement to pass on to the next group. I'm trying to do some of those things now. In the NYM, when we got into our late twenties, we didn't want to be youth anymore, we wanted other things. But we didn't train our replacements, and that was a mistake.

What I learned through all of that activity was that people are people, they are human and fallible, and you have to account for that. You've got to deal realistically with the personal insecurities and egos of everyone involved. I had to be aware of that later in life, and I was more prepared, because I had seen it with Adam Clayton Powell and Jesse Jackson and others. I was expecting it. A lot of people act like they have political differences, but it's not political at all, it's personal. It's envy, jealousy, it's a desire to be the one in the spotlight. It can be extraordinarily frustrating, because you have to contend with political issues and problems and these personal hang-ups simultaneously, and it's like walking a tightrope.

History doesn't record the personal beefs, it records the public outcomes, and sometimes events that seem to involve heavy theoretical, philosophical, and ideological arguments really boil down to personal animosity based on something that happened somewhere and that has nothing to do with all those heavy things. We don't want to think that men and women who appear to be giants could be so petty, but they are.

In the early seventies we were trying to challenge the corporate structure of America, and company by company make them put money in black communities, give blacks franchises, give jobs that could support black families, get blacks on the board, get blacks millions in contracts. We were winning more than we lost, and we blew it fighting over personal issues. But that's how it was. And I've seen it again and again in my career.

But the other thing I learned was *persistence.* The most important thing to do, *no matter what,* is persist. Had I not learned that at an early age, from watching that stage of the Civil Rights Movement, I couldn't have handled what happened to me later. I would have never survived Howard Beach, Brawley, or Bensonhurst. I have a saying now, "When God made me, he forgot to put reverse in the motor." I don't back up. Whatever comes, I'm going forward. No matter what the confusion, the accusation, keep focused.

We used to sing a song in the movement, "Keep your eyes on the prize and hold on." I used to combine that with an old hymn in church about how sometimes you've got to walk by faith if you can't walk by sight. Even if you don't know where you're going, you hold on and keep moving ahead. It will clear up after a while.

IV.

I graduated from high school in 1972, receiving the Community Service Award at commencement from the same principal who had considered me a trouble-maker. Before he handed me the award, he said, "I never in all my years as principal have been so glad to give a student his diploma." Everyone laughed, including me. Then he hugged me. I was also upset because I saw that all my friends' families were there, and I didn't know where my father was. I hadn't heard from him in years.

My mother was upset that I was upset. She said, "Boy, I scrubbed floors to see you graduate high school and get you accepted to Brooklyn College. When they call your name and you walk across that stage, if you don't smile for nobody but me, you smile, because I fought to see this day." I remember that. When they called my name, I

looked out at my mother and smiled, because I was the first one in
my immediate family to get a high school diploma.

This was 1972, and in the fall I went to Brooklyn College. I was,
of course, also the first in the family to go to a university. At this
time I was still going around preaching every Sunday, and at home
it was just my mother and I. I entered the Brooklyn College School
of Contemporary Studies at what was then a new campus in downtown Brooklyn, and I majored in contemporary politics. There were
some outstanding teachers there, and I enjoyed myself, but looking
back I now see my course of study was a mistake; I should have
studied something I didn't know, something that would have made
me push my thinking, maybe even something scientific like biology
or math. Much of what we studied I knew better than the teachers,
because I had been out there on the front lines doing it, and I knew
personally many of the people we were talking about. This caused
me to get bored, and I dropped out after two years. But I liked
college, I really, really enjoyed myself. I was active in the Black
Student Union and on the debate team, where I think I sharpened
my skills. I've never feared debate, and Brooklyn College only
sharpened those skills. I love the back-and-forth. And it's strange: to
this day, I still get nervous, butterflies in my stomach, before I
preach, but never before a debate in any kind of political situation.

Even though I dropped out of college, I was still growing intel-
lectually. I saw Jesse Jackson reading *Love, Power and Justice*, by Paul
Tillich, and so I went out and bought all of Tillich's books, *The
History of Religions*, all the ontology, everything I could find. I was
imitating my mentor, but also expanding myself as a person. It was
the same as when I read about Adam Clayton Powell and found
Marcus Garvey. I was a young Pentecostal preacher, how would I
have heard of Marcus Garvey? That's why it is so important whom
you choose as your mentor; their heroes become your heroes, their
ideological bent becomes of serious interest to you. That's what
happened to me. Because of Jesse, and Reverend Jones and others, I

started reading Walter Rauschenbusch and Paul Tillich and Harvey Cox and others. And I tried to use it. I was going around to these storefront churches preaching and trying to incorporate the most current contemporary theology.

In 1975 I started running around the country trying to start up National Youth Movement chapters. This also hardened me against school, because I was telling myself that I didn't need school, I'm building a national organization, I know all these heavy hitters, what do I need a degree for? I'm saying this to make clear one of my profoundest regrets: *I should have stayed.* I think one of the reasons I read so much is to try and compensate for that loss. And I must say, at the time the only people who really, really leaned on me to stay in college were my mother and Jesse Jackson. I'd be around Jesse and he'd get very sarcastic, saying things like, "Here come the boy wonder, ain't gonna be nothing but a Harlem fanatic." At the time I resented it, but now I know he realized what I would need for the long run. I thought he was trying to stifle me, that all the people applauding were the ones who cared. But it was the opposite, wasn't it? He never gave me undue credit; with him I had to earn everything twice, which is what any young person needs.

When I look back upon the men I was able to get to know when I was young, it astounds me whom I had access to and how good they were to me. In Bishop Washington, Adam Clayton Powell, and Jesse Jackson I could watch some of the greatest black leaders of our time very closely and learn from them.

When I was growing up in Hollis, Queens, in the late fifties and early sixties, I was aware of another, quite different but equally great, black man, the legendary rhythm-and-blues singer James Brown. He lived in the same neighborhood as we did, and by then he had become the number one black artist in the country, both on the charts and by popular acclamation. The kids in Hollis knew who he was, of course, and we would go and stand by the gate to his big house—it actually looked like a castle—and sometimes he'd come out and talk to us and sign a few autographs, and tell us stuff like "Stay in school," "Don't do drugs," "Be proud of being black," things like that. So I'd met him a few times before I got to know him seriously.

In 1973 we were trying to raise money for the National Youth Movement, and James Brown heard about it, and called a disc jockey I knew and offered to help us by doing a benefit. James had heard about me. He knew I was a preacher and an activist. James thought I was his kind of guy, and he had me brought to a concert in Newark to meet him. They took us backstage. I was awed. When I was a kid, I thought that when I'd seen Adam Clayton Powell I'd seen God, but after I saw James Brown I *knew* I'd seen God.

Right as we shook hands, he went into this overpowering monologue. "Young man," he said, "I understand you've got a lot of authority"—he meant spiritual power—"and if you listen to me, you might become the biggest young man in the country." That's how he *started*. Then he said, "But you can't set your sights on nothing little with me, you got to go for the whole hog." I had no idea what he was talking about, but I just kept nodding and saying, "Yes, Mr. Brown, yes, sir." He was telling me all the ways he was going to help the youth group, asking me all kinds of questions, and then he starts walking out of the dressing room. I'm walking along with him, talking, nodding, not paying attention, and then I look up and he grabs a microphone and starts singing. I was out on the stage with him. The people in the audience are excited, screaming for James, and I'm standing there not knowing what to do, so I just started dancing and worked my way back to the wings. I think people thought I was part of the show.

We talked some more after the performance and kept talking the next few weeks. James had a show scheduled in Brooklyn, and he asked me if I wanted to help him. This would be a show for

NYM. Of course I said yes, and he said if I did exactly what he said, we could sell the place out. He was in a little slump right then and hadn't been selling out in New York, but I took all the money the Youth Movement had and spent it on this date, ran spots on the radio the way he told me to, hung the kind of posters he told me where he told me, just did everything exactly as he said. That night he pulled up in a limousine, and there were kids lined up blocking the street trying to buy tickets. We ended up doing two shows that night, over eight thousand people.

In between the shows James called me backstage and said that because I had followed his instructions so well he was taking me with him to California. He took me all over the country that summer. He took me on *Soul Train*. Everywhere we went we tried to promote the Youth Movement, get young people involved. We had an L.A. chapter, chapters all over the country. I'm a kid, flying around in a private plane with James Brown, the emperor of blackness. He has been the number one artist in the world and has a quarter of a million dollars in his suitcase.

I think there were any number of reasons why I was so eager to drop my life in New York and follow him, including that I wasn't exactly dropping my life, I was raising money for NYM and learning a lot about business. But I also think that I was badly in need of a father figure at that time, which he willingly provided, and that my being in his presence, strangely enough, brought me back to my best memories of my own father, when we would stand in line for hours outside the Apollo waiting to see James. Not only was James good to me and I was learning, but it enabled me to feel good about my family in a way that I hadn't previously. My father loved James Brown so much, and it was like I was living his dream.

We became very close, and in the middle of our getting to know each other well, James's son Teddy, who was a good friend of mine, was killed in a car accident. I think in his grief, James came even closer to me, and in some ways I took the place in his life that

Teddy had occupied. And I was open to this. Since the summer of
'73 we have been like father and son. Even when he was in jail in the
eighties he would call me collect from jail four or five times a week.
Sometimes he called every night. This was when things were getting very hot for me, Howard Beach, Tawana Brawley, and such,
and he would watch me on television and call me and critique my
techniques and style. "What are you doing on *Morton Downey*, that's
a circus. Be more deliberate when you're talking on camera." Things
like that.

In 1974 James says to me, "Reverend"—when he was feeling
good, he'd call me Reverend—"they won't let me play Madison
Square Garden. They say my crowd's too rowdy. I want you to go
down there and book it for the National Youth Movement. Tell
them that if they won't let you, you'll picket the Knicks games." I
did what he said, and the managers laughed and said, "Look, kid, it
costs sixty thousand dollars to rent the Garden." I said, "I didn't ask
you how much it cost. I want to rent it." They said, "All right, here's
the contract. You have two weeks to pay the first twenty thousand.
You've got to put up forty thousand two weeks after that."

James gives me a certified check for $20,000 from Polygram
Records, and I signed the contract. They wanted to know who the
artist was. I told them. They said they didn't want James Brown, but
they had the signed contract and the check and had no choice. I
told them I wanted the Fourth of July, and the management said
that was very unwise because everyone would be on vacation.

When I mentioned that to James, he just laughed and said,
"Reverend, our people don't have the money to go on vacation." We
sold out that night and had about three thousand people standing
outside trying to get in. James gave NYM 12 percent of the gross.
We walked out of there with $30,000. With my promotion cut of 10
percent of the $30,000, I went and rented four suites at the Essex
House on Central Park West and asked my mother to come and
stay with me but she wouldn't. She thought it was crazy. But I

stayed there until I spent all my money, every dime. By September 1, I was totally broke, and I caught the No. 2 train back to my mother with about five dollars in my pocket. James kept telling me, save thirty-three cents out of every dollar you make, live on thirty-three cents, and spend the rest on making more money. I never did get that down.

A short time after that, Joseph Mobutu, the president of Zaire, said the only black Americans he'd ever heard of were James Brown and Muhammad Ali. So Mobutu wanted to promote a prizefight— which became the Rumble in the Jungle between Ali and George Foreman—and he wanted James Brown to do a concert before the fight. That's how I met Don King. Don was promoting the fight, and he had to use a friend of mine to get to me so I could talk to James. King offered James $100,000, and James just laughed, saying, "Reverend, ain't no black folks got that kind of money."

But we met with Don, who was then just this wild-haired guy from Cleveland, and they cut the deal. The day James and the band are leaving we're riding to the airport, and halfway to Kennedy, James says, "Reverend, where's the money?" I said I didn't have it, that I didn't think they could give it all to us at once. James said he wasn't leaving until he was paid. He made Don King's people come up with the money, a hundred thousand, cash, and they did.

The day of the fight I get a call from James's secretary, saying, "Mr. Brown would like you to meet him at the airport." I couldn't believe it. The fight hadn't ended yet. But I went to meet James and asked him why he didn't stay and enjoy the fight and he laughed. "Reverend, how many times do I have to tell you that this is a business? I did my show, I made my money, I got things to do." And strangely enough, Mobutu put everybody connected with the show and the fight under house arrest afterward because of high hotel bills, but James was here in the States, counting his money and booking new dates. All business.

In 1980, after years of working together on and off, we were in

England, and James got this idea that he and I would do a gospel record together, which we eventually did, "God Has Smiled on Me." While we were there, James's manager, Al Gardner, had a heart attack and had to go home. James asked me to stay on the road with him and act as the manager—I was mortified, I didn't know anything about the business at that level—because he could at least trust me to collect and hold the money. People often wouldn't pay black artists in those days, and James knew I wouldn't steal from him and would do as I was told to by him.

One of the things I had to do on those English trips was to figure out how many pounds we were supposed to be paid in equivalence to the dollar figure on the contract. We were playing the Hammersmith Odeon, one of the great clubs of London, and the manager walks up and hands me the money before James goes on— our standard operating procedure—and I turn to James and say, "We've got our money," and he says, "Good, Reverend." And then I said, "Yeah, twenty thousand pounds," or whatever it was. And James said, "Pounds? Where'd you go to school at, Reverend?" I said, "Samuel Tilden High School and Brooklyn College." James said, "And where were these schools located, son?" I didn't understand what he was getting at, but I said, "New York." Then he said, "Did anyone in any of those schools say anything about 'pounds'?"

Then he said, "Reverend, they'll drop the value of that pound overnight. You go tell them I want American dollars or there will be no show tonight." That's what I tell the promoters. They say, "Are you kidding? It's ten o'clock at night. Where are we going to get fifty thousand American dollars this time of night?"

I went back and told James of this problem, but all he said was, "Reverend, one thing I'm trying to raise you on is, don't mind other folks' business. Mind your business. Your business is you want American dollars. Let them worry about how to give it to you." Then the promoters came in. James had this big red comb and he was combing his hair and looking in the mirror. James said, "Can I ask you a question?" The main promoter said, "Yes, Mr. Brown." James said, "Can you sing 'Get up on the Goodfoot'?" The promoter said, "Well, no." Then James said, "You're going to sing it tonight unless you come up with some American money." Forty minutes later they walked in with the money.

Another thing I had to do at that time was find a new background singer. I had a recommendation from one of the band members, and James okayed hiring her, said we'd audition her on the road. James never held formal auditions. You'd go onstage and sing along. If you made it through the show, you'd do another show. If you messed up, he'd fire you standing there onstage. This particular young lady, Kathy Jordan, from Niagara Falls, New York, made it, and eventually became my wife.

I don't know what happened between us, it just worked. I fell in love. And it's kept working. She's from a small town, real religious from a strong church family. She has stood by me in some very rough times, which should be obvious to any observer. She left the band after we were married to come back to New York City with me, with no security, and she never flinched through Tawana, indictments, hoaxes, and the FBI hassles. We had two little kids through all of this, and I was gone most of the time. She has been more than a wife, really; she's been my partner through everything that I've built and everything that's happened.

James Brown taught me more than anyone in the Civil Rights Movement about how to stand up, not compromise, be a man and push things as far as they can go. So in 1981 Ronald Reagan invites James to the White House to meet with George Bush, for Martin Luther King's birthday. He said he'd come, but he had to bring me. Before we go, he takes me to this lady in Georgia who does his hair and says, "I want you to do the Reverend's hair like mine, because when we go to the White House there's going to be a lot of press, and when people see him I want them to see me, like he's my son." I agreed, and she put the relaxer in my hair, then started rolling it. Halfway through, James says, "Reverend, I want you to make me one promise. I want you to wear your hair like that until I die." I said okay. Even when he was in jail and he'd call me, he'd say, "Rev, how's your hair?" And I'd say, "Just like you." People often say that wearing a process indicates self-hatred and imitates white people, but my hair has nothing to do with that; it is symbolic of my bond, very deep and intensely personal, with James Brown.

When we were in the meeting with Bush, James started speaking very strongly about how he felt things were going very wrong in the country. He kept saying, "You've got to do something," and Vice President Bush kept saying, "Tell us, Mr. Brown, tell us what to do." Finally, James points to me and says, "Reverend, you tell him." This was the first I'd heard of this, and I had to improvise a policy on the spot. But James was always doing things like that. Later, he said, "My job was to get you in there."

James took me all over the world with him. I introduced him to his present wife, just as he was responsible for me meeting mine. Pound for pound, he is the strongest, most courageous man I have ever known. Even when he was in jail, he didn't break, he didn't back down. There were many stories about him over the years of domestic violence and drug use, but all I can say is that I didn't see it. I can't say that it didn't happen, but if it did, he shielded me from it. James's father, Joe Brown, used to say that I brought out the best in James, because he wanted to live up to my admiration of him. Maybe that's true. All I know is that I've learned more about manhood, and being a man, from him than from anyone else. And he's a musical genuis. He can do every single job on one of his records, and those records are among the most influential in the history of popular music. What a man.

After working with James, we decided to focus the National Youth Movement in on the music business. There was a tremendous amount of racism in that business. Black concert promoters couldn't get major contracts. This was an issue because black artists were beginning to cross over into major venues like stadiums and arenas, but all the dates were being controlled by the Bill Grahams and the Ron Delseners. Amazing amounts of money were being made off black acts, but not by black promoters. And those black promoters, by definition, didn't have access to the top white acts. I wanted to organize the promoters, break down some of those barriers, and keep some of that money in the black community.

Also, I was beginning to understand that entertainment had an incomparable influence on young people. I thought that it could have a tremendous impact on black people as well, if they could begin to think about show *business* rather than just the show, that they should not consume entertainment, should not spend a dollar unless there is some form of return to other blacks, through black promoters, black managers, black accountants. I think that I and NYM made a significant contribution that many overlook in making the black community more aware of these issues and encouraging consumer accountability. And it worked. When I marched on Whitney Houston, five hundred young people came and stood with me. If I had marched on Merrill Lynch, it would have been me and two others. Carnegie Hall and Radio City were much more immediate to me than Wall Street. Young people don't understand those issues, and I was trying to lead a youth movement.

We had different kinds of experiences picketing and trying to gain concessions. Marvin Gaye was extraordinarily upset at us and went so far as to say publicly that we were trying to put him out of business. He never cooperated. Whitney Houston, on the other hand, was upset as well, but asked to meet with us, listened to our explanation of the issues, and agreed to begin hiring black promoters. She kept her word, and each time I've had the opportunity to see her since then she's been very respectful and cordial. She understood that we were trying to help *all* black people and that we have to stick together and pool whatever resources we have if that goal is going to be advanced.

V.

T hrough all this activity I never stopped preaching, every Sunday and sometimes during the
week. I had a traveling circuit of churches
where I regularly gave sermons that I had developed by the time I was sixteen, and was often asked to
other black churches throughout the tristate area and
sometimes beyond. I was known from my boy preacher
and Breadbasket days, and I had enough of a reputation
that I was often booked, even then, two months ahead.
Those churches knew when I preached that the church
would be full. I haven't, since I was fourteen years old,
had to call and say that I'd like to preach somewhere on
Sunday. Now, as an adult, having led the protests and run
for the Senate and such, I'm booked six months in advance and have preached at virtually every major black

church in the country. And I've been invited to Riverside, the pre-eminent white pulpit in the country.

I must say, however, that I still enjoy preaching at little store-front churches in Brooklyn or Harlem or Newark or somewhere more than those big pulpits. Those storefronts are more authentic, the people really worship. They come, as black people say, to *have church*. There's no pretense, no posturing, no competition. And to move them, you really have to reach into your heart and soul and preach, because they're so sincere themselves. For a lot of those people, church is all they have outside of work and family, and to worship with them, to preach for them, is an honor and real plea-sure for me.

I've always been more James Brown than Johnny Mathis. And the other thing is, those storefront churches keep you in shape. If I'm at the Holiness Church of Jesus Christ on Hollis Avenue in Queens, the parishioners don't care that I'm Al Sharpton, a big man on television. A lot of them are deliberately not worldly and don't watch TV. They don't really care about the paper. They want to know, "Can he preach? And if he can't, what is he doing here?" That is good for keeping your ego in proper balance. In a storefront, either you can "say it" or you can't.

There are several ways I develop a sermon. Sometimes a certain verse in the Bible, a certain passage of scripture, hits me, and from that notion I'll develop a theme that interests me. Most of my sermons are built from a text theme, and then I tell two or three stories around that theme. Then I end with some personal experi-ences that fit in with whatever I've said already. Take, for example, the 23rd Psalm, the most familiar text in the Bible, "The Lord is my shepherd; I shall not want."

I'll start out talking about how David was the reject in his own house, in his own family, how his father didn't even call David into the house when the prophet came to reveal who was to lead Israel. The prophet said bring David in, he is the new king of Israel, and anointed him. Then I'll talk about how David fought Goliath when everybody else was afraid, how the Lord protected him and was a good shepherd. The second illustrative story might be about how God sent Nathan to correct David after Bathsheba, how the Lord admonished him but also loved and forgave him. The Lord, the good shepherd, wants what is best. The third story might be about the Lord's comfort of David after his sons fought and destroyed the family. Then I'll talk about times when I was lost, or down, or discouraged, and I'll testify as to how the Lord was my shepherd, how I know that myself.

Another way I develop a sermon is what I call "being a sponge." I listen to people everywhere I go and get ideas. I could be on a plane or in the car, or listening to a tape, or the radio, and something will strike me, I'll get a thought and turn it into a sermon. That has led to some of my better sermons. There is a sermon I've preached many times involving Shadrach, Meshach, and Abednego when they were cast into the fire by Nebuchadnezzar because they wouldn't bow to his god, but the true God protected them. That came to me during my fraud trial, when an old black woman yelled through the crowd to me, "Don't bow, Sharpton, don't bow!" I got a sermon from that.

The other way I make a sermon is through sermon books. I read all the time, whatever free time I have, on airplanes, late at night, early in the morning. I read a lot of sermon books, which are collections of great sermons by important ministers, to see how it's done. I study C. L. Franklin, Gardner Taylor, Dr. King, Howard Thurman, Jesse Jackson. Sometimes I'll recast a classic sermon into my own experience.

At any given moment, I have five to ten sermons in mind. I never decide, *never*, what I'm going to preach until I'm already sitting in the pulpit. I have these various topics floating around in my head, and they'll shift and change over time and according to events. But when I go into face a congregation, I want to gain a feeling from them, try to decide who they are before I determine what I'm going to say. If I walk in and sit down and see that the audience is made up of sensitive people, sensitive in attitude and spirit, I'll know which one of those sermons to preach. A different, more lively, what we call "whooping" congregation may require a different sort of text. I try very hard to be aware of those issues. Then, right before I'm ready to speak, I may make a few notes to myself to underscore the points I want to make, but I have never, since I was eight years old, preached from a manuscript. The most I'll have is a few talking points, not even an outline. So next Sunday, if I'm preaching somewhere, and I will be, I couldn't tell you what I am going to say until I sit down in that pulpit at that church, look at the crowd, and decide, *"This* is what I think I need to preach here."

I remember the first time I was asked to preach at Adam Clayton Powell's church, Abyssinian. For all of my life, for black preachers, that has been considered the Cadillac of pulpits. I thought about that sermon obsessively. Abyssinian as a church is basically quiet, conservative, and I thought that's what I would do, but then when I got there, while I was walking in, the place broke out into spontaneous applause. I'd never seen that there. I sat down in Adam's chair and I made up my mind, I decided that I was going to whoop and holler and do what it is that I do, and by the time I was finished it felt like we were in a Pentecostal church. People were jumping and swooning, and even Rev. Calvin Butts, the pastor of Abyssinian, was standing and waving his hands. I had never seen that at Abyssinian.

The reason I did that was that I realized that what those people wanted was Al Sharpton. While I was sitting there getting ready to preach, I thought about a time I was with James Brown and he was working on the Blues Brothers movie. They asked James to sing a gospel song, and he was being all polite and everything, very proper, and John Belushi interrupted him and said, "Mr. Brown, with all due respect, we want you to put your soul into it, we want the screams, the wow. We want *James Brown.* If we had wanted Frank

Sinatra, we would have booked him." That's what I realized at Abyssinian. If they wanted Cornel West, they would have asked him. They wanted Al Sharpton. So I'm trying to be there, be *me*, whatever the church. At some white churches I may not go into the full singsong or whoop, because you need the full call-and-response from the audience to maintain the rhythm, and whites are not trained in that "amen" pattern the way blacks are. Middle-class black churches may downplay it, but they know it. You can bring it out. But even at a white church I treat it as the same service, the same Christians, the same fire, because if they don't want Al Sharpton, they shouldn't have asked him to come preach.

I am most comfortable, of anywhere else in the world, in the pulpit. Most people think I'm most at home on television or leading a protest march or something, but that's not so; there is something for me about standing behind a pulpit on Sunday morning with a robe on, in front of a congregation, talking about faith and over-coming the odds, overcoming any obstacle, that gives me the most contentment that I've known in my life. No politics, no racism, just straight-up "God will make a way for you." If God said to me today, "Al, I'm taking you tomorrow at noon, but you can do whatever you want from eleven-thirty until twelve," I would ask for a church of about three hundred people and preach my way into the hereafter.

In the early eighties I began to look more seriously into the music business. I was growing increasingly aware of how black people are exploited in entertainment, and I wanted to learn more. The music business is an extremely dirty endeavor, because it is a cash business and it is a street business. Most of the talent is uneducated, unsophisticated, and just off the street. The gray-flannel guys feel those people are beneath them. So the business is overrun by hus-tlers, con artists, black and white, who go into these clubs and bars and churches and find the talent. Music is a street business, and that's where organized crime is, on the street, on the ground. So it's very dangerous to young people. Intimidation is used, people's money is just taken. We know all the stories of musicians who worked all their lives for nothing and died broke. With NYM we tried to get training programs, profit sharing, community purchasing, things like that, from the big record companies, with very little help. We tried to boycott companies and artists, we went up against stone gangsters, with no help. I have often wondered why law enforcement, the FBI, haven't been interested in cleaning it up.

Spring Records, which was owned by two brothers, Julie and Roy Rifkind, was located at 161 West 54th Street. It was a small, inconsequential company, but they had cut a very big deal in the seventies when they helped set up James Brown with a worldwide deal at Polygram. There was a man who worked for them named Joe Medlin who had been a singer in the fifties and then became one of the first blacks to work in the business in an executive capacity. He and I became close, he was sort of another mentor to me. They'd let me use office space at Spring from time to time, as a donation to the community, and they'd introduce me to other people in the business and encourage them to help me, do events with me, and such. The people at Spring would also buy tickets to NYM events I was sponsoring.

Across the hall from Spring Records, a theatrical booking agent named Benny Cohen had an office, and he pulled me aside one day and said that the city was getting ready to begin giving contracts for private garbage collection, and why didn't I form a black company to claim some of the set-aside contracts? I thought it was interesting because the garbage business in New York City is extremely lucrative. He said that he could arrange for me to buy a company that was already into Consolidated Edison, already had the contract. When we began negotiations with Con Ed about assuming the contracts and how all that would be executed, their attorneys warned us of the mob connection and that our silent partner would be Matty "the Horse" Ianniello, and how it was all a Mafia ploy to maintain absolute control of garbage collection, and we backed off.

Then Julie Rifkind said he wanted me to meet a friend of his who was a filmmaker, Michael Franzese. This Franzese wanted to meet Don King. They knew that I knew Don and might be able to get him in. They had an investor, they said, who wanted to back Don and put on fights. But Don wouldn't return their phone calls. I set up a meeting with Don the next Wednesday and met with Franzese and his investor at the Atrium Club on the Tuesday before. They told me what kinds of projects they wanted to do, and they said that they would donate part of the profits to NYM. We met the next day at Don's office, but Don wouldn't let the investor in the meeting. It turned out that the investor, Victor Quintana, was an FBI agent, running a sting operation, and his partner, Reggie Barrett, was an ex-con let out of prison to set up this sting on Don King.

There was another time when I was talking on and off with Danny Pagano, of Third World Records, about getting more seriously into the music business. There were rumors that Pagano was mobbed up, but it wasn't proven. One day we were sitting in his office and another "investor" who had approached me about the music business came in, but he only wanted to talk about drugs. Pagano said, "I don't know what *your* thing is, but we're not into that shit," and we got up and left. An FBI tape of that meeting was later released to try and discredit me during the 1992 senatorial campaign.

That "investor"—Victor Quintana—kept trying to get me to introduce him to someone, anyone, but after the business with Pagano I didn't trust him. I didn't mess with drugs and was scared to be around anyone who did. Finally, Joe Spinelli, an FBI agent, came around with other agents, they show me badges and say that they wanted to talk to me about Don King. They claimed they had us in a sting and that there was nothing I could do about it but cooperate. I said, "Prosecute." I hadn't done anything. I was angry, actually, and

I asked them why they didn't go after the drug dealers selling to kids on the street, that I would happily work with them on *that*. We went back and forth for several months, I think they thought I would come over, and I kept hoping they would do something about crack, which was just coming in then, and which was worse than anything we had seen to that point.

I called Spinelli in 1986—he was working in the Southern District U.S. Attorney's Office—to try and get help setting up an 800 number for drug enforcement. This was cited when the allegations of my being an FBI informant became public in 1987. It was alleged that I had worn wires against friends, most notably Don King, that I associated with organized crime figures, and that I may have myself been involved in organized crime. The media, *The Village Voice* in particular, ran with this and smeared me without foundation.

What I have never understood in all the accusations and discussion of my involvement with the FBI is why it has never been noted that *they* were trying to sting *me*, entrap me, really, and why were they trying to include in drug deals a young minister who had never in any way even been rumored to be involved in drugs?

That should have been the story. Why hasn't the liberal establishment questioned that? If the FBI had tapes on me and my associates, why didn't they use them? When the tapes were finally released, they clearly showed that the FBI was trying to entrap me; *they* were the ones talking about drugs, about money, about criminality. I don't know if Pagano and those guys were gangsters, but I do know they were operatives in the music business. I was a young black kid hustling in the city, and they were on the inside, they were willing to talk to me. They had Italian surnames, yes, but what does that mean?

We are talking about the real world, and in the real world, the Mafia doesn't need black preachers to do anything illegal, because they've got that covered. They need them to do *legal* things, the things they can't do, things that appear to clean up their act. Now, I will confess to a certain amount of naïveté during this time and in these matters, but that's nothing like the naïveté of those who would wish me into La Cosa Nostra.

The final thing is, why, when all this happened in 1983, did it not become public knowledge until 1988? And if I was, in fact, on the FBI's payroll, as has been accused, why did they assault me then? Wasn't I courting death by providing electronic surveillance against mobsters and Don King, if he was who they said he was? The reason for the attacks is that by 1988 I had a profile, I was moving against the system. To me the greatest proof of my innocence is that none of my close associates, not Alton Maddox, not C. Vernon Mason, not Jesse Jackson, ever questioned, suspected, or turned against me. Why wasn't I subpoenaed to testify against Don King when he was tried for tax evasion in 1985? Shouldn't I, if I was an informant, have supplied all the inside information? Don King himself said publicly that I was one of only two people who supported him throughout the trial. These charges and attacks were clearly designed to discredit me.

My last big foray in the music business was the Jackson Family's Victory tour in 1984. Michael Jackson was coming off *Thriller*, the biggest album of all time, and it promised to be a huge tour worth millions and millions of dollars to all connected with it. We held press conferences early, even before the tour was official, demanding that black promoters be involved.

Right after we started threatening protests and a boycott, someone who called himself Sal came to New York from Los Angeles and said he was speaking for various people in the music and concert businesses and that if I didn't stop interfering with the Jacksons and their right to make money, they would kill me. He came straight out and said that. He said, "You don't know who you're fucking with, Sharpton. I can pick up that phone and in one half hour your brains would be blown out of your head." Straight-up gangster. But I'm from Brooklyn, and I knew that the one thing I could not do was let that man intimidate me. So I said, "That might be true, but I want you to remember something, sir. I'm not afraid of you. Yes, maybe you can pick up that phone and get me killed, but first you've got to get to that phone, and before you do that, I will kick your ass all over this room." He didn't quite know what to make of me, and we stared at each other for a moment. Then I said, "If Frank Sinatra was touring with Tony Bennett and not one Italian was going to make a dollar from that, you wouldn't be picketing anybody, you'd be breaking legs. Michael Jackson is *black*, black folks paved his way to Hollywood. We are due some of this money, whether you like it or not." Sal looked at me and said, "I can't argue with that." And they got out of the way. We were allowed to participate.

Late one Sunday night, I got a call from Don King asking me to meet him in Los Angeles the next day. I was surprised, because we had been quarreling, but he left a first-class ticket at Kennedy Airport and had a limousine waiting for me at LAX. The limo took me to Michael Jackson's house out in Encino, where we had a meeting with everybody in the family, who were feuding. It had now developed that even the parents were being pushed out of the tour by the big-money people, and had turned to Don King. The parents, though their motive was self-preservation, were demanding black promoters, and that's where I came in.

We had a meeting the next day, of everyone, all the brothers, Michael, the parents, all the lawyers and accountants. Michael was lying down on the floor playing with a balloon while everybody talked and negotiated. Each brother had his own manager, his own lawyer, his own accountant, and they were all fighting. Then someone said, "Why do we need black promoters at all?" I spoke up and said, "You call this a victory tour, whose victory is it? Is it a victory for all those kids who supported them when they were on the black chitlin' circuit? Are the Jacksons forgetting them now that they've crossed over? What we need to do is, in each city, go to the hospitals and give the kids free tickets. They're complaining that the prices are too high, and the way to combat that is to give away tickets, to schools, to colleges, to churches, to make donations to worthy causes as we travel. And I would like us to hire some poor kids to do security in every city we go to, we can call it 'the Pride Patrol.' " In the middle of all this, Michael rolls up off the floor and says, "I like that. He's right. We'll do it. But I want him to do it." He pointed directly at me.

I was later accused of extorting money from the Jacksons, but on that tour I had a staff of three traveling, I had to establish temporary offices in each city, make donations, buy the tickets we were going to give away, and hire the patrols, all on a half million dollars. And that's what I did, and all I did. It's documented in various ways. Later, when New York State Attorney General Robert Abrams was trying to indict me, he talked to lawyers from the Victory tour, especially Joel Katz, who became one of the music industry's most prominent lawyers, pumping for information, but they all said I was on the level, legit, and that I did a hell of a job. And the feds couldn't find anything wrong either, though they certainly tried.

VI.

In New York City in the early to middle 1980s there had been several civil rights cases involving assaults on blacks in the metropolitan area. And nothing had come of them; they were in the news for a day or so, if at all, then they were never heard about again because there was no connection between black leadership and the people. Whenever something happened—Claude Reese, Michael Stewart, Eleanor Bumpurs—there were no sustained marches, no mass movement, nothing to keep these things in the public eye. I had learned from the experiences of my youth—A&P, for example—and the Martin Luther King movement in general that the only way to make the system move is by keeping events constantly in front of the public. In New York, in particular, everything changes every day, and if you don't make people aware of what you're doing, your issue will be ignored, forgotten, and die, and the status quo will remain.

So when I came back from down South and started working on the black concert promotion strategy and the Victory tour, I couldn't help noticing that there seemed to be no sense of black people standing up and demanding that their concerns be addressed. And they had concerns, all right, because when I went out into the community, I could hear them complaining about what was happening in the city. I'd go in churches and restaurants or just be walking down the street and people would walk up to me and say things like, "Reverend, did you hear about that boy they shot on the subway?" Or, "They're evicting people for no reason over in Crown Heights!" There were all kinds of concerns and issues, but no one to address them.

I had a little office then that was donated to me by Saint Mary's Hospital in Brooklyn. Only the space was free; I had to provide my own phone and staff. I had about four kids working with me steadily, and we started having meetings on Saturday, Breadbasket-style, to talk about issues and try to organize. I was trying to give them a sense of empowerment and to show them some of the techniques that had been used by black people in the past to confront the established order and gain concessions.

The next Christmas, 1985, a white man named Bernhard Goetz shot four black kids asking for money on the subway, and everyone in the city seemed to treat it as an act of heroism. I didn't see it that way. In fact, I thought it was crazy. The only thing that made these kids muggers rather than beggars was the color of their skin. No one disputes that they asked him for the money, but all kinds of people ask for money on the subway. Whether they were robbing him or not, we don't know, but his response was to stand up and shoot to kill. He permanently paralyzed one of them. And he became a folk hero because he played to the same mentality of scapegoating blacks that was later seen in Boston in the Charles Stuart case and in South Carolina in the Susan Smith case.

I became aware of the case from reading the newspaper. I read the story sitting there in Saint Mary's, and it really struck me because I had some young men whom I was really fond of working with me there, and I realized that this terrible situation could have easily involved them. That shook me up. So I called a news conference on the steps of City Hall and denounced the situation. As a result I started feuding with Curtis Sliwa of the Guardian Angels, who supported Goetz, and Roy Innis, who did the same. That made me very suspicious of the Guardian Angels, that they would support vigilantism based on race, and I also realized that there were blacks who didn't understand the dimensions of the issue.

I decided to go to Manhattan and start marching on Bernhard Goetz. I went to his apartment house on 14th Street, and immediately we started getting press coverage. We held prayer vigils, we went to all the court proceedings. I had learned those things from the civil rights manual, so to speak. Those techniques had never been used in New York before. We had never gone to white people's houses or to their neighborhoods to picket and march. We created drama. That became my technique, to dramatize issues and events until something had to be done about it by the authorities. That's one of the things it means to be an activist in the media age. That means someone in authority, in the judicial system, has to answer. There had been no indictment of Goetz before we started, not even a gun charge. He only had to say that the threat from the black boy was imminent; he never had to prove he was actually in danger. We were the ones who agitated until he was indicted on the gun charge. It was a mixed victory, but at least he spent a year in jail on the gun violation, carrying a concealed weapon.

There was a very simple reason I was so concerned about the Goetz case while so many others were cheering him on: anytime you justify vigilantism you create an ongoing situation where it becomes very difficult to draw the line as to what is called for and what isn't. There was never any evidence presented that Bernhard Goetz's life or person was being threatened. One kid asked him for five dollars and he made an assumption. Goetz himself never stated that he was threatened. Should someone be executed for five dollars? If we applaud or condone something like that, we're setting up a situation where none of our kids, white or black, are safe. Who knows where they might find themselves, and whom they might scare? Most people don't know half the time where their kids are or what they're doing. We have the police and the courts to adjudicate these matters.

Some people have said that there is a problem with black crime, but to the extent that that is true, it is in the most part a situation of blacks committing crimes against other blacks. And it begs a question: why is everyone so obsessed with crime committed by blacks as opposed to that committed by whites? What gave Bernhard Goetz the right to make the assumption he did? It was a racial assumption, and that cannot be condoned. Would Goetz have made a similar assumption of a white teenager? In 1994 a gang of white kids beat a New York City police officer so badly that his family could not recognize him. Or think of Bensonhurst, Howard Beach, what those gangs of white kids did. Does that give me the right to shoot the next white kid that startles me on the street? A white kid stabbed me in the chest; does that give me the right to pull my firearm and start blasting every time a white man walks up to me now, as many of them do, and offers me his hand to shake? The law has to work for everybody. Bernhard Goetz tried to legalize racial assumption, which is commonly known as prejudice. That's why I felt I had to go after him. Who was guilty and who was innocent wasn't so much my conern; you can't make prejudiced assumptions and then defend them with deadly force.

Regardless of your political viewpoint, and despite what the Ed

Koches and Michael Levins of the world proclaim, there is no way to justify black kids being treated differently than white kids. I have spent countless hours in prisons and schools talking to black young men, telling them that they have to respect other people, their property, right and wrong. I challenge them not to put us as black people in a position where we are wrong and trying to defend the indefensible. Two wrongs do not make a right, and those boys did not have the right to ask Goetz for five dollars, but they did not deserve to be shot for asking. If the forces of fear think that such behavior is correct, and they want that kind of country, then everybody is going to be shooting everybody. If you look at the FBI data, any white person in this country has much more to fear from being shot by another white person than by a black.

I think about it this way: Whites go into black Brooklyn every day. They collect rent, utility bills, package payments, they carry around large sums of money every day. They go into Bedford-Stuyvesant, East New York, Brownsville. They're postal workers, policemen, doctors, nurses, firemen. They do the same thing in South-Central, the West Side, the Fifth Precinct, Overtown. We don't hear of heinous crimes being done to these people. So in my opinion a very exaggerated stereotype has been made calling young black males the source of all crime and trouble in the country. The other groups, including whites, play as large a part in it.

Much of the perception of blacks as the sole cause of crime in this country extends from certain structural flaws in the way the judicial system works. For instance, the judicial system does not incarcerate whites at the same rate as blacks for the equivalent crimes. This is not an excuse; studies by the government and white university professors have shown this to be true all over the country. There are more whites arrested than convicted per capita than blacks, and the whites convicted are sentenced to and do less time.

There's also the inherent unfairness built into many statutes along racial lines. Why is crack cocaine punished so much more harshly than powder cocaine? Crack violations carry long minimum sentences while the equivalent powder offense, more likely to be committed by a well-off white, can be handled with probation if the judge cares to. That's why there are so many more blacks in jail. It doesn't mean more blacks are guilty, it just means more are sentenced. And there was a famous case in Maine recently where a white drug dealer convicted of smuggling eleven tons of marijuana into the state was not only allowed to attend law school but was hired as a clerk by a Maine Supreme Court judge, which is supposed to be a very high honor for a young law student.

Blacks, poor blacks in particular, generally don't have the contacts and finances needed to secure good legal protection. The O. J. Simpson case, it goes without saying, is an example of how the legal system functions. If you know the right people or you have enough money, lawyers can change night into day. So you have, in my opinion, a system that is prone to let whites go home and incarcerate blacks. This feeds into and backs up the Goetz mind-set that says it's open season on young black men.

Once you accept the demonization of these young men, you can kill them at will, because the system is not supposed to protect demons and devils. Once you devalue someone's being, you can eliminate them at your will. They're nonbeings, nobodies. So on one level Goetz was shooting nobodies, and justified in thinking whatever he chose to think. It spreads out over the country, and everybody begins to look the same. All blacks are devalued. It's a pathology in this country, the criminalization of young black men. Let's blame *them* for the escalation of crime, blame *them* for the lack of urban programs that would provide training and opportunity and build a social order that's equitable. They are the victims of this society, and in this society the easiest thing to do is blame the victims.

There is a lot of loose talk in this society about "victimization-chic" and the like, but the fact is there are large numbers of African

Americans whose families have not ever in their experience of life on this continent had exposure to real opportunity. White folks can talk about their struggle, but they were not systematically denied access to opportunity and education based on the color of their skin. The Irish, for example, suffered terribly, but they did not have to struggle against institutionalized racism. In fact, they were able to join in on the side of the oppressor and use that to their advantage. It was not against the law for Irishmen to go to the good schools, it was not against the law for them to use public accommodations, they were not prohibited from where and when they could go. They had to struggle against economic disadvantages, but not legal apartheid based on who they were. If they could break out, they could make it. The possibilities for them are self-evident today. Meanwhile, blacks were falling behind. They were *held* behind, more truthfully. You can't compare the groups.

What really happened in the Bernhard Goetz case was that he became a thug himself; he got on that subway predisposed to do what he did. He had a gun loaded with dumdum bullets, bullets specially designed to do maximum lethal damage to a target. They explode on impact to create even more trauma than is usual with gunshot wounds. So to my mind Goetz was the thug there that night—he was the one looking to damage and destroy—and New York City embraced him as a hero. But he was in reality a psychotic racist who went looking for trouble that night and found it, maybe even created it, and I'm proud to say that I contributed to getting him the time in jail that he did receive.

Around the same time, I was involved in leading a group of protesters in sitting down on the tracks at Grand Central Station during morning rush hour to draw attention to the fact that there were no blacks on the board of or involved in the upper management of the Metropolitan Transit Authority (MTA). Millions

of blacks rode public transportation every day, particularly the subway and buses, and there was not one black person involved in any
of the decision making. We had warned Governor Cuomo that
there would be protests if he didn't act, but he didn't think our
threat was credible and ignored our appeal. After the sit-down, he
asked us to his office. This was the first time I met with Cuomo face-
to-face, and I asked him, "Why is it that eighty percent of the riders
can't have one vote?" He and I debated there in front of everyone
for an hour and a half, and finally he said that he would do it, he
would appoint a black (who turned out to be Laura Blackburn).

After we concluded our agreement Cuomo said, "The media is
out in the lobby. Go out there, tell them that you've had your
meeting and gotten what you wanted and that there won't be any
more sit-ins on the tracks." This was a trick. He didn't want to
appear with us because he didn't want to be seen in the media as
kowtowing to blacks, so I said, "I was better trained than that. You're
coming out there with us and *you're* going to announce the agreement." He says, "What?" He was very startled. I said, "If you don't
come with us, I'm going out the back, and I'll let you answer whatever questions the media wants to pose by yourself." As a result he
agreed, we made a joint statement, and I have photos of Cuomo
standing with me and the other black leaders.

Another thing we did in early 1986 was to march on crack
houses. This was at a time when no one had ever heard of crack,
when it was very new in New York. We would go right up to the
doors of these places where they were selling drugs and would paint
a big red "X" on the house to say that "this is a drug house." We went
so far as to send my assistant, Simeon Kitt, and a producer from
Channel 4, Robert Dembo, into a crack house to buy cocaine and
film the transaction with a hidden camera. That footage was later
aired. We tried to get the FBI involved as well, to raid these places
and put them out of business, but they didn't listen. We needed the
FBI because the cops were involved with the drug traffickers and

wouldn't do anything. We were accused of making false statements against the police, but what we said was borne out by the Michael Dowd case and the Mollen Commission years later. I was given a citation by the Brooklyn borough president, but what might we have accomplished if our charges had been taken seriously?

This phase of my life was when I realized that things were really changing for me, in an irrevocable way. The growing notoriety didn't affect me very much, because I'd always had some sort of notoriety in my circle from the time I was a little boy. I was a celebrity of sorts in the black church world, and I had been a leader in school. It seems like I was always prominent in some way.

What was different about what was happening to me in 1986 was that I was incurring the wrath of people in the wider world because I was controversial. And because Kathy and I were starting our family, I suddenly had all kinds of concerns that I'd never had before. It's one thing when I'm out there by myself and I say what I mean and let the chips fall wherever they may. It's something else when you're out stirring up trouble and you've got a little baby sleeping at home and you're worried if somebody is going to try and do something to your house or if they're going to try and do something to your wife. I became very cautious about that. It was years before I let my family be photographed by a newspaper or magazine. Kathy and Dominique and Ashley would be in marches with me and I'd never let them be identified as being with me. I was very sensitive about their being publicly exposed.

I do think that during this time I became conscious of the price that I was going to have to pay. In the years since, I have faced tax trials, I've had fifteen or sixteen arrests and jailings, I've spent as much as thirty days in jail at one time for demonstrations. Once I had six different trials going at the same time for demonstrations, Days of Outrage, stopping the Brooklyn-Queens Expressway, closing the Statue of Liberty. I don't think people see the downside of all this. I've spent as much time in courts and jail as I have anywhere else in the last ten years.

That is how my life has changed. This is not fun. I can't do the things that normal people do without seriously considering what I'm doing. I can't take my family to a movie. If I do, I have to go to some out-of-the-way place and have two or three men with me because anything might happen there in the dark. If I take them out to dinner, it means either getting into debates or shaking hands all night. Plus, I've got to remember, at all times, that the hand reaching out to me might be offered in friendship or it might be hiding a knife. No one subjects himself to that kind of threat and tension unless he believes in and is serious about what he's doing, and I'd like for those who disagree with me to at least give me that. Right or wrong, I'm serious about my life and my work.

What I have realized is that I will always be Al Sharpton. I can't get up tomorrow morning like the average person and say, "Okay, I've done that, now I'm going to try something else." I will be Al Sharpton until the day I die. The door back to normal life is closed to me now. I know that. I think I've given my identity up to the cause. I'm intertwined, I've even become a stereotype for a certain kind of activism. My kids were watching a show one night, and a guy puts on a longhaired wig, and somebody says, "Oh, now you're going to go protest like Al Sharpton." So, yes, I'm known, my name's out there, but what it really means is that I spend a lot of nights in hotels by myself, because nothing—going for a walk, getting something to eat, meeting friends for coffee—is simple anymore. Life has changed.

VII.

I n the summer of 1986 I was working out of my office at Saint Mary's Hospital in Brooklyn, working on the Disciples of Justice, a subway patrol group we started because of the bias shown by the Guardian Angels in the Goetz case, and what we called the War Against Crack, painting houses and trying to alert people to what was just beginning to happen. Because I was right there in the neighborhood, I could see firsthand the devastation that was beginning to result.

We continued with this work through the fall, and late that year one of the kids that was working with me, Derrick Jeter, who was also known as Sunshine, because of his disposition, called me at home in the middle of the night. He kept saying, "They killed my friend out in Queens," and then he asked me to call this friend's mother and go out to see her in Queens. The man who was killed, Michael Griffith, was so close to Derrick that he was wearing Derrick's jacket the night he died, and as I listened to Derrick crying I decided to take the number and the address, and I told him that I'd go over in the morning and find out what had happened.

In all honesty, I assumed that it was drug-related or something like that. We had seen the violence escalating daily in the black neighborhoods as the battles for turf and crack heated up, and we were noting more and more criminal activity. When I got to Jean Griffith's, Michael's mother's house, Mrs. Griffith was there along with Cedric Sandiford, her boyfriend and later husband, who had just gotten in from being questioned by the police. He just sat there, bleeding from cuts and bruises with his clothes dirtied and torn. It turned out that he and another man, Timothy Grimes, had been in the outer Queens neighborhood of Howard Beach with Michael Griffith the previous night, when their car had broken down and, trying to walk and find a phone from which to call for help, they came upon a crowd of whites that started taunting them racially.

They then went into a pizzeria, and thirty minutes later, after eating and leaving the restaurant, they were followed by the group of whites with whom they had had the verbal altercation, and about a dozen reinforcements, who started explicitly calling them "nigger" and other names and taunting them. A fight broke out and the blacks ran for their lives while the whites gave chase armed with baseball bats, bricks, rocks, and knives.

This was the beginning of the notorious Howard Beach incident. Pummeled and screamed at every step of the way, Griffith, Sandiford, and Grimes ran and made it several blocks, ending up at a fence next to the Belt Parkway. They looked behind and saw that the mob was still chasing them, with sticks and rocks and everything else. Sandiford and Grimes ran to hide—Sandiford was caught and beaten within an inch of his life—while Griffith went through the fence and ran into the highway with the mob chasing and screaming, "Kill the nigger!" "Kill the nigger!" Griffith was struck by a car in the middle of the road and killed instantly.

I became furious as I sat there listening to Cedric. And beyond anger I felt humiliation, everything from what had happened to my father in North Carolina on our trip to Florida when I was a child to the Goetz shooting came to me, like it was flashing before my eyes. I was enraged. I told Mrs. Griffith and Cedric Sandiford that whatever we could do, they could count on us doing it. I had no idea what was possible, and I didn't know what, exactly, to do at that moment, but I knew we were going to do *something*. I got up to leave, and as I was heading out, the older Griffith son, Chris, was coming in, and we talked briefly, and I asked him if the family had a lawyer, which they didn't, it was too soon.

I went outside, where there were press gathered, and they started asking me questions. I called the situation a racial murder, which it was, and told them as much as I knew about the events. I also told them how horrendous I was feeling as a result, and how this confirmed the danger inherent for blacks in certain sections of New York. Later that day the news reported that I had been at the house, as had Mayor Koch and Police Commissioner Benjamin Ward, the first black person to hold that job. Koch had announced that the city considered the incident a bias attack, and put up a reward for information leading to the arrest and conviction of the guilty.

But I thought there was no reason to leave things in the hands of the Koch administration. Koch had been hostile to us in the past, during the Goetz situation, for instance, and I didn't think he could be trusted. He was trying to quiet things down, chill them out, make it look good, and then let it drift away and die a slow death like every other bias case in New York City up to that point. But we'd had some limited success in the Goetz situation, and I also thought it was time for the black community to take responsibility for itself and show some effort.

I went back to the Griffiths' house the next day and told Mrs. Griffith that I wanted to put up a reward for information through the National Youth Movement. She gave her permission, and I held a press conference in front of the house. The reward was $1,000. I also said that we were going to press this case to the end because we could not live in a city where blacks were barred from traveling through or spending time in certain neighborhoods. I got angry, saying, "The nerve of these people to tell us we can't be in Howard Beach." I remember thinking, here we are, in New York City in the North in 1986 and white people are still telling black people what they can and cannot do. This young man, who did nothing to anyone, is dead because white people refused to recognize him as a human. It was like the entire story of our life, blacks keep hitting these false ceilings, these imposed limitations that are determined by others, others who do not intend any good for blacks.

These overwhelming emotions that I felt standing there in the yard led me to spontaneously announce—at the time I had absolutely no idea of how I was going to pull it off—that I was going to have a rally in front of the pizzeria in Howard Beach. I wanted the world to know that black people in New York were going to go wherever they pleased. I called for a motorcade, for people to meet me with their cars, the next day, Monday. I said we were going to drive from Mrs. Griffith's house to that pizzeria. People started calling, saying they wanted to support me, and we got it out on the radio. (That was the first time I dealt seriously with WLIB.)

When I got to the house at the appointed time, 11:00 A.M., I was stunned: there were over a hundred cars waiting, each one filled with people ready and waiting to head to Howard Beach. This was extremely important in the history of blacks in New York, where, outside of Adam Clayton Powell, there had been very little overt civil rights activity. It was also important to me personally, because it symbolized my transition from working with and leading young people to leading adults. I looked around and saw all those adults in their cars—ironically, I didn't own a car at the time—and I thought, I can do something.

We tied red ribbons on everyone's antennae to help with staying in line, and I got in the lead car with Jim Bell, the labor leader, and we pushed off for Howard Beach. We got out there and turned onto Cross Bay Boulevard, which is the main strip of the neighborhood. To our amazement, there were several hundred people in the street—whites—screaming and yelling, "Niggers go home! Get out of here!" It was just like the films I've seen of Mississippi in the sixties. We rode down the street, and, to my surprise, the taunts and the insults from the crowd angered rather than frightened me. I looked at those enraged, contorted faces, and I never thought about the danger. I thought about the ignorance and the arrogance of those people, and perhaps I went back in my mind to that day in North Carolina when my father was refused service. Sometimes I think that I have always wanted, subliminally, to even that score, to somehow wipe out my father's and my family's humiliation. I was thinking more about that than the danger.

Then my own rage started rising, rage that must have always been there in the past but that I had never really felt or tapped into. I can remember it quite specifically, sitting there in Jim Bell's car in Howard Beach and just simmering, getting really mad in a way I had never known. I think it was because in the past, even with Goetz, there had never been face-to-face confrontations of masses of people. But this was like Selma or Birmingham or Ole Miss. This was like a Freedom Ride.

We parked across the street from the pizzeria. And there were more white people *there*, with the media, screaming and making threats. Then I look in the rearview mirror and I see the Reverend Herbert Daughtry, a longtime and extremely respected leader in the

black community, and his assistant Charles Barron—who was later
to become a close friend of mine—pulling up unannounced. I hadn't
known they were coming. They hopped out and got in the backseat
of Jim's car, and Reverend Daughtry said, "We came out here to
support you, young man, because you're doing the right thing." I
knew Daughtry from Operation Breadbasket when I was a teenager,
but I had never really worked with him.

We sat there for a minute, and then Jim Bell says, "Well, now
we're going to circle around the pizza place and head on back,
right?" And I said, "No." He was worried about the mob, but that
was exactly why we had to get out of the cars. I felt we had come to
prove our right to be anywhere, and anywhere meant inside the
pizzeria. I opened up my door and got out with the mob right there
and walked across the street to the restaurant. The crowd went nuts.
Everyone else saw me, and they all got out of their cars and followed me.

So we've crossed the street, the mob is howling, they've crossed
behind us and they've surrounded us, but the media have surrounded *them* and are filming everything. I stood in front of the
pizzeria—I'll never forget it—and I made a speech about how nobody was going to tell us where to go, that we had fought too hard
and come too far in history to ever accept other groups saying that
we couldn't walk the streets. I said that I came to proclaim that we
would walk wherever we wanted, and that those people that killed
and maimed on Friday night must be apprehended and made to pay
the price for what they'd done.

Then we walked inside the pizzeria, I took out a hundred-dollar
bill, and ordered pizza for all those with me. To this day I don't
know if the hundred covered it or not, but the guy at the counter
kept dishing out pizzas and we stood there before the cameras
while everybody who wanted had some, in the very place where
sixty hours before, Michael Griffith had been chased down and
killed.

After we finished we came back out and got in our cars and went back to Brooklyn. The next day the *New York Times* had us on the front page, and we were big news everywhere around the world. We had no way of knowing that this was going to become such a big case, which is important, because I'm often accused of being a media hound, deliberately creating sensational events. But I had handled many situations before that young people had brought to my attention, and some got a little notice in the paper, some didn't get any notice at all. We had several big demonstrations that no one ever noticed. I had no way of knowing that the cameras were coming to the pizzeria, I never have any way of knowing that. And how can I "exploit" something that I in fact created? I'm the one that called the motorcade. For all I knew, no blacks would show up, and maybe the media wouldn't care. In the case of Howard Beach, I was responding by reflex to racism, as I had my entire life.

Howard Beach became a big case because the rest of the world didn't think that the crowds and the craziness could happen in New York. On that day at the pizzeria we were able to show everyone— really those people there did it themselves by how they acted—that what had happened that night was not an isolated incident of some bad kids chasing some other kids, but that what happened was a logical outgrowth of the sorts of attitudes and practices that were commonplace in that neighborhood. The nation saw that there was a bastion of racial hatred right there in the most famous metropolis in the world. When people turned on the news that night and saw grown-ups, homeowners, taxpayers, standing out on the streets of New York City yelling, "Nigger! Nigger! Nigger!" they couldn't believe it.

We made Howard Beach into "Howard Beach." What happened that night would have just been another scuffle involving teenagers if the world had not seen those images. And they would not have seen those images if we had not gone there. We provided the occasion for the world to see the truth.

The next day there were calls from the New York State NAACP about doing a bigger demonstration that weekend. We had a press conference and announced we were going back with hundreds, if not thousands, and that we were going to march all the way through the neighborhood. That Saturday Benjamin Hooks, the national director of the NAACP, came up from Washington to march with us. We started lining up, and it seemed like people came from nowhere. We had about three thousand out there, ready to go. There must have been just as many whites from Howard Beach waiting for us, screaming, jeering, uglier than the day we went to the pizzeria. If we had three thousand, they had three thousand.

The police were there, in force. Ben Ward, the commissioner, was there, personally working at keeping the crowds separated. That was another big moment for me, because I was standing there at the head of the march of thousands, arm in arm with Laura Blackburn and Ben Hooks, and I'm the one who has called the march. I had arrived as an activist, and even the most respected members of the community were standing with me.

When we got the front of the march to the starting point, in front of the same pizzeria that we had been at a few days before, there was a crowd of teenage white kids standing in front of the restaurant with a big poster of me with a noose around my neck. They were yelling, "We're gonna hang you, Al!" I must admit I was taken aback, but then Ben Hooks punched me playfully and said, "They don't like you out here," and laughed, and then I laughed and it broke the tension.

Howard Beach was the beginning of me becoming for whites a symbol of hate and derision, and for blacks a symbol of standing up and going into these racist areas. We marched that day about two miles down to a high school athletic field, and it was ten times worse than earlier in the week. I had let my wife, Kathy, accompany me with our new baby, Dominique, that day, which is an indication of how little trouble I had expected, but I had them stay at home on

Saturday. Looking at the crowd tormenting us that weekend, I was glad I had.

People were yelling nigger this, nigger that, they had signs and placards and bullhorns. I, of course, was a center of attention and hecklers pointed at me and threw things. They even attacked Benjamin Ward, the police commissioner, who was standing there supervising the cops. Some white kids were pointing at me and yelling, "Nigger, we'll get you, we're gonna get you," and Commissioner Ward looks at the kids and says, "That'll be enough of that, quiet down." A little kid, a white girl about twelve or thirteen, comes up to Ward and says, "Who do you think you're talking to? You ain't nothing but a nigger yourself." Ward is the police commissioner, in full dress uniform, and he just deflated. I don't know if he was humiliated at being treated with such disrespect or if he was upset that I had seen it—he and I were political enemies, I had called him an Uncle Tom for not fighting police brutality—but in that moment he and I were united as blacks, Mr. Inside and Mr. Outside, behind the wall of racism.

When we got to the field, we had a rally. All of the leaders were there, along with several thousand people. Laura Blackburn started singing "The Star-Spangled Banner," but the crowd started booing, refusing to sing that. She didn't understand what was going on and got a little scared, so she handed me the mike and said, "You better handle this." I started singing, "Lift Ev'ry Voice and Sing," the NAACP Negro national anthem, and the crowd joined in. The crowd received me so warmly that I ended up emceeing the rally.

What I think leaders of Laura's social class and generation didn't—and don't—understand about that black crowd in Howard Beach refusing to sing the national anthem or participate in other patriotic rituals is that though those people *were* African Americans, America hadn't worked for them. They had just walked two miles being called niggers, with eggs and rocks being thrown at them, and they had seen the black police commissioner, presumably the most inside and trustworthy (from the point of view of whites) black man in the city, disrespected and humiliated by a child. That child was Italian, like most of those whites out there waving American flags and cursing us. How many Italians were killed in the American Revolution? How many blacks? How about the Civil War? World War I? World War II? Korea and Vietnam? This is not name-calling, merely a question of who truly has purchase on this country. All these groups, Irish, Jews, Koreans, whatever, that are constantly into it with blacks and complaining about them are, strictly speaking, Johnny-come-latelies. But those same groups claim the flag and the national anthem and all that, and I think the crowd that day felt that singing "Oh, say can you see" would have represented aligning themselves with the forces they had just confronted, and I agreed with them. America, that day, seemed to be the last entity interested in the rights of Michael Griffith. We were the real Americans, but couldn't deal with symbols from the past that were so closely identified with our opponents.

The Griffith family informed me the next week that they had retained Alton Maddox to represent them. I knew Alton only in passing—I'd bumped into him at Don King's trial, read things in the paper about him—but I knew he was committed to and deadly serious about his work, and he had a growing reputation as an extraordinarily brilliant defense attorney. C. Vernon Mason, another gifted young black attorney, was representing the other victim, Timothy Grimes. I knew Mason from the Goetz case, where Mason had represented the victims.

We were to work together, the three of us, as a team protecting the families' interests. There were some grumblings—mostly petty jealousy that refused to take into account that all the news coverage and political heat had resulted from my initiative—in the community at the time about my role, but the Griffith family in particular was comfortable with me, so we moved forward and prepared for the next area of conflict, which would involve the grand jury.

Cedric Sandiford had said from the outset of the incident that he didn't trust the police or the Queens County District Attorney's Office because of the way they questioned him that night after the attack, as if they didn't believe him and were trying to protect the perpetrators. John Santucci, the Queens D.A., had said that he was going to come back with charges, but Cedric could not be mollified, and that's one of the reasons Maddox, Mason, and myself were brought in.

The night of the incident Sandiford was left sitting bleeding in the police station out in Howard Beach, and no one was brought in to take care of him or tend his wounds. Then, when they finally got around to talking to him, the cops questioned him more about what he and the others were doing in Howard Beach, as if he were out there to rob someone or break into houses, than what had just occurred, who the suspects were, what they were wearing. There was absolutely no concern for the personal attack he had just endured, or for the tremendous personal loss—the son of the woman he was to marry—he had suffered. "Was this about drugs?" The autopsy did reveal later that Michael Griffith had cocaine in his system. "Were you getting high? Selling?"

At the precinct that night, Cedric Sandiford was the suspect, not the victim. Here was a man who had been beaten senseless, as had Timothy Grimes, and had watched a close friend murdered— think of what must have been going through Cedric's mind about what he was going to have to tell Michael's mother—and not one question of "What did the killers look like?" Not "How many were there?" Not "Which direction did they run off in?" Only, "Why were you in Howard Beach?" *And these are the authorities.* This is what Cedric Sandiford told us in the days and weeks after the attack, and Alton Maddox, to his eternal credit, stood up and said, "There is no way we are going to cooperate with this."

So we—the victims, their representatives, the police and prosecutors, the news media—all assembled at Queens County Courthouse to hear the D.A., John Santucci, release the indictments. This
is after the first two marches, and there was much tension, some of
it legitimate, stemming from the anger coursing through the black
community and the streets of Howard Beach, some of it ludicrous,
such as the super militants who were shouting to reporters that I
had forfeited my right to be an African American leader because
they didn't like my hair.

We're all there in the courtroom and Santucci comes out with
"reckless endangerment." Maddox and Mason are on their feet.
"That's ridiculous!" And it was. Reckless endangerment is what you
get charged with for yelling "Fire!" in a theater. We left the courthouse, angry but undecided in how to proceed, and as the press
closed in on us, I decided to step forward and say, purely on instinct, "We're not going to take this, we're going to fight, and we're
going to get justice."

For the next several days we met at Jim Bell's office in Manhattan plotting and planning. Maddox developed his legal strategy of
withdrawing cooperation of the witnesses with the authorities to
force appointment of a special prosecutor. We decided Santucci's
office was compromised and too close to elements in Howard Beach
to be trusted to work with vigorous impartiality for complete justice. We didn't want hands slapped, we wanted punishment, significant jail time, a recognition that a young man had had his life stolen
from him for no reason other than that he was black.

We needed leverage. Maddox and Mason's job was to counsel
their clients in noncooperation with the investigation, refusing to
talk to and avoiding police and prosecutors. My job was to keep the
community focused on what had happened, rallying and marching
so that the events we now know as Howard Beach would not fall
out of the public eye. If Michael Griffith's murder became merely an
administrative judicial matter, there was grave danger of a cover-up.

Sooner or later, with the marches galvanizing blacks and the subsequent ugliness being broadcast into everyone's living room, Mario Cuomo, the governor of New York, had to come to the table. He decided to meet with a group of black elected officials and ministers—the same sort of group who had let this sort of outrage pass unchallenged in the past—and refused to meet with me or Maddox and Mason, but he did after a few days acquiesce and appoint Charles Hynes as the special prosecutor for the murder and assaults at Howard Beach.

We didn't know Hynes, but Mason didn't like him. Charles Hynes was New York City fire commissioner during an affirmative action war in the fire department. Whites fought viciously to keep out any hiring goals, and largely prevailed. Because of this we didn't trust him. After Cuomo's announcement we immediately reconvened at Jim Bell's office and strategized. My job then became to keep as much pressure as possible on Hynes. The only way we could have a hope of being able to trust him was to keep a mass mobilization on his head, literally. We had learned that from the civil rights leaders in the South—you only get what you want by keeping the heat on and large doses of nonviolent force.

So we marched and marched and marched, keeping the issues out there, deliberately provoking conflict and attention, and finally Hynes came down and indicted five people for murder and manslaughter. Charles Hynes got murder indictments out of the same Queens grand jury that John Santucci could only convince of reckless endangerment. It's never said, but I think that alone vindicates our attitudes and strategy.

It's funny how these things work. I think Hynes's political ambitions (he later ran for and won Brooklyn D.A.) were whetted by the cause célèbre of the case, and this motivated him to work harder and more fairly. If we had not made it a cause célèbre, it wouldn't have been politically advantageous for him to come in and get indictments and convictions. But with the racial undercurrent in all this, the white media would still rather say that Hynes did the crucial job, make him into some kind of folk hero, than say that if we had not done what we'd done, Hynes wouldn't have wanted or needed to do a good job, he would have never been appointed special prosecutor, *in fact, there probably would not have even been a case.* There never had been before. Black folks had been killed in bias cases in New York City for years to very little notice.

I can't emphasize this enough. We, by energizing the community and the international media, forced Cuomo to appoint Hynes, and Hynes, in the spotlight we created, treats the case with the gravity and gets the indictments we want. But the white media don't come back and say that Sharpton and Maddox and Mason were right, or that we had a good strategy that worked as planned. The white media come back and say that Charles Hynes is a great man, a folk hero, New York's new Saint Patrick driving out the snakes, defending the weak, and comforting the afflicted. And while the saint prepares for trial, Maddox, Mason, and Sharpton are depicted by that same media as charlatans and rabble-rousers.

It took about a year to prepare for the trial, and that whole year I was fighting every racial case in New York. *Anybody* who had a racial problem—or thought they did—is calling my little office at Saint Mary's. And the liberal establishment—white and black—is going crazy, because I'm not the anointed black leader, I'm not the black man they want to be dealing with. White and black politicians are angry with me because they've all had their carefully laid plans and their protégés that they wanted to build up, and I'm coming along and overturning all that.

They thought of me as some jive Brooklyn jackleg preacher, and they couldn't see why victims and everyday black people were gravitating toward me whenever there was trouble. But what they didn't understand was that the people—*particularly poor and average people*—saw me as the person who would do something about whatever had happened.

Your famous borough president sitting over at the U.S. Open wouldn't stand up for people like Michael Griffith. I would put the issue on the front burner and turn it up as hot as I could, and if you do that, something will happen. People have to respond. If you're just an average black man in the community, if you're Yvonne Smallwood's husband—she was a black woman killed by the police—are you going to call a bureaucrat whose main interest is covering his butt and keeping his job, or are you going to call that man you saw on television leading marches through racist white neighborhoods and getting indictments and convictions?

But for the longest time the system didn't want to see that. Those in power were hoping that I would go away. The ruckus I was causing threatened all the interrelationships that had grown up over time as the way of distributing power. The important black politicians don't want to go up against their white friends, the borough president doesn't want to challenge the D.A., because they're all elected out of the same political clubs, they socialize together, sometimes their families are friends. Simply put, they run together.

That, however, is not the only way black politicians are compromised. They are also the victims of their own personal ambitions. They think, if I keep my head down, I make this move here, then that one over there, I can get from the assembly to Congress, and I'm going to need the county Democratic machine who won't back me if I cause problems for the Democrat district attorney or the Democratic mayor or the Democratic governor. I had none of those considerations. I was outside of all that. I had a youth group, I earned my living preaching, my wife had a job with the army. So I couldn't care less if the district attorney was offended by me, or the mayor, the governor, or the president. I wasn't funded by the insiders, so there was nothing, on that score, they could do to me. They couldn't cut me off because they had never cut me in.

Whom were they going to call? Those thousands of poor black

folks giving me a quarter or a dollar or a five every Sunday because they were moved by how I preached? Those people had known me since I was a little boy—the Wonderboy—and you couldn't tell them anything negative about me. In fact, whenever I was under pressure in the media, they struggled and went out of their way to give me *more* money so that, as they would say, I wouldn't have to bow down.

So the establishment blacks saw me as a serious threat. The mere fact of my independence was a threat. In their hearts they could not disagree with me, they knew I was right on, but the fact they couldn't control my actions was a threat to them. I was altering the comfort level, showing their white allies how little power and influence they actually had. And what worried some of them the most was, "What's he going to do? What's he want? With all this limelight he might decide to run against us." Back to self-serving career concerns. They're not looking at the fact that this beautiful young black man just got killed and the perpetrators might get away with it, and that I was trying to make sure people went to jail. They're wondering, "How does all this noise affect *me?*"

There have always been these various kinds of intragroup conflicts, rivalries, and diverging agendas in black liberation movements—in any movement, really. As things heated up in New York in the second half of the eighties, there were many different ideas of how to best do things, from the sort of Marxist-Leninist "overthrow the government" point of view to totally pacifist pray-and-fast silent witness. A lot of the differences do simply come down to jealousy. Everybody wants to be the leader. As time went on I was increasingly the one in the paper, on television, and there was a lot of discontent and arguing about this. I was ready to deal with it because I had grown up in the movement, I saw Adam Clayton Powell, I saw the battles between Jesse Jackson and Ralph Abernathy, it's all to be expected.

Some of this is because the establishment media have absolutely no understanding of the gradations of thought and opinion in the black community. They lump us all together, Sharpton with Farrakhan with Chavis with Jackson with Edelman with Wilder, and they ignore that we have some serious ideological and personality differences among us, and that we're not necessarily all together. After Howard Beach I was increasingly out front, and I became responsible for anything said in the crowd. For example, I'm on the news and the news says, "The Reverend Al Sharpton led three thousand marchers through Howard Beach last night," and they show a black man in the line yelling, "The white man is the devil," and the message that is transmitted is, "Sharpton and three thousand angry black people stormed through Queens last night stating that the white man is the devil." I, Al Sharpton, decidedly *did not* say that. But that becomes the effect. That one man expressing his, in my opinion, misguided viewpoint may not have anything to do with the other 2,999 people marching, but the media can't resist. Some of it is the media's naïveté, some of it is their duplicity.

I have been doing this since I was fourteen years old, whether the cameras were there or not. There were no cameras at Tilden High School or at A&P, I wasn't in the paper, but I did the same thing every day: preach and agitate. I didn't do anything different at Howard Beach than I had always done. The difference was that now it was on television and everybody could see me do it. And that was what was amazing to me about the media and how I was covered: nobody bothered to look up who I was and what I had done. I thought I had a pretty consistent track record.

We started meeting and getting ready for the trial. One of our first decisions was that a huge priority of ours had to be keeping the courtroom packed every single day, and various community and church groups agreed to do that, planning and organizing who would take days off when and such. Our goal was to keep the pressure on Charles Hynes, so that every time he turned around and looked at the gallery he knew that black New York was watching him. Every day.

We had Jean Griffith sit right up front, so the jury could see her, the grieving mother. And we kept anyone who was remotely controversial away from her, including me. We didn't want a white member of the jury to look out and see me with her and say, "I can't stand that jerk, I'm voting not guilty." So I was there, but far from the family.

The trial itself was rudimentary, open-and-shut. There were twelve members of the chasing mob indicted, and shortly after the indictments Hynes announced that Robert Riley, one of the attackers, had agreed to turn state's evidence in exchange for leniency. In the first, and most serious trial, Jon Lester, Scott Kern, and Thomas Pirone were charged with murder, and Jason Ladone was charged with manslaughter.

Everything went as expected, the trial lasting two and one-half months. But I was still worried, and when the jury went out I called a meeting at Junior's in downtown Brooklyn, and representatives from virtually every black group came, from the Brooklyn Republicans to the black nationalists. At this meeting I said that I thought we needed to do something dramatic while the jury was out, to underscore that we, blacks, weren't going to take this anymore, and wanted justice. Someone suggested prayer vigils, and Timothy Mitchell and I agreed to organize and do that, which we did. But I also thought we needed something a little more direct. We needed another Day of Outrage.

On December 21, 1987, a year and a day after the killing, we went down into the subway station at Brooklyn's Borough Hall, planning to hold the doors of a train open and thereby block the tracks. Rev. Herbert Daughtry was with me, as were Benjamin Chavis and about three hundred others. Borough Hall was chosen because it is the nerve center of the entire Brooklyn transit system, and blocking there would block everything. But while we stood there, all the trains just passed us by, and when we went over to the other side, the same thing happened. They were ready for us and were planning to keep us from holding the doors and stopping the train. I realized that the only thing to do was to do what we had done during the MTA fight, which was jump on the tracks. Which is what I did. Then Ben Chavis jumped down, Reverend Daughtry jumped down, Charles Barron jumped down, several more. The police ordered us to get off the tracks or face arrest, and when we didn't, seven of us were arrested. As they pulled us up, I knew we had won, because, by law, if someone is on the tracks, they have to cut the electricity to the third rail. When they cut the juice to the main artery, that stopped all the trains from the Bronx to Brooklyn, which is exactly what we wanted. We stopped mass transit in New York City.

We wanted people to stop and say, "What's going on?" Then we can say that what's going on is that a boy was killed in Howard Beach a year ago and the jury's out and it looks like it might come back without a conviction. We wanted people to understand how outraged black New Yorkers were and how tired they were of the usual way things were conducted. The cops took us to central booking in Brooklyn, and they kept bringing people in after us, because, though we didn't know it or plan it, people kept jumping on the tracks, one after another, once they took us away. Adelaide Sanford, a black woman and a member of the New York State Board of Regents, jumped. C. Vernon Mason jumped. Lawyers, preachers, nurses, all kinds of people. By the end of the day, seventy-three of us were in jail.

Black people all over New York, of every station and walk, finally had this feeling that enough was enough. I think black folks in New York City had been seething for years, but no one had ever given them a way to express it. We just didn't know what to do. And that day, finally, they said "Okay." People did all kinds of things:

one group blocked the Brooklyn Bridge, and there were other subway protests. Black New York had been waiting to make a statement
for years, because urban blacks in the North were used to limiting
themselves to rallies and elections, politics, while I was thinking of
Breadbasket, SCLC, Dr. King, and civil disobedience. I had listened
to Jesse Jackson and Jim Bevel and those men sit and tell stories
about the Freedom Rides and lunch counters, and I'd always
thought, "Why can't we bring that to New York?"

The problem was that the New York media were so inept on
black and civil rights history that they couldn't analyze and understand what I was doing. *I was in the tradition.* But the media didn't
understand that, and, frankly, they went nuts. "What is going on
here, keeping people from getting their suppers, stopping traffic and
all that?" *We are trying to get your attention. One time, look at us and listen.*
Any sixteen-year-old in the Mississippi Freedom Democratic Party
could have thought up these moves. But the biggest city in the
country is filled with people who've never been challenged before,
people who are sure that if they don't know of something, it doesn't
exist. They think I'm "manufacturing" this rage, as if such a thing
were possible, and it has been there for fifty years.

But that's how I became demonized and, I'll say, inflated. If all
this had happened in Birmingham, the establishment whites would
have known much better how to handle it. Instead, this was New
York. People are already upset because they've had to admit that
some of those nice little bungalows with manicured lawns and
Christmas lights housed some of the most vicious racists in the
world. Then you've got blacks blocking bridges and subway trains
and throwing everything out of whack, some of the most accomplished blacks in the city included, and your map doesn't work
anymore. Why? This maniac, Sharpton. This nut is trying to destroy the city, our way of life. But that wasn't it. I'm saying *listen:* I
want these people to go to jail for what they did. They committed

murder. All we want is justice. I guess that makes me a revolutionary and a communist.

New York, as I've pointed out, is the center of the world. It is the home of Wall Street, the home of the entertainment and news media, the entrenched arbiter of everything fashionable and au courant. These world leaders had never been challenged until us. They had handpicked their opponents. They decided who the Left was, not the people; it was like a gentleman's agreement that those protesting would only do certain things. You would not interfere with the normal flow of life in the city. And the leaders, including the blacks, went along. They got a patronage job here, a neighborhood program there, a substance addiction or an illicit arrangement with a woman overlooked. They all had their little arrangements. Then here comes somebody who says, "The hell with that, put me in jail," and alters the arrangements, who wouldn't be mad?

The other unsaid problem, which I also pointed out earlier, is that it's easy for a white New Yorker on the Upper East Side, even a Village liberal, to mail a check to Martin Luther King down South. He can do that and feel quite smug and superior. It's more difficult to accept that your kid, or someone you know, is going to jail for breaking bias laws. That's not a thousand miles away. If Mr. Channel 4 News Director sees his cousin on the tape out there throwing rocks, it's more complicated than running the film on a bunch of rednecks in Texas. Free South Africa, fine. Black liberation in South Africa is a fine thing. Somebody you know, people you empathize, even identify with, going to jail, that's another matter. I'm forcing these people in New York to confront their own true feelings about blacks, which they've never done. I'm not marching down Highway 61, I'm on their block. The facade is exposed. The great northeastern liberals aren't so liberal anymore. And you've got people across the country and around the world saying, "How could this be happening in *New York*?"

Kill the messenger. Destroy him in the press. He's a buffoon, look at that hair, he's an informant, he's a tax cheat. That's what has always been done to "uncontrollable" blacks. Howard Beach was the beginning of that for me. We were exposing the truth of white racism in New York City. And for that, I can't be forgiven. But it was, and is, the truth. Bernhard Goetz, I must say, did not stand up and play the race card. He played "crime," and his slick lawyer, Barry Slotnick, was able to keep the rhetoric gray. There was no gray in Howard Beach. The white kids ran through the night yelling, "Kill the niggers," and the adults, the people of responsibility in that community, rallied around those kids.

But strange as it may sound, I don't totally blame those whites. Their rage came from years of white politicians, Nixon into Reagan on through Bush, telling white folks that the reason the country doesn't work is blacks. This led to the reenergizing of racism and race scapegoating. "Why are your taxes so high? Blacks. They're all on welfare and they're bankrupting us. Why is there so much unemployment in Howard Beach? Why can't the young people get meaningful work? Blacks. The niggers have your jobs and affirmative action is helping them do it." Howard Beach was 1986. The heart of the Reagan-Bush epoch. "Them, them, them. It's their fault. Next thing you know they'll be wanting to move in, and after that they'll be screwing your lovely daugh—Look! There they are! Them, them, them! Get them. Kill them!" The media were no help, but of course they have trouble dealing with their own racism.

As we sat in jail that night after the Day of Outrage, we didn't know what was happening with the jury deliberations. They had the leaders all in one cell, and about one o'clock in the morning Al Vann came into the jail and said he had talked to the Brooklyn D.A., Liz Holtzman, and that she had agreed to let the leaders go. But I said, "No. We all have to go or nobody goes." I remembered

Fannie Lou Hamer and them, you don't leave anyone in jail. So then the authorities said, "If you won't go home we're going to transfer you to the jailhouse, to the cell behind the courthouse. You'll be arraigned in the morning." They put all of us—Herbert Daughtry, Timothy Mitchell, Ben Chavis, Roger Green, Charles Barron, and myself—in a paddy wagon and took us to Brooklyn Criminal Court. We sat in the big bullpen cell until nine o'clock, when the judge came.

At about 5:00 A.M. the morning shift came on, with new black corrections officers. A guard walked up to the cell and said, "Hey, Sharpton, you really showed 'em, man." I said, "What?" He said, "The verdict came back, they're all guilty." We had no idea that the jury had come back that night. This was the first we'd heard. I can't help but think that our demonstrations helped jump-start the jury by underlining the seriousness of what they were about to undertake. Another guard came, and he had a *Daily News*, and I'll never forget the cover: "GUILTY!" with a picture of those who were convicted, while across the bottom it said "OUTRAGE!" and a picture of me being arrested.

Jon Lester, Scott Kern, and Jason Ladone were convicted of manslaughter in the second degree, while Thomas Pirone was acquitted on all charges. Lester and Kern were given maximum sentences, ten to thirty years and six to eighteen respectively, while Ladone was given five to fifteen years. For the first time, whites were going to do serious time for assaulting a black in a bias case in New York City. Black lives were worth something in the eyes of the law. Several other members of the mob—Harry Buonocore, Salvatore DeSimone, William Bollander, James Povinelli, and Thomas Fario—also were convicted or pleaded guilty in the case, and Dominic Blum, the driver of the car that killed Michael Griffith, was found guilty in an administrative hearing of hit-and-run.

VIII.

On November 24, 1987, in the middle of the first Howard Beach trial, a fifteen-year-old black girl was found covered in racist graffiti and dog feces in a plastic garbage bag on the grounds of an apartment complex in Wappinger's Falls, New York. The girl, Tawana Brawley, was rushed to the hospital and treated for trauma and sexual assault. Tawana told a story of having been abducted by a group of white men, held captive, and tormented, raped, and sodomized for several days. The local and state authorities apparently took her accusations at face value and initiated an investigation that went in circles and was unsuccessful, stalling after several weeks of dead ends, contradictions, and recriminations.

I didn't hear of any of this until several weeks after

the incident, when, at one of the planning meetings for the Howard Beach Day of Outrage, a woman from Orange County told us of some problems they were having up there around racial conflicts in the county jails, and as a sort of addendum she told us about a very young woman who was saying that she had been kidnapped and raped by law enforcement personnel in that area. Though I didn't know it at the time, I was about to be drawn into the most complex and trying time of my life.

On December 12, 1987, nine days before the Howard Beach verdict, there was a rally in Newburgh, New York, in support of the county prisoners and Tawana Brawley. The rally was held at Baptist Temple, a church pastored by Rev. Saul Williams, an old friend of mine who had known me since I preached there for him and his congregation when I was nine years old. The speakers were Louis Farrakhan and myself, along with various other more militant groups that had been involved in the Howard Beach protests. At the end of the rally we went out of the church and marched through the streets of Newburgh. Farrakhan marched with us, which was unique because he had never before been on a march; the Nation of Islam disapproved of them.

By this time the Brawley investigation had apparently bottomed out, and New York State NAACP President Hazel Dukes accused the local authorities of engaging in a cover-up. Almost a month had passed with no concrete developments. Tawana had made statements to the investigators to the effect that at least one of her attackers was a policeman, and had also, in an apparently trauma-induced mute state, scrawled a note saying, "I want Scoralick. I want Scoralick dead." Frederick Scoralick was the longtime sheriff of Dutchess County, where Wappinger's Falls was located.

Dutchess County is located about seventy miles north of New York City, the third county east of the Hudson River, north of the Westchester suburbs and Putnam exurbs. Dutchess is largely rural, the only true city being Poughkeepsie, the home of Vassar College.

The population, just under 300,000, is overwhelmingly white and middle-class, with the largest employers being IBM and the New York state government, particularly the corrections and state hospital systems. Like most places in upstate New York, Dutchess County seemed to be a quiet, even sleepy place, but close scrutiny would reveal many of the same problems—drugs, illegitimacy, crime, racial conflict—plaguing urban areas, only at a lower volume. Blacks who lived there basically fit two categories: either commuters who had escaped from the city but still worked there or longtime residents who worked in some kind of service job like maid or gardener. There had been a history of low-grade police brutality over the years, police stopping blacks in cars, arrests that were without basis, two or three charges of excessive force.

Almost a year before the Brawley incident, a twenty-year-old black man, Jimmy Lee Bruce, had been killed by two off-duty white police officers across the river from Wappingers Falls in the town of Walkill. Bruce and several friends had been unruly at a movie theater and an argument led to the deadly scuffle. Bruce's death had raised racial tensions in general and had caused a deep suspicion of police in particular (blacks were grossly underrepresented on local forces) throughout the Middle Hudson Valley, as the area is known. Also, strangely, in a little-known case, a black woman in Newton, New Jersey, was left by a gang of white men in much the same condition as Tawana Brawley, with feces smeared all over her body, her hair roughly chopped off, and an "X" crossed on her head. This happened in February 1987, nine months before the Brawley situation, and there had not been any arrests. Was there some kind of sick gang on the loose, targeting black women? Given what was going on in the national media, Bernhard Goetz, Howard Beach, and the like, to say that Tawana Brawley entered her charges into a volatile environment is the grossest of understatements.

I met the family for the first time at the Baptist Temple rally, and several weeks later Alton Maddox, C. Vernon Mason, and I became involved as advisers. The Dutchess County NAACP had been representing the Brawleys, but the family, who had been talking to Maddox off and on about legal strategy, felt the NAACP wasn't aggressive enough and asked us to take over the case. I want to stress this: all I knew was what I had heard at the pre–Day of Outrage meeting, what I had seen on Channel 2 as it was reported by Mary Murphy in December, and what was said at the rally. This is important because it is often implied that we were in league with Tawana on some kind of conspiracy from the start, that she lied and we knowingly embellished and fabricated the rest. The fact is, the story was already public when we became involved—it was on WCBS, it was in various papers—and whether one wishes to believe Tawana Brawley or not, it is erroneous to say that I used my media wiles to disseminate a tale that I was not even involved with until a month after it had been made public by mainstream media sources.

I think it is obvious why the family would ask us to become involved. We had just gotten the convictions in Howard Beach, a first in New York City, blacks across the country were aware of and proud of the Day of Outrage, and we—Maddox, Mason, and myself—were increasingly seen by the black community as unbought, unbowed, and unafraid. We were seen as able to get results and we were only concerned for the people we represented, not the system.

By the time we entered the case, early January, it was already a ticking bomb. On November 28 Tawana had been taken by EMS technicians in an ambulance from the Pavilion condominiums where she had been found in the garbage bag to the emergency room of Saint Francis Hospital six miles up the road in Poughkeepsie. She had been found by Pavilion residents Joyce and Lorenzo Lloray, who called police. Admitted to the hospital as a "Jane Doe," Tawana was examined and interviewed by doctors and police officers and a story began to emerge. Upon returning by bus from visiting friends in Newburgh, she had been abducted Tuesday evening by a gang of white men, held, drugged into unconsciousness, and brutally attacked for four days, then left defiled and in the garbage bag in front of her old home on Saturday morning.

I cannot describe the horror I felt upon hearing the full details of this story. No black person is without historical memory of the outrages visited upon black women throughout slavery and into the twentieth century. I was interested in this case because I felt someone had to stand up and defend this young girl; I felt like I was defending my mother, my wife, my daughters, my sisters, all the black women I know and love, black women in general, even. Something had to be done. I had spent some time up in the area talking to people, interviewing the family. I personally talked to the EMS technicians who had brought Tawana into the hospital. According to ambulance records, she was unconscious, unresponsive, and 30 percent of the hair had been torn out of her head. Eighty percent of her body was covered with excrement, and she had burns. She could not speak. For some unstated reason, Tawana was not taken to the closest hospital, but all the way to Poughkeepsie.

I also finally met Tawana personally—I hadn't actually met her at the rally in December—and talked with her in a serious manner about what had happened. I was totally convinced that Tawana Brawley was telling the truth, that she had been raped and kidnapped as she had said. I didn't believe that she could just make these things up. She was describing law enforcement suspects who resembled actual persons, and other aspects of the case seemed to be lining up just as she said.

We were getting up to speed on the particulars just as William Grady, the Dutchess County district attorney, withdrew from the investigation without explanation to the public. Apparently, Grady felt he was caught in a possible conflict of interest because one of his assistant district attorneys, Steven Pagones, was rumored to be a suspect in the assault. Those rumors were complicated by the further rumor that Harry Crist, a part-time police officer from the town of Fishkill, was identified by Tawana Brawley as one of her abductors. Crist, a close friend of Steven Pagones, had apparently committed suicide on December 1, three days after the girl was found. Crist carried a gun and a badge, and had admitted riding around with New York state trooper Scott Patterson on the night Tawana disappeared, and his car, a decommissioned silver four-door Plymouth police car, was similar to a car carrying four white men that postman Timothy Losee thought he had seen cruising the parking lot of the Pavilion condominiums on the morning of November 28.

These admitted activities on that Tuesday night corroborated parts of Tawana's story. Crist's car also matched Tawana's description of the "unmarked police car" that carried her abductor, which could have also possibly been an unmarked police cruiser. Grady's withdrawal seemed to lend substance to these suspicions, which were further roiled when the first special prosecutor appointed to replace Grady, David Sall, himself withdrew from the case within thirty-six hours of having been appointed. After reviewing the case, he said that "no local attorney could possibly prosecute this case."

That left it to Governor Mario Cuomo to appoint a special prosecutor, as he had done in the Howard Beach case and as he had resisted doing in the Brawley matter. He chose New York State Attorney General Robert Abrams, whom we weren't crazy about because we preferred someone who, like Charles Hynes in the Howard Beach case, could give his full attention to the matter. And, as we had suspected, shortly after Abrams had been appointed, he delegated the day-to-day supervision of the investigation to his assistant William Ryan. We had nothing against Ryan, but we didn't know him, he had no visible civil rights record, and in our minds, we wanted someone who would be publicly accountable.

This public accountability had another twist as well. In the Howard Beach case, Charles Hynes, as special prosecutor, was totally independent of even a temptation to slant the case toward the whims of public opinion. As became evident, Hynes had his political ambitions, to be sure, but he was not an officeholder who would face a referendum on his action the next year. This was my biggest problem with Robert Abrams, and it led to the breakdown of trust and cooperation that so complicated the case. I was worried that the Attorney General's Office would try to score points with the public to build Abrams's political profile. That was very disturbing, given that this was the most sensitive bias case in New York State history. I think there became times the authorities were as interested in nailing Sharpton, Maddox, and Mason as they were in finding out what happened to that girl those four days.

The Tawana Brawley case quickly took on an aspect of "through the looking glass," Alice in Wonderland, nothing-makes-sense, as everything that was said was quickly and easily contradicted by the other actors in the situation. For example, Abrams stated unequivocally near the end of the investigation that Tawana had not been raped, and this is what was submitted to the grand jury. He said there was no finding of rape in the hospital examinations, but there are problems with this analysis. First of all, there are two sets of records, one that says "rape," another that does not. She was bathed before her pelvic examination, which is not supposed to be done in a rape situation, because you can destroy evidence. Bathing her was probably just a humanitarian response to a very bad circumstance; the person who so acted was not trying to participate in a cover-up or anything like that, but rather wanted to make Tawana more comfortable and remove the filth. So an act of kindness complicates the investigation and contributes to "he said, she said" conflicts in the situation.

Abrams insisted his version was the only one possible, and we just didn't buy it. He said there was no rape, no abduction, the whole thing was a hoax staged by the girl and possibly her mother. But Abrams also said Tawana ran off with a boyfriend; where is he? The FBI, the state police, the entire State Attorney General's Office, and all of the deputies and local police in Dutchess County, working together for over a year, couldn't find this boyfriend, couldn't find where Tawana was. Abrams is asking us to agree with him that she lied without his being able to offer an alternative of what happened. The *New York Times* investigative team also posits a hoax theory, but it is built on the hearsay testimony of a purported friend of Tawana's, Daryl Rodriguez, and can't be given any more weight than that.

If Tawana Brawley lied, if her provision of plausible descriptions that were never followed up on was merely circumstantial, then why can't all that law enforcement firepower tell us where she was? All other accounts are hearsay, or circumstantial themselves, at best. Mike Taibbi of Channel 2 came out with a story where he said Tawana spent the time that she was missing in a crack house in Newburgh, utilizing two witnesses who were discredited and later recanted, and that's the closest anyone has come to a definitive account.

While Bob Abrams released a report saying that he believed the case to be a fraud, the grand jury said only that there was not enough evidence to indict the accused. They did not say that it was a fraud. Two voted in support of Tawana. And, again, *no one ever said where she was.* This was not a person with resources or options, this was a fifteen-year-old black girl. She had six dollars in her pocket, not a credit card. People, including the *New York Times*, have spun theories. Why hasn't all that collective investigative power proven it?

I had to make a decision. I'm faced with this story, one of the most horrible things I have ever heard, she's backed by her parents and aunt, and there are other things that fall into place surrounding the story. There was, for example, the young white boy who said he saw a car with a license plate that matched the accused assistant district attorney's leaving the apartment complex where Tawana was found. He testified to that, then later said he didn't know whether he could remember anymore, and he and his family moved suddenly to Virginia. There were a lot of things like this that just fit in, but I was asked to call her a liar, and meantime believe in and trust the same criminal justice system that has told me lies all my life.

This is a tragic consequence of American life that I only began to understand during the Brawley case. If ever there was a situation that cried out for cooperation and community trust, this was it. But it couldn't occur, because the reservoir of goodwill was empty. No one had done any work in building it up, and the case dropped into a vacuum, which led to mistrust and recrimination. How could it have happened any other way?

For example, people ask me if I really believe that law enforcement personnel, who swear their very lives to the pursuit of justice, could possibly be involved in something like this. It may sound flip, but I say, "Of course." Law enforcement men sworn to uphold justice killed Eleanor Bumpurs, killed Michael Stewart, beat Rodney King to within an inch of his life. Law enforcement officer Michael Dowd sold drugs out of his police cruiser, DEA and Justice Department men go over to the Colombians. Law enforcement people are human, sinners, and as susceptible to becoming criminals as much as the rest of us. The perception on the Upper East Side of Manhattan, in Westchester and Dutchess counties, might be that a prosecutor, by definition, could not be involved in something like this affair, but that is decidedly *not* the perception where I come from.

We only wanted to ask a simple question, of the assistant district attorney, of the state trooper, of the man who died, Harry Crist, of their friend Eugene Branson: where were you? Tawana implied that they were together, and the accused freely admitted to spending those days with each other, but said they were shopping, in Danbury. Their corroborating witnesses were each other. One of the men, the prosecutor, offered a detailed alibi to the grand jury under oath, but the others did not, though there was exculpatory information placed before the grand jury on their behalf. But again, assuming those four are innocent, where was Tawana? And another curious question: how did she know they were together?

So we began to wonder if someone was being protected. Tawana's story seemed coherent, and there was a lot backing it up around the edges. But there were a lot of conflicts. Besides his status as an elected official, Abrams had a house in Dutchess. Also, how could the attorney general go against the state police? He needed their cooperation on most of the activities in his office. The prosecutor's father was an influential judge in the county. Who would want to cross him? That's why we didn't want to cooperate. We thought the deck was being stacked, and no one was able to convince us for sure that it wasn't.

Then the bottom fell out. January 20, 1988, front page of the papers, ran the headline "SHARPTON FBI INFORMANT." Under normal circumstances, if someone works with the government, provides information useful to the apprehension of criminals, he's a hero. It remains extremely suspicious to me that I was suddenly set up as an informer—not only on drug dealers, which I've freely admitted, but on black activists and politicians. I was accused of "trying to meet" Black Liberation Army leader JoAnne Chesimard by contacting some low-level black revolutionaries; what was never understood is that if I wanted to find her I know how to do it, call William Kunstler. Why didn't anyone ask if the so-called revolutionaries were FBI agents? Has COINTELPRO (FBI counterintelligence program dedicated to destroying civil rights and black power movements) been forgotten so quickly? Why that timing, in the middle of Brawley?

Then, even worse. Out of nowhere, Channel 2 News did an eleven-minute story—I don't know when they've given the president of the United States more than three or four—concerning a man who claimed to be my chief aide, Perry McKinnon. McKinnon was a security officer at Saint Mary's Hospital where I had my office. He drove me around sometimes—I still didn't have a car—but did not work for me. He said that I had doubts about Tawana's story. On what did he base this? That I had asked him, concerning the case, "Brother, what do you think?" First of all, if I had asked him that I think it would have illustrated that I must have been seeking the truth, looking for other perspectives, but it doesn't imply anything about my view. Second, I asked a lot of people that, though not him. We never had any such conversation. The truth is, McKinnon had a lot of big thoughts, and one of them was that he wanted to form his own private security company, and he got it into his head that I should introduce him to and get him contracts with Don King and Donald Trump, which I refused to do. This was his attempt to get attention, and probably get even, in his mind, with me. And when he was found to have fabricated much of his past, to not be able to provide certain facts about me, to, basically, be lying, there was no eleven-minute retraction by Channel 2 and the rest of the media. There wasn't even an eleven-second one.

Things come in threes, and the third attack on my credibility during the Brawley affair was launched by an artful dodger named Samuel McClease. This time there was a twelve-minute story done by the same reporter as the McKinnon story, and it made all the front pages. McClease's tale was that he was a navy-trained electronics surveillance expert and that I had hired him to place listening devices in my house, Mason's house, and Maddox's office (not his house), so that if the Brawley hoax blew up I would be covered. I would have tapes and be able to prove that I hadn't concocted it and that Maddox and Mason were in on it.

Aside from the comedy of all this (if I'm a wired FBI informant constantly gathering tapes on everybody, why do I need to hire somebody to wire me?), the totality of these attacks began to seem incredible. If I'm cheek by jowl with the FBI, don't they know it's a hoax? Why don't they break it up? All this is being put out to the public, and I'm beginning to be sure that someone is being protected up in Dutchess County. Things were getting delirious.

For four days the feds did a dance with this McClease, whom I've never met, by the way, making all these charges and defaming me *and they haven't even heard the tapes*, all led by the venerable U.S. attorney, the current mayor and my chief antagonist, Rudolph Giuliani. Giuliani brought McClease to the grand jury and announced he was preparing to indict Al Sharpton, Alton Maddox, and C. Vernon Mason for this hoax. Then they found out that the tapes were blank.

There had never been any tapes. A logical question might be, why did CBS and law enforcement do all that damage without ever hearing the tapes? Mike Taibbi never said to McClease, "I need to hear the tapes before I give you half the six o'clock news." The U.S. attorney never felt the need to check either. So, if you're looking at it from where I am, you'd say somebody's seriously trying to discredit me. I must be a threat to something. And I'm still waiting for my apologies.

I attribute this massive attack to two things: someone in law enforcement did not want the Brawley matter pursued, and I think that after Howard Beach the powers-that-be were afraid that we might be building a movement that could move some rocks out of the road. Black folks in New York were doing things they had never done before. The power structure didn't want another victory by the poor blacks.

New York State, in the persons of the governor and the heads of the criminal justice system, was being exposed as having double standards where racial matters were concerned. The same person who tried to snare me into informing on Don King, Joe Spinelli, had by this time resigned from the FBI and become inspector general of the state of New York, appointed by Mario Cuomo. I was told that Spinelli was the one that fed Mike McAlary and *Newsday* the informer business. I've never been convinced of that. He always seemed fair and discreet. Coincidence? Timing? Rudolph Giuliani, as U.S. attorney, was the prosecutor who went after Don King, which was where that whole informant business started. Coincidence? Timing? As the old saying goes, just because you're paranoid doesn't mean somebody's not after you. Why was I such a threat? Hadn't I been *right* at Howard Beach?

The case careened through these issues with us refusing to cooperate until finally Robert Abrams subpoenaed Glenda Brawley, Tawana's mother. Abrams decided to coerce the family into cooperating with his investigation, though several of our qualms and questions had not yet been addressed. When Alton Maddox stood before Justice Angelo Ingrassia to answer the subpoena, he protested the few blacks in the courtroom, Ingrassia's impartiality, the exclusion of blacks from the grand jury, and the possible illegality of the actual impanelment of this grand jury. Maddox tried several other tacks, some right up to and maybe even over the line, but all trying to make the point of whether or not Glenda and Tawana Brawley could get fair treatment from this investigation conducted by these people, in this county.

Then he read a statement to the judge detailing our concerns and putting them into a larger context, which many whites refused to do with this case. "Four hundred years of oppression is riding on this case, and we have reached a point when the African nation in this country, and particularly those Africans in New York, are thoroughly disgusted with the way justice is administered and they are thoroughly disgusted with black victims of racial crimes being told by a grand jury that they are hallucinating and that what happened to them amounts to a hoax. I hope from this day forward we can wipe clean those four hundred years of injustices and begin to proceed into the twenty-first century like intelligent and civilized men and women. And because of that I would ask you to take all that into consideration and search your heart and your mind."

Whites in New York and across the country tended to want to see the case as one isolated incident in Dutchess County, New York, and without relevance to anything else. Blacks saw it as the latest in a series of outrages stretching back to Jamestown. *Why, given what has happened here in America, should we trust law enforcement? Is it completely out of the question that a cover-up might be occurring? Why should we trust the media, the institutions that have held us up to the world as monkeys for so many years? What is the advantage to cooperating?* Whites, perhaps, cannot even formulate these questions, much less understand or answer them. Perhaps such questions are too alien to their experience as the majority, the power. But they cannot use their power as the majority to dictate to the minority what reality is, what is and is not true. That freedom, or the promise of it, is what the country is built on.

Throughout my career my motives have been questioned, and even sneered at, but it all comes down to the old spiritual "How Long, Lord, How Long?" Or as Maddox said, we "are thoroughly . . . disgusted with black victims . . . being told . . . that they are hallucinating. . . ." Particularly when all the public, much less private, facts don't add up. But as blacks we have to reserve the right to see what we see, to make our own judgments and form our own opinions, and to proceed as our interpretations compel us. To do otherwise would be less than human.

Maddox decided that he did not want to cooperate any further in the proceedings. There was no room for us, the Brawley supporters, in the courtroom, and he was suspicious of the procedural arrangements. Glenda Brawley became a fugitive from justice, having been sentenced to thirty days in jail for contempt of court, and there was a warrant issued for her arrest.

We decided to place her in sanctuary in a black church and see if the state of New York would break into a church to arrest her.

After a long night with me making phone calls and conducting negotiations while Maddox and Mason drove throughout the tri-state area with Glenda Brawley, we landed at Ebenezer Baptist in Queens, Rev. Timothy Mitchell's church, at about six o'clock in the morning. After we got her inside, I called the media and they all came, and then the police knew and they came, and we had a standoff, because the state troopers wouldn't go to the church, but they wouldn't leave, either. We had a big rally that night. Everything was galvanized.

At midnight the deacons of the church come in and say we have to leave the church. I was stunned and said, "What do you mean? The whole world is watching us, and you say we have to leave?" Then they said that Reverend Mitchell had left town for a few days, and as deacons they were now in charge and they wanted us out. We were absolutely at a loss, because we were going to look very stupid after making a great stand. We still refuse to submit Glenda Brawley to arrest, but we're losing our sanctuary. In fact, we've been evicted.

Maddox and Mason started working the phone, trying to find Reverend Mitchell so he could overturn the board's decision. I decided to do what I had always done when I got in trouble: I called Bill Jones. I said, "Reverend Jones, here's the situation." He said he would call me back in the morning, and I asked him to make it early, because we would soon be on the street. Then at about ten o'clock in the morning, who comes walking in but the Rev. William Augustus Jones, saying, "Pack her bags, you're coming to Bethany." I don't know why, but Bill Jones was just always there for me. He was my beginning in the outside world in many ways, and here he was in a time of deep crisis. A guardian angel.

We got in the cars and drove to Brooklyn. Somehow—luck, I guess—the police never got wind of what we were doing. We made it to Bethany without incident and stayed there for the next three weeks. Phil Donahue came out and did a live show from the church about the case. I stayed in the basement with Glenda and four or five security guards, and in many ways I was right back to where I started from when I was fourteen, when we used to do Breadbasket rallies in that very same basement.

Some were surprised by the level of support we received, but I think the majority of the black community always believed Tawana, from the beginning up until now. I think that the way the media approached the situation—trying every possible way to discredit us—affected the way some people saw it. But most black people understood us and what we were trying to do. What I don't think most white people understood was that there is some Tawana in most black people, almost like a collective memory, as Jung described it, that corresponds to the event. On the *Donahue Show* Phil Donahue said to me, "How can you possibly believe that these men you've accused could do such a thing?" And I pointed out to the crowd and said, "How could you ask me that, when you're sitting in a church with five hundred black people and every one of us has a different complexion? Where did that come from? How could I not think it possible that white men might rape black women?" Then it occurred to me that whites probably didn't understand it, *couldn't* understand it, but it was something blacks understood all too well.

And maybe we did bring a lot of that to the table in the Brawley matter. Maybe in my case it also had something to do with what happened between my father and my sister, all the emotions that were involved. Maybe the harder they attacked Tawana, the more I saw a vulnerable black woman, like my mother, that no one would fight for. At some point it stopped being Tawana, and started being me defending my mother and all the black women no one would fight for. I was not going to run away from her like my father had run away from my mother, like so many other black men had run away. This was going to be one time, if I lost it all, that I was going to go all the way down.

I am sure that there are those who think that these factors may have pushed me past good judgment, but I think that my best judgment had already been exercised. I think that was what made me passionate about it. I think people might like to explain my ferocious involvement as overemotional zeal, but the fact is, Tawana was never disproved. Can I say that I know beyond a shadow of a doubt what happened? No. Neither can my critics. We haven't proved anything definitively, but it hasn't been dismissed. Who has conclusively proven her to be false? Not Abrams, not the FBI, not Dutchess County. This is unarguable.

Tawana Brawley provided descriptions and names she should not or could not have known otherwise, and she was found in a condition that was, to me, evidence enough. I firmly believe that if those facts had been allowed to get through the secret grand jury to a public trial, there would have been evidence enough for a jury. There was no eyewitness, but there was no eyewitness in Howard Beach, either. There's another factor here as well: I have never fought a case that someone somewhere didn't say was a hoax. I deal in matters that people, by definition, do *not* want to deal with. So they say that nothing happened that night at Howard Beach, that Michael Griffith was high on cocaine and ran out onto the Belt Parkway of his own volition.

Right after Tawana's case there was a young black woman raped at Saint John's University, and one of the rapists turned state's evidence and the others were still acquitted. When do you have enough evidence? Whites have never believed us. In the Brawley case I believe it was a combination of the authorities in Dutchess wanting to protect law enforcement people and the state powers-that-be wanting to derail our movement that made them dig in. What else can be made of the fact that, at the end of the case, not only did Robert Abrams hold a press conference to announce his findings in the investigation, he announced at the same time that he was starting bar disciplinary actions against Alton Maddox and C. Vernon Mason, and a criminal investigation of Al Sharpton, which led to a seventy-count indictment?

If Bob Abrams is playing fair and being thoroughly objective, then why should he want to penalize those who believed in the case and merely sought to see that it be conducted openly and honorably? Let's speculate that Tawana lied. Why should the whole power of the state be put behind sending me to jail? Because I, like most others, believed the lie? Again, these were the same dynamics that were involved in the Howard Beach scenario—that it wasn't true, we were pushing too hard, why couldn't we butt out and leave it to the authorities? Those were the conditions that led Santucci to file no indictments. And our strategy and tactics led to a satisfactory conclusion. That is all we were trying to do in the Brawley case. I thought Abrams was going on a vendetta, and that proved to me that the system, as it did against Marcus Garvey, Martin Luther King, and the Black Panthers, will stop at nothing when threatened by blacks.

As far as I'm personally concerned, the Brawley case comes down to this: some believe, some disbelieve. But even if those who disbelieve are convinced beyond the shadow of a doubt that Tawana lied, how do they justify Perry McKinnon and Samuel McClease and their absolute deception, along with, at best, the willful blindness to the truth of the attorney general of the state of New York, the United States attorney, and the FBI? Remember McKinnon slandering me for eleven minutes on broadcast television? Remember the blank tapes? Remember the seventy-count indictment and my acquittal on all charges? Not one charge made against me by the state of New York stood up in court, not one. How do they justify taking Maddox's and Mason's licenses, their livelihoods, when Abrams and Giuliani can be forgiven their incompetence and mistakes? They can be forgiven, but they are also so high and mighty that they can beat up on a little girl who they feel is incorrect? Why should anybody believe what Bob Abrams says about anything? I believe Tawana, to this day. I have always believed her and always will. And I believe Robert Abrams lied on me. As a matter of fact, I know he did. I was there in court, and I heard what he said.

I don't know if it is possible for us to deal with these racially charged cases in the United States. The Rodney King case would be the second biggest hoax of all time—no white person would have believed Rodney's story—if a white man named George Holliday hadn't been standing there with a video camera. And, *even with the tape and a white man swearing what he saw,* twelve white folks out in Simi Valley still thought it was a hoax. If you look at the Brawley situation through the eyes of Al Sharpton, it might look different.

People say, "Can't you see how this looks fishy?" and I say, yes, I can see that; I've always had to look at Tawana Brawley through their eyes, but they've never had to look at her through mine. They see another black telling lies, disturbing the peace. But what I don't understand is why there couldn't be a trial based on what had been discovered and uncovered. What everyone forgets is that the grand jury is secret, we don't know what happened unless it goes to trial. We don't know what was said by whom. And everything that happens is only the presentation of the prosecution. You don't get to hear what the defense has to say.

Why do we have trials in this society? There's an accusation made, there's prima facie evidence, it's examined. In the Brawley matter there were three men (and one dead) accused who cannot account for their whereabouts other than to say they were with each other, and this girl is able to establish independent knowledge of them and that they were together. That's enough for a trial. There was destruction of potential evidence in the bathing, the hospital didn't follow the procedure, there's all kinds of room for doubt. There were too many conflicts of interest, in my mind. If it *was* a hoax, why not bring it out into the light of day? Why did it take three prosecutors to figure that out? Why were the first two alarmed enough to withdraw? Why didn't Grady and the hospital announce it right away? Obviously the district attorney went through the initial records and found them creditable enough to move forward. And, to beg the question, how did he have a conflict of interest if, because it was a hoax, there was nothing to conflict?

I don't know if the definitive truth will ever be known. I examined this case, and in my best judgment, I believe I came to the right conclusion. I'm aware that I would be an instant folk hero in some circles—particularly now that I'm taken more seriously by the mainstream—if I were to say that I was duped and made a mistake. But I don't believe that. If I was in a race for a U.S. Senate seat and was two points from winning, and my pollster said, "All you've got to do is say Tawana tricked you and you'll go up five points and win," I would lose the race. I'm not going to say something I don't believe. I'm often accused of being opportunistic. It would be more opportunistic to say what everyone is waiting to hear. But that's not what I think, and I'm not going to say it.

Why was everyone so focused on Tawana Brawley, so obsessed with her? Why, if Al Sharpton went out tonight and dived in front of a bullet intended for the pope, would a bunch of white guys stand up and say, "But what about Tawana?" I think Tawana represented a real problem for Americans, and it didn't have anything to do with whether or not it was all a hoax. What it has to do with is a psychosexual dilemma that America still can't get past. If they simply thought she lied, that could be handled. It's this racial/sexual psychosis that's become part of the fabric of the country that they can't get past. Tawana Brawley calls up too much in everybody's memory, white and black, for there to be any rational discussion of the facts and issues.

Tawana Brawley was the O.J. Simpson case before O.J. Simpson. You're into the murky swamp of taboo "race-mixing" and it all hit a nerve, a racial/sexual nerve, and it has nothing to do with whether anybody believed her or not. That's why there's been such a reaction to the O.J. situation. If O.J.'s wife had been black, the soap operas would have been in full swing, there would have been no CNN, and Mr. Simpson would be just another black man sitting up in San Quentin.

The whole thing goes to my credibility. I was right about Howard Beach, which was before Tawana Brawley, I was right about Yusuf Hawkins, which was after Tawana Brawley. I was right about Phillip Pannell. I proved Robert Abrams and the state of New York wrong in open court, humiliated them, beat seventy counts. Why didn't anyone say Abrams was perpetrating a hoax? If they were fair, they'd at least say, "Sharpton was lying through his teeth about Tawana, but what the state did was wrong as well," but I think I'll be in glory before I hear anyone in the establishment or the media say that.

The way I've come to understand extends from something Jesse Jackson once said to me. We were in my car listening to a talk show on WABC—we call it "hate radio"—and there was a guy on who was really running me down. And Jesse said to me, "Before you even say anything about this, let me tell you something. This used to happen to me in Chicago all the time. But have you ever been in a football game?"—Jesse was a great high school and college football player. "If you've played football, you noticed that the players, the offense and the defense, they're all thinking about one thing. The guy with the ball. If everybody's after you, it must be that you have the ball. Nobody's chasing anybody that doesn't have the ball." So I have learned to be flattered by everybody being after me. If I'm the one they all want to tackle, it's because they're afraid that I may score.

I represent an element that is rising up in this country and saying that all the problems are far from solved. People haven't liked me saying it, but more and more are coming to agree. The problem is still the color line, the problem of race. The American Dilemma.

From Du Bois to King to now, it's still the American Dilemma. And I won't let them ignore it. Jimmy Breslin wrote a story several years ago about me being the black man that haunts suburban living rooms with "Hey, it isn't over yet. Racism isn't over yet." And rather than working at solving the problems, they try to wipe me off the screen. And every time they start doing that, it only makes the screen dirtier, more opaque, more difficult to see. But they're not going to wipe me off. Whether it's Bernhard Goetz, Howard Beach, Bensonhurst, Tawana Brawley, or anything else, I'm still there.

IX.

In December of 1988 or January of '89, everyone I knew started calling me, saying that they were getting subpoenas from Robert Abrams and being grilled very closely about my activities. Then they started telling me they were being brought in front of a grand jury.

Then I got a call from James Brown. He had gotten into trouble and was in jail, and he called me collect at least five nights a week from jail. One night he says, "You'll never guess where I am." I said, thinking he was joking, "In jail in South Carolina?" He said, "Albany!" I said, "Albany, New York?" Then he told me what had happened. "They came and got me, two New York state troopers, and flew me up here. I've got to go before a grand jury against you in the morning."

I knew from all of this that Bob Abrams was trying to

build a criminal case against me. Everybody was called before the grand jury, including Don King, who would presumably have reason to retaliate because I had supposedly informed on him. Federal prosecutors opened a probe as well, and I didn't know who would ultimately come after me, the state attorney general or the U.S. attorney.

One afternoon while the investigation was widening I received a phone call from my old *Village Voice* nemesis Jack Newfield, who was then writing for the *New York Daily News.* After a few pleasantries, he says to me, very matter-of-factly, "I understand you're going to be indicted in a week or so." I said I didn't know, because I didn't. He said, "My sources in the Attorney General's Office tell me it's going to be a tax indictment." I said, "Well, if it is, then I guess I'll join the black leader tax indictment Hall of Fame. Martin Luther King, Adam Clayton Powell, Marcus Garvey all had tax indictments. I guess I should be honored to have reached that level."

Newfield kind of chuckled, and the next day the *Daily News* had the headline "SHARPTON TO BE INDICTED." The story didn't really tell me anything, but I stayed around the house that day, and at about one o'clock the phone rang, and someone said, "Mr. Sharpton, I'm so-and-so from the Attorney General's Office and we're outside your home this very moment and we've come to arrest you because you have been indicted. We've closed off all the streets, and we'd appreciate it if you would open the door and cooperate." I said I would.

I was wearing a jogging suit, and I just put on the jacket and went downstairs. I will never forget how many cops they had down there and the way the neighborhood was sealed off. You'd have thought they were bringing in Al Capone. But no press was there, and we rode over to central booking in Brooklyn without incident, where I was fingerprinted and held for a short time.

Then they said they had to take me over to Manhattan Criminal

Court for arraignment. Two troopers were in the car with me, and they were being real respectful—they hadn't handcuffed me—and we were having a nice, light conversation, talking about the weather and the Mets and the like, when, as we drove over the Brooklyn Bridge, the car phone rang, one of the troopers has a short conversation, and after he hangs up, turns to me and says, "Al, I hate to do this, but I'm going to have to cuff you. That's from downtown. They've got all the press down there, and that's how they want it." I told him to do whatever he had to do. He said, "Well, at least we can wait until we're almost there."

So we went on, and just around the corner from the courthouse they stopped the car and handcuffed me. Then they eased around the corner and brought me out for the cameras. The whole thing was set up for the media, the whole thing was political. They thought they were shaming me or something. I didn't even know what I was being indicted for, I don't know if they've called my lawyer, nothing. They brought me in through the gauntlet, but I didn't say anything because I didn't know what to say. They put me in the bullpen behind the judge's chambers. Then, about twenty minutes later, here comes Alton Maddox walking through the gate. I never found out who called him, Abrams or one of my people, but I was glad to see him.

The first thing I said to him was, "Alton, what is it? What are they saying I did?"

He said, "I don't know, they didn't give me anything. But we're going to have to go in front of this arraignment. All I've heard is sixty-seven counts, a lot of counts." All I could say was, "Okay." Then they came and got me out of the bullpen and took me in front of the judge. The courtroom was packed with media and, surprisingly, a lot of my supporters who had heard what was happening on the radio. That made me feel very good, and I knew everything was going to be okay because my people were with me. Black radio has always been one of the keys to our movement, WLIB and WWRL. These radio stations and their DJs have been like the drums of the contemporary black community.

Victor Genecin, one of Abrams's top lieutenants, was there to handle the case himself. He announced the charges, sixty-seven counts, including fifty-three felonies. The judge turned and looked at Maddox, and said, "Counselor, for the purposes of this arraignment, how does your client plead?" And before Maddox could respond, I looked at the judge and said, "I plead the attorney general insane." Everybody in the courtroom—except the attorney general's people—burst out laughing. They had something of a problem getting the court back to order, and that was the arraignment.

To everyone's surprise, given all those felony counts, the judge released me on my own recognizance. This was a signal to me that he didn't see the indictment as completely serious. Sixty-seven counts, you're supposed to put up some bail. Right after he released me, I was immediately rearrested, to be taken to Albany and arraigned up there on the three remaining counts, the tax indictment. They brought me out the front door of the Manhattan courthouse where the public walks in, which was unusual. They never bring prisoners out the front. But I think they planned on humiliating me in front of the whole city, so when we got to the revolving doors and were getting ready to go through, my defiance got the better of me, and rather than walk with my head down or cover my face like I was some guilty criminal, I stepped through the door into the cameras with my handcuffed fists up and shouting, "They did this to King! They did this to Powell! They did this to Garvey! This is my inauguration! I have arrived!" All the way to the car. The law enforcement guys, cops and prosecutors, kept saying, "Be quiet, be quiet." I said, "Be quiet for what? You the ones that brought me out here in front of the press, so let's talk to the press, this is what you wanted."

Then, when we finally got to the car that was waiting for me at curbside, an officer reached up to push my head down—which they do as a courtesy when you're cuffed—but before I got in the back-seat, I popped back up and yelled, "He's messing up my hair!" Everybody out there was laughing and shouting, and I got in the car.

I know a lot of people at that moment thought, "There goes that fool again, making a mockery of the legal system and law enforce-ment," but I had two very serious reasons for what I did: sending a message to Robert Abrams that he wasn't getting to me, and concur-rently, sending a message to the black community that I was all right, and that this was all frivolous, cooked-up nonsense. If I had come out of the courthouse in a somber mood and looked like I was trying to hide, it would have given the impression to my people that there was something to be concerned about, there was some valid-ity to the accusations, and that I wasn't all right.

We started driving the three hours to Albany, and the troopers escorting me were laughing and making jokes, saying, "They should have known that you know how to deal with the media, you really outsmarted 'em." I had deflected Abrams's intended spin. The next day the front page of the *Daily News* said, "67 COUNTS—SHARPTON PLEADS ATTORNEY GENERAL INSANE."

When we got outside the city limits, they took the cuffs off, and we rode all the way to Albany with me relaxing in the back, them in the front, talking and laughing like we were going fishing or some-thing. That's how serious they took the situation. After we'd gone about halfway, they said, "Al, you hungry? We're going to get some Chinese." I said, "Fine." We went in and sat down, and during the entire meal people were coming over to get autographs and make conversation, all the while I'm sitting there under arrest, on my way to my second arraignment that day.

Then something happened that has always stayed with me. I had excused myself and gone to the rest room, and when I came back, one of the troopers looks at me and says, "You know, Al, I worked on the Brawley case. I'd like to ask you a question. What really happened to Tawana?" I said, "You're one of the state police investigators, you all handled the case, you released a report calling it a hoax, and you're asking me what happened?" It hit me then that there had been a party line developed that everyone in the police was told to go along with. Here's a veteran detective in the state police admitting he didn't know what had happened. I knew then that my own beliefs on the matter were not without some foundation.

By the time we arrived in Albany it was late, and they put me in the Albany County jail overnight. I thought a lot that night about what was going on, as I had been arrested many times on civil rights charges, but this was the first time I had faced any criminal situation. But I wasn't worried. I really believed what I had said in New York, that this trial, literally and figuratively, was a symptom of my growing effectiveness as a civil rights leader.

Maddox arrived the next morning, and when I was brought in to see the judge and be arraigned, I simply pleaded not guilty, was given a bond that was guaranteed by John Beatty, the owner of Harlem's Cotton Club (we didn't have to put up anything), and released. We went back downstate, and that was that.

Maddox asked for an immediate trial, and we had to decide whether to hold the New York City or Albany trial first. This led to our returning to Albany one day, and while we sat in the courtroom, waiting to see Judge Turner, there was another trial going on, a black man accused of some crime. The black man was sitting there with a white defense attorney in front of an all-white jury being prosecuted by a white prosecutor, and then they call as witnesses a white cop and a dog from the canine squad. The prosecutor would ask the cop a question, and then the cop would ask the dog, and the dog would howl once for "Yes" and two howls for "No." I looked at Maddox and said, "If I'm in a place where a black man can be put in jail on the word of a dog, then I'll take my chances in Manhattan."

We almost ran out of that courthouse, went to the Red Lobster down the road, called the judge in the city, and said, "Try it now. We want the trial *now*. We waive all our rights for discovery and everything else."

We got ready for trial. First of all, they had to go through jury selection, in one of the biggest courtrooms on Centre Street. I was told that the only jury pool that was larger than mine in the history of the county was for John Gotti. Maddox did a masterful job with his preemptory challenges, and we ended up with a largely black jury. Most of the whites in the pool admitted that they probably couldn't be fair in a situation where Louis Farrakhan or Jesse Jackson might be called as witnesses for the defense. Not to mention that I would be sitting there at the defense table looking at them throughout the entire trial.

We went to the first day of the trial, and of course all the cameras were there. We were scheduled in a courtroom that held about three hundred, and we said that we needed an even larger room to accommodate all of my supporters who wanted to be there. I told the press, being provocative in a way that I now regret, "If y'all are gonna lynch me, you're gonna have to get the biggest tree, no small tree will do, 'cause I'm a big nigger." They gave us the largest courtroom in the city of New York, and everybody piled in.

The prosecutor opened his case by saying that he was going to prove that I had committed various kinds of fraud, and he asked the judge that he be allowed to keep nine witnesses under secret seal, like I was a mobster or something and was going to kill the prosecution's witnesses. I was a preacher, the leader of a nonviolent movement. Of all the things I had been accused of, being a killer was not one of them. I was very offended.

As the trial started and progressed, it quickly became evident that the attorney general couldn't come up with the money that I had allegedly stolen; they couldn't show any trail of where money that had been given to me had disappeared or been misappropri-

ated. They couldn't produce one witness to corroborate their allegations, and, in fact, every person they called to the stand said the
only reason they were testifying was that they had been subpoenaed. Maddox would ask them on cross-examination, "Did you
report this misbehavior to the authorities?" and witness after witness
said, "No, the attorney general came to me and asked if I knew
anything."

One kid that worked for me broke down on the stand and
started crying. He said, "Reverend Sharpton didn't do nothing but
try to help us. He helped us make a little money." Another young
woman who was one of the sealed-list witnesses told Maddox that
she had worked for the National Youth Movement. He asked, "How
much did you get paid?"

She said, "A hundred seventy-five, two hundred dollars a week."

He then asked, "How many words a minute can you type?"

"I can't," she said. The courtroom tittered. "I answered the
phone. They taught me what to say and how to take messages."

Maddox zeroed in. "What job did you have before answering
the phone?"

"None."

"Then why did he hire you?"

"I was a friend of a friend," she said, "and I had a baby and no
way to make a living, and Reverend Sharpton told my friend that
because he'd asked him he'd try and look after me. That's why he
gave me a job. To help me so I wouldn't have to be on welfare."

Maddox said, "And that's why you're here to testify against him,
because he tried to help you?"

She broke down weeping. "I'm here because they told me I had
no choice, otherwise I'd be in trouble."

There was another guy they had who was almost comical. He
said, "Sharpton appropriating money? I don't know about that, but
he made us do all kinds of things that we didn't want to do. We

wanted to have a basketball team, but he wouldn't fund it. He made us march against drugs instead. And he made us do the Disciples of Justice thing, but we got paid straight up every week."

And the attorney general never got around to presenting those witnesses who would say that I was in the mob, none of those people who were to prove that I was getting money, shaking down promoters and all that. No Bill Graham or Ron Delsener. Not one. The trial lasted four months. The prosecution presented eighty-three witnesses, not one who said I strong-armed them, extorted money, or anything at all like that. Just bank records stating that much of our money was withdrawn in cash. If they had bothered to do a real investigation, the attorney general might have learned that the reason for that was as so many of the kids testified: I paid everybody in cash because most of them were young black kids who would have a hell of a time going into a bank in New York City and cashing a check. They didn't have accounts, they didn't have IDs, the banks didn't want them in there. You can't buy subway tokens with a check. You can't go to the movies, buy records or groceries, with a check. All of those questions could have been settled in grand jury, but the attorney general didn't want that, he wanted an indictment. He figured with seventy counts, one or two had to stick.

Something else related to all of this that has always been very interesting to me: why didn't any of the mobsters I was supposedly involved with, Michael Franzese, for instance, ever turn me in? Franzese became a federal informant against other mobsters, he turned his own people in, why wouldn't he turn me in? I was the least threatening person for him to betray if he needed to make a deal. In his book he said that I was a good, sincere guy who fought his union to make sure blacks got good jobs. He said he didn't know if the other things said against me were true or not, but in his own personal experience he thought I was okay. That was the mob snitch talking. So where were all these stories coming from? The usual "unnamed sources"—i.e., some reporter's overactive imagination.

The trial wound down, and as their last big gun the prosecution brought in Monsignor O'Brien of Daytop Village, whom they said I'd defrauded of thousands of dollars. Monsignor O'Brien is justifiably revered for his work with substance abusers, and we'd had a "Dinner Against Crack" to raise money for his organization. Monsignor O'Brien was asked if there had ever been a dinner. "There certainly was," he said.

"Do you think you've been defrauded?"

"No," he said, "the Attorney General's Office told me I'd been defrauded. We couldn't get the kind of attention we received before that night. Reverend Sharpton had a celebrity host at each table, and he gave us six thousand dollars."

The prosecutor pounced. "But the dinner grossed forty-two thousand, shouldn't Daytop have gotten twenty?"

And the monsignor said, "I don't know what his expenses were, he had to pay the Waldorf, and we had no risk, no bills. He had all the risk, paid all the bills, gave us six thousand dollars and a new life among the wealthy and celebrities, some of whom have become regular givers. We feel we were way ahead."

This is when even the press started to say, "What? What's going on here?" Monsignor O'Brien was asked, who introduced you to Sharpton, who brought him in to con you? O'Brien said, "The chairman of the House Subcommittee on Narcotics, Charles Rangel, who ought to know who is doing what in the fight against drug abuse."

As the trial was about to end, Maddox took me aside and said, "I'm going to do something very risky, but I want you to trust me. I'm going to rest. I'm not going to call any defense witnesses.

They've put on a very weak case, they haven't proven anything, so why let them tear at our defense?" I did want the thing over with, I was exhausted from being involved in the Bensonhurst trial and the Phillip Pannell protests over in New Jersey, but I wasn't sure. Maddox said, "Trust me," and as I've said, he is a brilliant attorney so I let him follow his hunch.

We got to court the next morning, and with me the only person aware of what was coming, Maddox, instead of calling his first witness, looked at the judge and said quietly, "We rest." The lawyers from the Attorney General's Office almost passed out. There was nothing for them to rebut. It came time for closing arguments, and I asked Melba Moore, whom the prosecution had alleged I'd defrauded, and Don King, who was supposedly my biggest victim, to come to the courtroom and sit near me.

When the verdict came down, we were waiting in the hall, and I looked out the window and saw the judge come running across the street. Then the court officer said, "Mr. Maddox, would you bring the defendant in? We have a verdict." I felt like my whole life was right there, that it had come down to that moment. I walked in the courtroom and sat down, and started flipping through a Bible my mother had given to me when she moved back down South. I opened to a passage from the 37th Psalm, "I have been young, and now am old; yet have I not seen the righteous forsaken, nor his seed begging bread." I thought to myself, is this a sign? Then the jury came out, and the foreman said they were ready.

The judge read the charges. "Count one."

"Not guilty."

"Count two."

"Not guilty." They got all the way to number thirty-seven, not guilty, and I knew I was safe, because the rest were umbrella charges related to the preceding. The attorney general's lawyers just sat there like rocks, and when they got to number sixty-seven and said, "Not guilty," cries and cheers broke out through the courtroom. My wife started crying, Rev. William Augustus Jones started crying. Then the prosecutor said he wanted to poll the jury, make each juror state how he or she voted on every count, and I just sat there. The judge finally said, "Reverend Sharpton, you're free to go." I got up and walked out, right past a stone-faced Jack Ryan, the head investigator of the Brawley case and the head of the Criminal Department of the Attorney General's Office. He had come to personally take me into custody once I'd been convicted.

Outside, the press came running up, and I told them I'd talk to them at the Cotton Club. I'd eaten lunch every day during the trial at a restaurant owned by Peggy Doyle, an Irishwoman, and as I looked up she came zooming down the block like the Flying Nun and hugged me, almost knocking me over she was so happy. Then one of the members of the jury, an older black woman, walked up to me and said, "You be careful now, son. They're after you. I saw with my own eyes that they didn't have any evidence. I got up one morning during the trial and just fell out, I had lost all my strength, and my daughter said, 'Mama, let me get you to the hospital.' I said, 'No, I got to struggle on, 'cause I got to stay on this jury. They're trying to destroy that boy. He fought for us, and they're trying to destroy him. I can't let 'em replace me with somebody prejudiced. I got to struggle.' And that's what I did, I came here to make sure you got justice." What that old lady said made all of it, the headlines, the criticism, the nights in jail, worth it.

After that trial, we went back upstate to deal with the tax evasion charges, and the judge tried to revoke my bail. This was not successful, but the matter dragged on for three years, with me having to report my whereabouts and get permission to leave the state from the judge. So all through Bensonhurst, my first Senate run, anything I did until early 1993, I was under those indictments and having to report my whereabouts. Finally, in one of his last decisions, Thurgood Marshall, sitting on the Second Circuit, ruled that I could not be indicted on tax charges because of double jeopardy. A young black attorney, Michael Hardy, argued the case for me, pro bono. If the state had determined that I hadn't stolen the money, how could I evade taxes on it? So the Attorney General's Office offered a fine for not filing state income tax for one year and said they would drop the matter. I paid the fine, and it was finally over.

X.

In the middle of my trial maneuvering in the summer of 1989 I received a call early one morning from Moses Stewart, who was the father of a young man named Yusuf Hawkins. This was the month of August, and David Dinkins was closing in on winning the Democratic primary for mayor—which everyone was excited about because he was the first black to achieve this in New York City—and I had just gotten out of bed and was listening to the radio like I do every day. I heard on the news that a young black boy had been murdered on the street in the Brooklyn neighborhood of Bensonhurst the night before. I was in the process of making a few calls to reporters and ministers I knew to see if I could find out what had happened in more detail when my special private number rang, and it was the boy's father, who had gotten the number from a reporter. He was distraught and said the media had surrounded their house and were harassing the family and would I come out to East New York and help them? I said yes, of course.

When we got there, *everybody*—television, radio, newspapers, national magazines—was there. I had to push through them to get to the house—which caused even more of a clamor—and I went inside. The entire family was crying, weeping, really, and it was a heartrending sight. They asked me if I would represent and advise their family during the coming months, and I said that I didn't know if I could do it, maybe I wasn't the best person because I was currently under indictment, I had just come out of the Brawley situation, and my involvement might harm their position in the media and with law enforcement. And Moses said, and I'll never forget this, "That's why we want you, we know you won't sell us out. You stood up for that girl and for the Griffiths." So I agreed to do it.

People forget that at times of crisis like these killings and attacks the families are often overwhelmed with grief and duties, not to mention the media, and the victims are not the sort of folks who can hire Madison Avenue public relations consulting firms to manage and coordinate the circuses they find themselves caught up in. They're not spokespeople, they don't know how to control the producers and reporters, and they are overwhelmed with sadness and grief. The last thing they want is to be tricked by some Ivy League–trained journalist who is only trying to advance his or her career. That's where I come in. I have often been accused of manipulating or exploiting these situations for media exposure, but that's wrong. I'm there to aid and protect, and the people who call must like what I've done in the past, because they called me.

The first thing we needed to do in the Hawkins case was go on the black media and let the community know what had happened. We decided to go on WLIB live, and we let into the house the LIB reporter, Dominic Carter, and the only print journalist we knew and trusted at the time, Peter Noel, of the *City Sun*. Moses and I did two hours live on the radio with Imhotep Gary Byrd (who pioneered black talk radio and who I have often had to turn to in crisis) by phone hookup explaining the details of the incident and the evolving situation. Byrd preempted his regularly scheduled show to broadcast Moses and me. Moses announced that I would be the family's adviser and supervise their interactions with the authorities. This was crucially important in this case because so much was at stake, there was a mayoral election on, and every side had its own motives, interests, and angles, which did not necessarily coincide with those of the family.

By the time we got off the radio the house had filled with relatives. The grandmother, who was a staunch Holiness believer, didn't really want me involved; she was against "politics," and she was sure that I would drag all kinds of negative possibilities into the case, maybe even alienate the police and prosecutors. But she was the only family member who objected; everybody else really wanted me, was very enthusiastic. Then we heard that David Dinkins was on the way, and one of the cousins said, "That Uncle Tom. He's just coming out here after votes." About an hour later the doorbell rang, and there he was, looking me in the eye. I think he was surprised, and dismayed, because he had been so critical of me through the Brawley episode. He didn't want to have to deal with me.

When he rang, we had been planning for Yusuf's funeral. The family had no insurance. I promised to raise the money and make the burial arrangements. Dinkins came in the room and stood next to me, and said to everyone, "I'm here to give my condolences. I'm going to be the next mayor of New York, and when I am I promise this sort of thing will not happen." One of the younger cousins lit into him, saying, "What the f—— do you mean, once you become mayor, who gives a f——, you Tom motherf——. Who can help Yusuf now? What are you doing for us? At least Sharpton is talking about raising money for the funeral." The others jumped in, calling him "Uncle Tom" and accusing him of using them. Dinkins's assistants were getting nervous because every reporter in the city is sitting outside and the family is cursing him out and creating a mini-rebellion.

I let them ventilate their emotions (Dinkins, to his credit, took it and didn't engage them), and then I asked the family for a favor. I said, "We all have our various feelings about Mr. Dinkins here, but we don't want to destroy the possibility that he can become mayor. Let's appear supportive, let's let him go out and say what he has to to the press. We'll stay inside, and we won't attack him later." He went outside and made his statement and left, and I think we helped him there, because if a black family that had suffered such a devastating tragedy at the hands of whites had come out and publicly denounced Dinkins and accused him of betraying them, he would have lost the black community and the election.

We stayed at the house throughout the day, and the calls started coming. Governor Cuomo called, and the family demanded that I talk to him. Here me and Cuomo were, after the Brawley case and my tax indictment and all that, having to talk and be civil and think about the interests of this family and the city. Then Jesse Jackson called, which pleased and touched everyone, of course. Mayor Koch's office called next, and says that he wants to come and give his condolences. About ten o'clock that night, a police sergeant knocks on the door and asks to see someone from the family. He and some others come in and ask to speak to Moses Stewart alone. They tell Moses that the mayor's on his way in a helicopter from City Hall and that he's going to land at a school nearby and come to the house. But he would like Reverend Sharpton to leave before he comes in. Moses says, "Hell, no. He's our adviser, and if he won't see Sharpton he won't see us." We stepped out on the back step and saw that helicopter turn around in midair and go back.

The next day Koch, trying to salvage the situation, sent money to the family to help with expenses and he offered Moses Stewart a job as a bus driver. They were trying to keep the family quiet, keep them from making a public fuss. But by then I had announced that we were heading for Bensonhurst the next Saturday, where I would be leading a march of blacks right through the middle of that neighborhood. We had to assert the right of blacks to be anywhere in the city, to come and go as they pleased as law-abiding taxpayers without fear or apprehension. It had gone on too long in New York City that blacks were limited in their travel, and worst of all, it was as if *nothing* had been learned from Howard Beach.

W e will never know for certain what actually happened that evening, August 23, 1989, in Brooklyn at Bay Ridge and 20th avenues. Yusuf, sixteen years old and by all accounts a good, average kid, was with three friends of his from the block in East New York—Troy Banner, Claude Stanford, and Luther Sylvester—who had taken the subway out to Bensonhurst to look at a used car, a 1982 Pontiac, listing for $900, that one of them had seen advertised in the *Byline*, a kind of penny-saver paper out there in Brooklyn. They had called the seller, told him they were coming, set up a time to meet, and gotten directions. It was so simple, so routine.

Their first tragic mistake was that they got off the outbound N-train at the wrong stop in Bensonhurst, and they came out of the subway and walked into the neighborhood. They now had to walk much farther than they would have otherwise, but they didn't know that yet, and they stopped and bought some candy before continuing. The second tragic and absurd thing to happen was that they walked past a block where a gang of youths, thirty-two in all, had gathered in an agitated fashion because they had heard that a neighborhood girl, who was white and Italian, was dating a black man. The neighborhood toughs didn't like this, and they had threatened the girl, who, in another tragic instance, loosely threatened the neighborhoods that her black boyfriend and *his* friends were on their way that evening to get the Italians.

When the neighborhood boys saw Yusuf and his friends, they gave chase, and shortly thereafter Yusuf was shot twice in the heart. The black boys had been surrounded, and it is said that Yusuf had been knocked to his knees and was begging for his life before being cold-bloodedly executed. Police later found seven baseball bats and four spent .32 automatic shells at the scene. Yusuf was dead on arrival that night at Maimonides Hospital.

As long as I can remember, that had been how it was in Bensonhurst, that any black person who went there was taking his or her life in his or her own hands, even in daylight. Someone would stumble in there by accident, get lost or something, then get beat up, hurt, and no one, not the mayor, not the police, not mainstream black leaders, ever said anything. At the end of the Howard Beach trial and the beginning of Tawana Brawley—Christmas 1987—there had been a typical attack. Two young black men, the Lamont brothers, wandered into Bensonhurst while they were scavenging for empty pop bottles to return for the nickel deposit when they were attacked and beaten by a white mob. We had a march for them the next week, and it was much worse than anything that had occurred in Howard Beach. (It was also an example of how the media select what does and does not become an issue. There were no cameras there that day, and the ugliness of Bensonhurst remained masked for almost two more years.)

That's why we had to march, over and over again, in grief and outrage and support of Yusuf Hawkins. We had to prolong our protests and activities to say unequivocally to the whites in Bensonhurst that this was the end. This was not going to be brushed under the rug or explained away. You have to remember, this was 1989 in Brooklyn, New York, not Birmingham, Alabama, or Jackson, Mississippi. The Bernhard Goetzes, the Howard Beaches, the Bensonhursts, had all gotten away with these attacks in the past because there had never been any sustained agitation. It had to end.

Just during the Koch administration, we had seen Yvonne Smallwood killed by the taxi police, after protesting how they were interrogating her husband. She was beaten to death, right in front of her husband's eyes. Nothing happened. Michael Stewart, a young graffiti artist, was painting graffiti in the 14th Street–Union Square subway station and got into an argument with police. The police started beating him and later testified that Stewart had taken his own head and banged it on the cement six times and killed himself. Eleanor Bumpurs, a sixty-eight-year-old grandmother, had a mental illness problem and had been fighting with her landlord. When the police came with an eviction notice, she held out a butter knife in her hand and a cop shot her twice in the heart with a shotgun. Richard Luke, who the media alleged was a strung-out heroin addict, got into a disagreement with police and was shot for "resisting arrest." Nobody went to jail for any of this. All of this the mayor, Ed Koch, justified. We had to get white people in jail for attacking and killing blacks, it's that simple. Those whites who were inclined to act in such a manner had to have it put in their minds that they would be punished, that they wouldn't just walk away from the incident. We did that, and it's one of the things I'm most proud of. Who knows how many lives have been saved?

I will never forget the first march in Bensonhurst. We met in Bedford-Stuyvesant at the Slave Theater that morning, and I had to tell Moses Stewart and his wife, Diane, that they couldn't go on the march. Moses got a little upset—standing up to those people was very important to him—but I told him that he had no idea what might happen out there, that Yusuf wasn't even in the ground yet, and that his mother didn't need to experience all the hatred and foul behavior that we would encounter. After a moment he relented and decided to let his sons represent the family.

We got on the buses and rode out to 20th Avenue and 67th Street, got out and marched eighteen blocks to Bay 22nd and Bath Avenue. This march made Howard Beach look like summer camp, with thousands of whites lining the sidewalks, yelling obscenities, and holding up watermelons. There were several fistfights that had to be broken up by the cops, and I remember one woman in particular, in response to our chant, "We want the killer," screaming at us, "We want to kill *you!*" It was like Mississippi in the sixties, and it got worse each time we went back for several months, thirty-nine marches in all. But we kept going; we had to. We had to prove that every street in New York was our street.

At one of the first marches, *Newsday* columnist Mike McAlary, who had written the story accusing me of being an informant, came along to Bensonhurst to cover the march. He had written a story the week before saying that those who had killed Yusuf were cowards and deserved the electric chair, really castigated them. He started marching with us, and the crowds were yelling the usual "Niggers!" and throwing watermelons, but when they see McAlary, they stop with the race-baiting and start shouting, "McAlary! Traitor! Dog!" I had the security guys bring him over by me and guard him. I was afraid they might actually hurt him. But that was an example of how much those reporters—McAlary and the other media—didn't know, and didn't want to know, about racism in the city. Blacks put up with it every day.

Meanwhile, the police were after the killers and arrested five right away: Stephen Curreri, Keith Mondello, James Patino, Pasquale Raucci, and Charles Stressler. Mondello was considered the ringleader and given $100,000 bail. All of them were charged with assault, riot, civil rights violations, menacing, aggravated harassment, and criminal possession of a weapon. Mondello was later charged with murder, as was Raucci. Joseph Fama, the suspected gunman, surrendered several days later after fleeing to upstate New York. Fama, Patino, and Serrano were subsequently charged with murder. The police were building a case around the testimony of John Vento, but Vento mysteriously disappeared in December, shortly before the trials were to begin. Vento, who had been promised immunity in exchange for his testimony, had connected Serrano and Fama to the gun, which was key to the prosecution's strategy.

I will always be ambivalent about what happened next. The trial was delayed while the search for Vento proceeded, then began a month late on April 2, 1990. Vento surrendered to the FBI but refused to testify. Separate juries were impaneled for Fama and Mondello, with Fama found guilty of murder and sentenced to thirty-two and two-thirds years to life, while Mondello was cleared of murder and assault charges but convicted of several lesser offenses for which he was sentenced to five and a third to sixteen years in prison. We were satisfied with the Fama conviction, but it seems as though no one else was truly punished.

Mondello got off lightly considering that Yusuf had lost his life. Vento and Serrano were convicted of minor charges, with Serrano receiving only probation, while Stressler's trial ended in mistrial and Patino was cleared of everything. We had continued the Goetz and Howard Beach precedents of holding those who attacked black people in New York City accountable, but only so far. Only one was convicted of murder, and as many as thirty other young men were out there that night who never had to face justice. So it was a mixed victory.

In a sad and ironic counterpoint to the Bensonhurst matter, during the trial of Fama and Mondello something else happened that seemed to underscore that black life was very cheap in the New York area, or that, at the very least, blacks had to be on their guard *everywhere*. In the commuter suburb of Teaneck, New Jersey, a sixteen-year-old black boy, Phillip Pannell, Jr., was shot in the back and killed by a white policeman as he ran through a neighbor's yard. He had been playing with friends when a cop investigating a distur- bance came upon them. The officer, Gary Spath, said he thought the boy had a gun. Pannell, who had already been wounded in the incident, had his hands above his head and was pleading with the officer for mercy and yelling for his mother when the fatal bullet was fired.

A grand jury refused to indict Spath, until the New Jersey attor- ney general, responding to our pressure in the media and twenty- nine marches, called a second review which led to Spath standing trial, where he was found innocent. Yusuf Hawkins was from the mean streets of East New York, Brooklyn, while Phillip Pannell lived among the bucolic avenues of the New Jersey suburbs; they were both, however, young black men, and they lived in a society where, by all appearances, their lives were not worth a dime. That's some- thing I think a lot of people, particularly the media, have refused to see and understand about our movement; we got started protecting black people from harm, insult, and degradation, and that is largely what we've done ever since. It makes me sick to think of people being mistreated anywhere, especially if it is because of who they are, which they cannot help, and I am of course devoted to black people, my people. Those who profess to not trust me or my mo- tives need only think of those two boys, shot down for nothing, save that they were black.

There is another aspect to the Pannell matter that I think is crucial to the current situation of blacks in America, the schism between blacks of different social classes. The upper-middle-class blacks in that part of New Jersey did not want me out there, and they certainly didn't want me agitating. But a local woman, Miss Robinson, who was an eyewitness—it had happened in front of her house—called and asked me to come out there because she was being threatened against testifying, including a brick through the picture window.

In the beginning, the local ministers deliberately kept the family from even meeting me, Mason, Maddox, and Louis Farrakhan, who had attended the wake. They thought I was a troublemaker, that I would disturb "the peace," upset the equilibrium, though they did meet with Jesse Jackson. This is something else overlooked by the media, and by blacks: the differences in temperament and ideology among blacks themselves, especially as delineated by economics. Those middle-class ministers in New Jersey basically wanted the thing to blow over, which it wasn't going to. Eventually the Pannell family also asked me to help, when they saw that the authorities were much more interested in protecting the police than pursuing justice.

I've regularly been called an outside agitator, but I have never taken a case, from Howard Beach to Brawley to Bensonhurst to Pannell or anything else, including the families I helped in the Central Park rape case, where the victims, or in the case of Central Park, families that needed help dealing with the system, didn't call and ask me to help them. I only become involved if I am invited. Patricia Garcia, Richard Luke's mother, said something to me that touched me more than almost anything anyone else has said to me: "I wanted the whole world to know what they did to my son, and I knew of nothing else but you to get that done." Sometimes it's the only way to get the criminal justice system to work.

I am a minister, and I respond to requests. Suppose Miss Robinson called me and said she needed my help and I said no. To me, that would be more of an indictment against my credentials as an activist than going into a strange place where I'm not a local. It's something like Mississippi in the fifties and sixties. Locals couldn't have settled it, outsiders had less to fear, and lose. Suppose Richard Luke's mother called me and I said, "Well, I heard he's a junkie, I can't do it." Does the fact he was a junkie change the fact that he was killed by the police for no reason? What if I had ignored Derrick Jeter and Moses Stewart? Would anyone know what had happened in Howard Beach and Bensonhurst, would anyone remember Michael Griffith and Yusuf Hawkins? I see my activities as part of my ministry, what I call my Christian walk, helping the needy, protecting the weak.

And it's not that everything in the integrated suburbs is safe; it's the exact opposite, in fact: those blacks know they're not safe, they're more insecure than anyone and don't want anything to happen because they know it will shake the ground and cause their thin roof of security to cave in on them. They *pretend* they're feeling safe, but in actuality they're more insecure than the guy in the project working three jobs because they have to be aware of how tenuous things are *all the time* and they're much more vested in the system. They look at me and say, "Loudmouth Sharpton, shut up, everything's fine, we don't need your mess out here in Bergen County," but deep down inside they're saying, "We're unsafe and barely getting by out here, and if you make noise, the white folks will cut off the little slack they're willing to give." Everyone forgets I spent the first ten years of my life in the black bourgeoisie, and I know that attitude. All of those upper-middle-class blacks worry that they're two steps from being back in the projects.

The black middle class doesn't make a claim on America. It's more like they are worried that they've gotten away with something. They're housebreakers, trespassing, and they hope if no noise is made, no one will realize that they are there. They look at me and are terrified, because my whole life is built on making *sure* white folks know we're here. I'm saying, "We ain't gonna shut up, we're gonna make noise, we're gonna break some dishes if we have to, because we have the right to be here. This is ours." The black leaders in Bergen had made their peace with the white power structure. Teaneck was a bedroom community, a "model of integration." Phillip Pannell was a poor kid from a broken home. On some level he's expendable.

But I understand that bourgeois attitude. If my father had not left us, I would have been one of them. I don't have contempt for striving black middle-class folk, far from it. Most of the historic black leadership and advance have come from that group, Martin Luther King being the preeminent example. All I'm saying to them is grow up. This racial thing is here, it has always been here, it probably isn't going anywhere, and we have to deal with it. Sooner or later it's going to hit you in the face.

I was there with James Brown on the private jets, I've had lunch with Don King at the top of Rockefeller Center. I've seen the big money, about the biggest money that black folks get. But I've also stood with those two in court. I saw James Brown brought in wearing shackles, and I saw Don King treated like a purse-snatcher. I've seen those illusions of black success burst in front of my eyes. *Every black person faces the same circumstances in America;* I've seen the wealthiest, most famous, most successful blacks face the same circumstances as Richard Luke, a poor man from Queens. So if any black person thinks they're transcending this, they're only fooling themselves. Something to remember about the Pannell situation: Eddie Murphy, along with many other rich and successful blacks, lived right up the road from where it happened. It could have been Eddie's kid.

The Phillip Pannell case was a turning point for me, because I saw that even suburban America was just as infected with raw racism when confronted with unnegotiable racial problems and issues, that the laid-back and well-mannered suburban whites would get just as savage, just as inflamed, as those blue-collar types. These people in Bergen County aren't washing planes out at La Guardia, they work at the accounting firms, they're law partners, they work in the financial district. But they acted just as vulgarly as a truck driver from Howard Beach. We came out to Teaneck the next Saturday after the funeral with ten buses and about five hundred people and had our first march down Teaneck Road. In response to our march the white police in New Jersey had a march, three thousand cops, selling

T-shirts that said, "We love you Gary." And I must say, a lot of whites who had been opposed to us up to that point were outraged.

The suburban whites are, on the surface, a little more refined. They like thinking of themselves as progressive, nonracist, but much of the reason for the very existence of the suburbs has to do with racism. Suburbanites say, "We get along with everyone," but what they mean is, "We have our blacks." And they make sure to only have a few, because only a few can afford it. Those few do everything in their power to not stick out, so it's almost the same as having no blacks, with the moral smugness that comes from self-satisfaction. *How can you call us racists?* They're content. But when it comes to locking up a white male for killing a black kid, then it's "Who do you niggers think you are?" The black kid isn't Stevie Wonder, he's Phillip Pannell, he's Richard Luke, he's Yusuf Hawkins.

So we had to do in the suburbs what we had to do in the city. We had to go out there and march and make our presence felt and say what needed to be said but others haven't had the power or the courage to say. And I used my natural in-your-face style. I didn't let it become a genteel matter. I didn't let whites take issues off the table. And I think it helped blacks out there feel better in terms of their self-worth, because they couldn't be discounted any longer, they couldn't be ignored. Particularly the poor people.

And something strange began to happen. When we started marching and the cops started marching and whites started standing out on the street in that manicured suburban community screaming at us just like they did in Brooklyn and Queens, a lot of the successful blacks who had been against us slowly started saying things like, "I didn't know my neighbor felt that way about me." After the fifth or sixth march some of the young people formed an African Council. By the tenth march all our critics were marching with us. They were starting to realize that otherwise, people would forget. The family also moved away from the local ministers and started working with me.

The most horrible thing about the way these cases were swept under the rug every time a black person was killed is that it became normal. It became the expected thing. It devalued everyone's life, whether it was Joey Fama's or Yusuf Hawkins's. So the more value I put on a black kid's life, enough to stop the city for a day, the more the killer has to think, maybe this is wrong. So even the upper-middle-class and rich blacks began drifting to me in Teaneck, as I made them aware of the other issues. That cop didn't request a W-2 on Phillip's family before he shot him, nor did he find out his social standing or what church he belonged to. He saw a black kid running through a yard, he stopped, he aimed, and he fired.

XI.

In the aftermath of the fraud trial, I was still facing the tax indictments in Albany. I'd spent the summer of 1990 protesting out in Teaneck and defending the boys in the Central Park jogger rape case whom I thought were innocent—let me underscore, I didn't dispute the case or the facts, only that some of the accused were clearly uninvolved and that could be proved and I didn't want them railroaded in the fashion of the Scottsboro Boys—as well as monitoring the Bensonhurst trials in Brooklyn. Both Joey Fama and Keith Mondello, the gunman and one of the ringleaders, had been convicted, but Brooklyn D.A. Charles Hynes—my reluctant compatriot at Howard Beach, now celebrated as a crusader—had started losing some of the secondary Bensonhurst cases, which was unacceptable. There had been two dozen attackers out there the night Yusuf Hawkins was killed, and we wanted two dozen in jail, not three or four.

It was time to put some heat on Charles Hynes. There appeared to be a pattern developing that as each of the lesser cases fell apart it would be progressively more difficult to get any of the lesser convictions. Once one was cleared, he could say he was innocent and testify in ways beneficial to the others. We were very concerned about this, and late in 1990 I took more than two hundred people to Bensonhurst to encourage the neighborhood to work with us and help bring the killers to justice. The Bensonhurst people kept saying that everyone out there was not a racist, and we urged them to cooperate with us if in fact that was true. Tell the authorities what you know, we asked, hand over the guilty, support these trials that seem to be losing steam. We need your help to administer justice, don't forget about the dead boy.

I went to mass at a local Catholic church out there, Palm Sunday 1990, and Mayor Dinkins joined us for a peace meeting, trying to open avenues of cooperation and fellowship with the community. This went on throughout 1990. Then, in January 1991, I thought the most appropriate way to celebrate Martin Luther King's birthday, the fifteenth of that month, was to go back to Bensonhurst with a huge march, to remind the community there that lip service about empathy and doing the right thing was not going to be acceptable, and that we, their fellow Brooklynites and New Yorkers, were not going to let them forget. Some of the guilty were walking free, awaiting trial, some of them had not even been identified or apprehended. Dr. King was a man of action, not talk and ceremony, and we were going to remember him on his birthday by doing what he would have done, which is go out to Bensonhurst and speak up for justice, confront racial injustice in a very direct way.

On Saturday January 12, the weekend before the King holiday, about five hundred of us got on buses and headed out. This was to be the twenty-ninth march in Bensonhurst, counting from the week after Yusuf was killed. The police, as they always had, met us on Fulton Street where the various buses gathered from around the neighborhoods. We rode the half hour out to Bensonhurst and parked in a barricaded schoolyard—this was standard procedure— and I was sitting in my car, talking to Moses Stewart, waiting for everyone to line up and get ready for the march.

Finally, my assistant, Carl Redding, walked over and said it was time, they were ready for me, and I got out of the car and walked toward the front of the line. We were still, remember, inside the playground, which was supposed to be a secure area, and I turned my head to say something to Carl, and suddenly I felt someone punch me in the chest. Out of reflex I turned my head back toward the front and I saw this face, a white male, flash past me. He had this contorted look of hatred on his face, a real look of hate, I'll never forget that, and before I could get a clear look at him I looked down and saw a knife sticking out of my chest. "Oh my God, he stabbed me!" I thought, and out of reflex grabbed the handle and pulled it out. Until then I hadn't felt any pain, just that punch or brush to the chest, but when I grabbed the knife, the air hit the wound and I felt it, it really hurt. I fell down on my knees and saw that I had blood all over my hands. Then people started screaming.

This all happened so fast, in a matter of seconds, like boom-boom-boom! The assailant was running away, and though there were over two hundred policemen standing around in that play-ground, none of them made a move to grab him. Somehow he had known the color of the jackets the undercover cops were wearing to be able to recognize each other that day, and that was how he had gotten into the frozen zone. So Carl Redding—a former college and pro football player—with Henry Johnson, one of my security guards, and Moses Stewart tackled him and held him down and *then* the police started beating *them* on their heads and backs and ordering them to let this man go until finally someone ran up and convinced them that this man had just stabbed Reverend Sharpton. It was pandemonium.

Then, after all that, it turned out that with all those policemen, all those motorcycles, all those mobile command units, they didn't have an EMS truck or an ambulance. There was no way to get me to the hospital. I'm on my knees, bleeding, people screaming and running around, and the first thing that hit me was, *get that knife.*

In the corner of my eye I can see Carl and Henry and Moses scuffling with the perpetrator and the police, people are rushing back and forth and there's all this noise and things are starting to swirl, and I can see the knife about three feet in front of me. I started yelling, in all the confusion, "Get the knife, get the knife!" And somebody, one of my people, grabbed it.

Then I hear Moses Stewart in back of me screaming and crying, "Ambulance, ambulance! What's wrong with you guys!" He was cursing at the police, who didn't seem to know what to do, and finally one of the marchers ran over and said, "Let's take him in my car." They carried me over, put me in the backseat of a car, and at that point the police said, "We'll put a car in front of him and behind him so he can use our sirens." They put a rookie cop in the backseat with me, and we roared off to Coney Island Hospital.

I never, ever forget what happened as we came flying out of that playground, bumping over the curb with all those sirens blaring. The rookie cop riding with me says to the men in the front seat, "Damn, I hope there wasn't any poison on the knife." Now, I was delirious, in severe pain, but I hadn't, *truly*, felt any pain until that moment. The first thing I thought was, "Is this cop here especially to torment me?" I mean, I had to think about it. The assailant was shrewd enough to get through the police line, to get to my chest and maybe my heart, he's probably shrewd enough to put poison on the blade. The Mafia had been threatening me, telling me not to come back out there, and *they* were certainly smart enough to use a poisoned dagger, an old Italian trick. So I'm sprawled there in the car, wondering, Am I poisoned? How deep did the knife go? Did he hit anything vital? I didn't know.

Ten minutes later I was in the hospital. They run out a gurney to the parking lot and throw me on. They started wheeling me to the emergency room, and right away they start cutting my clothes, which is standard procedure, of course, because you're in an emergency situation and they don't have much time. I had on a jogging suit and a full-length leather coat that my wife had given me for Christmas, and when I realized what they were doing—I guess the Brownsville was still in me—in the midst of my pain and delirium I made them stop and hauled myself off the gurney and took my coat off. I had always wanted a leather coat and was not going to let them cut it under any circumstances. The doctors and nurses and I all had a good laugh about that later, and they teased me about it quite a bit.

After they got me back down, they took X rays and all that, and they realized that blood was filling my lungs. The wound was more than three inches deep, very close to my heart, and they decided to operate immediately and drain the lungs. I have a significant scar on my chest from the draining, and another from the stab wound, and every morning when I'm shaving and shuffling around, I look at those actual, real scars on my body from racism—which is academic and theoretical to most people—and I think about Howard Beach and Bensonhurst and what we've been through. People always accuse me of preaching hate, but I see it every morning in the mirror, and will continue to see it every morning as long as I live.

When the blood was drained and they sewed me up, I was taken into recovery. I was just coming out of the anesthesia, semiconscious, and I sort of noticed four people standing in the room, and as my head cleared they gathered around the gurney and they all had masks on so I didn't know who they were. I didn't quite know what was going on, I didn't realize I was still in recovery and there was a danger of infection. One of the men with the masks reached for my hand and said, "Call for peace! Call for peace! Al, please, call for peace!" As he kept talking I realized it was David Dinkins. And with him is Deputy Mayor Bill Lynch, Deputy Mayor Milton Mollen, and Police Commissioner Lee Brown.

I'd known Dave Dinkins since I was a kid—he was the lawyer who incorporated the National Youth Movement—and we'd had our fallings-out and reconciliations down through the years, and there he was holding my hand and asking me to ask for nonviolence. I said, "What do you mean? I've never called for anything but nonviolence." He said, "There are people talking about burning down the city because of this." I still did not clearly know what had happened, just that I'd been stabbed and just had surgery. And that the first black mayor of the city is standing there holding my hand and saying, "Call for peace, buddy. Buddy, call for peace," over and over and over. So I said, "Of course I'm calling for peace!" Dinkins almost threw my hand back in my face and runs out the door, leaving Lee Brown and the two deputy mayors with me. I later found out that he ran outside and told the assembled media, "I've just left Sharpton's bedside. He's calling for peace!"

Lying there, I didn't know that day that Mayor Dinkins was under tremendous pressure to prevent serious threats of violence from becoming real. There were people at the hospital marching and saying, "Let's burn down Bensonhurst, let's burn down New York!" Some black kids had beaten a white kid on the train and claimed, "This is for Sharpton." There were other incidents. Dinkins was trying to stabilize the city, and I commend him for it, because things did not get out of hand, and they could have gotten very ugly, as was seen in Los Angeles the very next year.

But even in light of all that, I was slightly upset that the first people I saw as I was trying to figure out which end was up and if I was going to survive were the city fathers. They hadn't exactly been my running buddies. So I started asking, "Where's Kathy? Where's Kathy?" and they let her in. Kathy was in the Army Reserve, and that's where she had been that day, at Fort Hamilton, right near Bensonhurst. She came in in her army uniform, crying and extremely worried, and I tried to calm her down and comfort her. Then, while we were talking, Bill Jones—Rev. William Augustus Jones—came striding in with Rev. Timothy Mitchell and Rev. Darryl George. It seems like Reverend Jones is always there for me, whatever and whenever, and to this day I don't know how he found out and got there so fast, but there he was, with Mitchell and George, men who had stood by me in my darkest hours. I started to think it was going to be all right.

The doctors then came in and said that the operation was a complete success, they had cleared my lungs, that everything now indicated that I should pull through and that I was very lucky in that the wound was so close to my heart. Then another group of friends came in, Alton Maddox and C. Vernon Mason, and I talked to them. Maddox said that they wanted to finish the march the next day, they were determined to, and Reverend Jones thought that was the right idea, so I agreed. I said, "No violence, but we can't let these people get away with this. They can't think that this is the way to stop us."

Then everybody left, and I asked for a phone. I wanted to call Jesse Jackson. I don't even really know why, but for some reason I felt compelled to talk to him and tell him myself what had happened. We had not been as close recently as we were when I was growing up, but he was still my hero, Adam was dead, Jesse was the only minister whom I felt I could model myself on, look up to in that way—Bill Jones was more like a father—who was active and out there. I called him at home in Washington and told him what had happened. I said, "There's still too much racism in this country and if I survive I hope I'm going to be even more serious now in the true King tradition of opposing it." Jesse said, "Well, I'm on my way out of town, but I'll come to see you next week." I said, "I'd really like that, if you could, I feel like I need to talk to you." He said, "Okay," and hung up.

About an hour after that a nurse came in and gave Kathy a note. She wouldn't show it to me, and I could tell she was weighing something in her mind. After what was probably a minute or two—it seemed a lot longer to me at the time—she came over to me and said, "This is a message from a man in Orlando, Florida, who wants to talk to you, he says he's your father." This was the first time I'd heard from my father since I was a kid, in family court. I tried to tell myself that it was probably a prank, but I told Kathy to get the phone and we'd see. She dialed the number, and I knew immediately that it was him. He had seen what happened on the national news and was concerned about my condition. It was a strange situation for me, because there were all these things I had been waiting to say to him: "Where were you in my other crises, when I was getting arrested, when I was in jail, when I was on trial, where were you when I graduated from high school, when I needed somebody to tell me to stay in college?" But it seemed, suddenly, that none of that mattered. I just responded to his overture and returned the call. Then I called my mother, who had moved back to Alabama, and told her everything was all right. The last thing I did was have Kathy call the baby-sitter and tell her to not let the kids watch any television, because I didn't want them to see what had happened.

I was able to keep it from them while I was hospitalized—Kathy told them I was on a trip—and for about three weeks after I got out of the hospital, but then we had another baby-sitter in the house who hadn't been briefed and was reading *Jet* magazine, and Dominique, my older daughter, saw me in a photograph in the magazine lying in bed, stabbed with tubes all over the place, and she became hysterical, and started crying and had an asthma attack, and ended up spending a week in the hospital. After that, every time I would go out, Dominique and Ashley would fall out crying, wailing "Daddy's gonna get killed. Daddy's gonna get killed." That's what I had thought I was avoiding, but in retrospect I might have been wrong. Perhaps I should have sat them down and explained it to them, because they found out, inadvertently, anyway.

I fell asleep about 9:30 that night, and they gave Kathy a little cot and let her stay with me. By that time it seemed like every black and progressive group in the country was out there, plus the police, giving me protection. The Fruit of Islam, the security wing of the Black Muslims, was there, the New Alliance Party, my guys—there were twenty-five or thirty men standing out there guarding me—and I remember Kathy and I had a good laugh as I nodded off, saying how if I'd had that kind of protection at the march, I wouldn't have gotten stabbed.

I woke up at about 7:00 the next morning, and I still had the IVs and all that to deal with, and was waiting for the orderlies to come get me and take me to a regular room. I was expecting them at 9:30, but they came an hour early. They wheeled me down the hall, all the bodyguards surrounding the bed, and the moment I got in the new room, in walked Jesse. He leaned over the bed and started teasing me, and Chester Higgins of the *New York Times* took the picture that appeared everywhere, Jesse leaning over me, grinning, making me laugh.

What Jesse was saying that was so humorous was that the only reason the bad guys didn't get me was that I had seven inches of fat but it was a six-inch knife. It hurt to laugh, but I had to. Then we prayed, and after that we talked, and I told him how happy I was that he had come, and that even though we had had our disagreements, I'd seen myself as trying to work in the same tradition he'd been working in, trying to bring civil rights protest to the city. I

also told him that when I was released from the hospital I wanted to
sit down and have a real conversation, that I needed to spend some
serious and quiet time with him.

Though I hadn't yet said anything to anybody about my feelings, the stabbing had really shaken me up, and I was beginning to
realize that I was going to have to go my own way politically, that I
was going to leave the Slave Theater, where I had been participating in more nationalist-oriented rallies and organizing, and form my
own group that would be truer to myself and my roots. I also felt it
was time to start engaging in the electoral arena, which many at the
Slave did not believe in. They had, understandably, I think, given
up on the system, and felt that their time was better spent trying to
build the community. I understood their disappointments because I
shared them. I had been raised in the movement by men like Bishop
Washington, Adam Clayton Powell, William Augustus Jones, and
Jesse Jackson. I was thinking about that movie about Dr. King I had
seen when I was a kid, *From Montgomery to Memphis,* and the Nina
Simone song "What are you gonna do now that the king of love is
dead?" I had been terribly moved, and motivated, by that, and
somehow, in my night journey through the New York City of the
eighties, I had wandered away from it.

I didn't say all that to Jesse at the time, but it was running
through my head. After he finished praying and talking to me and
Kathy and the others, he asked me what I wanted him to say to the
press. He said, "They've heard things from the mayor, they'll hear
things from me, they need to hear them from you." I said to let them
know that I was still committed to protest, and that I supported the
march planned for later that day, but that I also denounced the
violent retaliations I was hearing about. I did not want that, under
any conditions. Jesse then asked my assistant Anthony Charles to
write it down and suggested that Kathy come downstairs with him
and read it to the press. And that's what happened. Kathy and Jesse
had a press conference. I was clamped down on by the doctors,

though I did receive a lot of visitors—even Howard Stern—and some of the community leaders from Bensonhurst. Cardinal O'Connor wrote a column about me in the *Catholic Journal;* one of the nurses showed me the piece, and she praised me for responding nonviolently. And something very nice happened: a group of fifth graders from the school where I was stabbed sent me flowers and made a card which they all signed. I was surprised and deeply touched by their gesture.

Mike McAlary—at that time of the *Post*—also came to see and write about me. He said that he had always wanted me to shut up but that he had never wanted me dead. Apparently, the stabbing was something of a catharsis for him. McAlary had written the FBI informer story, and I'd always felt that he was one of the major ones who contributed to creating the climate in which someone might think himself a hero for stabbing Al Sharpton. And ironically, McAlary became a victim of those antagonisms himself, as he was attacked by the crowd at a Bensonhurst march for criticizing them in the paper. So, as much as I was outraged by what I felt was his deliberate distortion of the facts in the FBI matter, I was also intrigued by and even empathetic to his curiosity about me, and I wanted him to really understand the depths of what someone like me—so different from him—went through.

After I stabilized, they started working on my recuperation, and it was more complicated and difficult than I could have imagined. They literally had to teach me how to walk; each morning and each evening I'd get up and struggle two or three steps and have to sit back down. I had no idea that the wound had hit me that hard, that it had caused that kind of effect. Then they'd wheel me down, or I'd be walking on a walker, for X rays. That must have been a sight, what with me surrounded by thirty security men opening doors, moving people, looking around corners, every trip, and that was also an ordeal, getting off the gurney, standing in front of the screen—I was incredibly stiff and uncomfortable even with the painkillers. It was a task. But every day I became stronger and stronger. Then after a week I went home and had a police escort over the George Washington Bridge.

Kathy and I had moved from downtown Brooklyn. I owed money to the landlord, which the papers, of course, gleefully reported. When I was raising money for Yusuf Hawkins's funeral, I was five months behind in my own rent, because I was on trial and I had so many unexpected expenses connected with that. Maddox and Mason may donate their time, but there are still things to pay for like copies and meals, and there wasn't a lot coming in—not that there has ever been—since I was preaching less and less. This is something that I can be faulted on to a certain degree, being so wrapped up in and distracted by the movement and my activities that I don't cover the home situation as thoroughly as I should. There are times, in crises, when we're working almost round the clock, and the urgency of the cause can drown out something as seemingly petty—I'm not saying it is—as the rent. My wife has been a literal saint about this on the level of money, and on the personal level as well. She's made a home for me and our daughters, gone out and made money, and, it goes without saying, remained unflinchingly at my side through episodes of my life that had to be incredibly painful and humiliating to her. Simply put, anything I've done, I could not have done without her.

With the help of our friends Ruth and John Beatty, the owners of the famous Cotton Club, we found a little development of town houses in Englewood, New Jersey, that was quiet and nice and safe for the girls, and decided to move there. Suddenly, this became national news: "REV. AL ABSCONDS TO JERSEY!" and all that. Everybody acted like I had bought some palatial house when I had simply rented a garden apartment. It was home after the stabbing, as I was forced to recuperate in bed and by sitting still, which, of course, I did not like. I had no choice, however, and little by little I regained my strength. And I thought I was being smart telling the kids I only had a cold, but a few weeks later they found out what had really happened.

When I came back on the scene, I went back to the Slave Theater in Brooklyn and was warmly welcomed by just about everybody. Maria Shriver was traveling with me, doing a piece for *First Person* on NBC, and the BBC—who had actual footage of the stabbing because they were there that day—continued filming me, doing this piece *Seven Days in the Life of Al Sharpton.* So I was back at the Slave. Yet I was beginning to wonder if I belonged at these rallies. While the overwhelming majority of those present gave me a hero's welcome, some of the activists in the movement— the hard-core super-militant group—were upset that I had allowed David Dinkins and Jesse Jackson to visit me in the hospital, and they were enraged beyond measure that I had allowed photographs to be taken and smiled and acted like they were my friends. They said they respected me, I was down for the cause, but I was dealing with Uncle Toms and endangering their movement. The super-militant thinkers feel that Jackson and Dinkins are integrationists, coalition builders, rather than only working for "the people," blacks. All I could say that night was that those men had known me since I was a boy, that, though we had our fallings-out, they had always tried to help me, and that they represented the tradition of black leadership that I had come from. What I was thinking, though, was, "Forget it. I've got to do my own thing."

Certain elements in the movement had become too small and dogmatic for me. As I said, this was a minority, but it was a very vocal minority, and I didn't appreciate having to explain myself and

vindicate my friends immediately after coming back from a confrontation with death. I didn't want to argue, and refused to, and so
immediately these hard-core black super militants, the truest of the
true believers, run to a white newspaper, *The Village Voice*, and start
in all over again. This is ridiculous. Dave Dinkins was buying me
sodas and answering questions I had when some of those so-called
revolutionaries were in grammar school. And *I* wanted peace. I
wouldn't have called for violence had it been feasible or possible. In
my darkest moments, the Mafia stuff, the FBI situation, Tawana
Brawley, Howard Beach, Bensonhurst, I never, ever even hinted that
violence was the solution. Pressure, yes. Giving as good as you get,
yes. But I learned my lesson, and I decided to find a space uptown in
Manhattan and organize a radio show.

I learned the Saturday morning radio rally from Jesse, who used
it to great effect with Operation PUSH in Chicago, where it was
the biggest thing in town. We also used it in New York with Reverend Jones when I was a kid. So we started the National Action
Network, live every Saturday morning, and my guests for the first
rally were Spike Lee and Dr. Betty Shabazz, widow of Malcolm X.
We broadcast from the auditorium of P.S. 175, which holds about
six hundred people, and for four years we've been there, live over
the airwaves, for an hour and a half. We never have an empty house.
And I've never looked back. We have two offices now, in Brooklyn
and Manhattan, our message reaches many more people. None of
this would have been possible if I hadn't decided to become more
expansive, to be more open to others, to look back to my elders and
forebears and listen to them rather than just my anger. It isn't that
anger isn't part of it, even now—you don't think on some level
Martin Luther King was angry?—it's just that it can't be *all* of it. So
my disagreement with some of those people was actually good for
me. And you know what? Some of those critics who had never been
comfortable with me, a Christian minister, participating in the activities at the Slave, ended up being among my most ardent

supporters as things developed later. Maybe it was supposed to happen.

It's important to understand the black nationalist position, to not simplify it and dismiss them as cranks. In many ways to me that worldview represents the tragedy of American society at its most melancholy, because some of these people are the most loyal, most naturally intelligent, most warrior-like—in the best sense of the word—of any humans I've known. These are, in many ways, men and women you'd want on your side in a fight or any other difficulty. They are like the Black Panthers from the sixties in that fashion.

But many of them are bitter, *and justifiably so*, at what white society has done, and allowed to happen, the nightmare of the past four hundred years that white people are responsible for by commission and by omission. So these nationalists want to have nothing to do with that white society, and on certain levels, it's a rational decision. For me, personally, I guard against using those feelings as a way of copping out. It seems so much easier (and more escapist) to me to say, "I'm going to just turn my back, I'm going to drop out, I'm going to give up and not deal with whites at all, I'm going to cover myself with a shell." It's a way of avoiding the issues. Some of it's out of bitterness, sure, but some of it's, I'm convinced, out of cowardice. Some of these people, maybe most of them, are *afraid* of white folks, they are afraid to confront them. They have internalized that sense of inferiority that society visits on black people, and are trying to veil it with bravado. And some of them, as an intellectual position, think that white people *can't* be confronted, they think that there are too many institutional and structural barriers for blacks to ever begin to think of taking on the white power structure in any serious fashion. So they don't want to be bothered, or they want to wait, to engage whites someplace else. But that's just a cop-out, a way of saying "I can't compete." Some of them talk about going back to Africa, but what is that going to do? Blacks don't control Africa, white folks do. It's an unavoidable fact that if you're going to live on this planet, you're going to have tó deal with the Western white civilization. Why pretend otherwise? And, to slip into the vernacular, we ain't got to be cute about it, just go at 'em straight up and try to empower ourselves.

We have to be very careful about all of this. Some nationalists and others argue that the persecution of white society has driven blacks to the point of killing each other, that what is happening is all their fault. At a certain rarefied level of sociological or anthropological analysis this might be true, but my thinking is that even if you have been knocked down and are suffering through no fault of your own, *you are still responsible for getting back up.* You are responsible for your life and your actions. The Lord is not going to ask you who did what to you, He will ask *them* that. He's going to ask you what *you* did. It's like the parable of the talents: those who use what they have receive more, those who misuse or destroy their resources lose everything. I'm not saying this to exculpate whites and white society from what they've done; my life and career are on record as opposing racism, both personal and institutional, vehemently. What I am saying is that it's imperative on every single black person in this country *to do whatever he or she can to advance our cause.*

So, if blacks are killing other blacks, if blacks are selling drugs to black children and other blacks, if black fathers are abandoning their children, the academic underlying cause might be the well-documented and long-understood racist society, but the actual action and effect have to be that we will analyze and attack the problem *in our own community.* Who is going to save us but us? Who else has the stake? Dare I say, who else cares? That's where I differ from some, in that I will acknowledge that there are many reasons for black people to give up on life and stop trying—I had several myself, my daddy left us, we were on welfare and in the projects, the whole bit, but that was no reason for me not to try, that was no excuse just to hand white folks what they wanted, which was me on the sidelines if not in the gutter. White racism did brutalize and even distort black people, that is an unarguable historical fact. What that means is that a black person should strive *harder*, have a higher moral code. Don't submit to the terror of your enemies, that's on them. When you give in, hate your own people, hate yourself, kill and corrupt the innocent out of greed and decadence, *then they have beat you.* It's that simple.

I came to understand those things as I entered the decade of the nineties. The stabbing changed me in the sense that I realized that your life can go, can be taken from you, just like that. I realized that if my life was so fragile, so contingent, then I had to be more serious about what I was doing and saying, I had to be more careful about the message I was leaving people with. Anything I said might be the last thing I said. I wanted to be known for more than slogans, and I wanted to be remembered for more than arguing with knuckleheads on television. Also, and perhaps most important, when I looked at David Walker, Frederick Douglass, Sojourner Truth, Ida B. Wells, Booker T. Washington, W. E. B. Du Bois, Charles Hamilton Houston, Marcus Garvey, A. Philip Randolph, Richard Wright, Walter White, Adam Clayton Powell, Roy Wilkins, Thurgood Marshall, Martin Luther King, Fannie Lou Hamer, Malcolm X, James Baldwin, Jesse Jackson, and all the rest, what was I doing to at least attempt to live up to that legacy? I realized that confronting American racism at its base is a very dangerous thing and not to be undertaken without serious spiritual and mental preparation.

In short, the stabbing is where I began to look at myself much more closely, to take my life more seriously. Who was I, where was I coming from? I realized I was a *Christian* activist, out of the tradition of Adam Clayton Powell, Martin Luther King, and Jesse Jackson, a minister. As Cornel West said to me, I come out of Martin's house, not Malcolm's. I began to see where I was rooted, in the New Testament, in the Christian Church, in a sense of belief that said the world could be better, that there was such a thing as progress. I began to remember my forebears, and, literally and figuratively, whose little boy I was.

XII.

When I got out of the hospital, it took about two months to get fully back into the swing of things. When I first got out, we had our annual march over the Brooklyn Bridge for Dr. King and I had to do it in a wheelchair, but by March I was up and around and allowed to fly, so Kathy and I accepted Jesse Jackson's invitation to come to Las Vegas for a prizefight and a birthday party for his wife, Jackie. We also were going to finally sit down and have that long talk we'd been needing to have. Jesse and I had been talking almost daily, but were too busy to just hang out. We spent five days together, just the Jacksons and the Sharptons, and Jesse and I were able to truly reconcile, to glue back together like we had when we were younger.

Jesse and I have been criticized for going to fights and associat-
ing with fighters and the like, but I don't see anything wrong with it.
That weekend there were two black men getting ready to fight in an
event sponsored by a black promoter—Don King—that these two
particular ministers had helped get and keep in business. We had a
right to go to a sporting event. Neither of us gambles, we just enjoy
the fights. Besides, Dr. King went to see Muhammad Ali fight, and
he went to see Sammy Davis, Jr., in Las Vegas. Of course, Dr. King
wouldn't be over at the crap table blowing on the dice, but neither
did Jesse or I. We were having some recreation, and anyone who
looks at our personalities might imagine that we like boxing. I think
about it like this: someone once asked me if Billy Graham would be
in Las Vegas with Evander Holyfield, and I said, "No, he'd be somewhere playing golf with Richard Nixon and George Steinbrenner,"
which in my book is more immoral and unethical.

It brings up the whole question of fame and infamy, and what
kind of life a public person, especially a minister, is allowed to have.
By 1986 I could no longer go to a movie—that had to stop because
my presence was too disruptive to everyone else, people would be
clapping and yelling and asking me questions—and once when I
went to a Red Lobster in Queens (I just wanted dinner), everybody
including the staff stood up and clapped. That happens all the time
now, and it's very gratifying, but it also means I can't just go over to
the mall and buy my daughters a snow cone.

Then there are the true negatives, which mostly involve the
media writing things that are inaccurate or untrue and which affect
your family and friends. That can be hard. Ninety-nine point nine
percent of the people who come up to me in airports or on the
street are positive and kind; those that dislike me don't say anything, except for one time I've never forgotten and will never forget:
I got off an elevator one day, and this eighty-year-old white lady
was coming in the other direction, and she peered at me and said,
"Sharpton?" I stopped and said, "Yes, ma'am?" She looked at me

again and said, "You're Sharpton?" I smiled and said, "Yes, I am. Nice to meet you." And she said, "You bastard," and walked away. But that's the only time like that I remember.

But fame has changed my life, and it has probably changed me. I don't worry so much for myself, but I am constantly aware of the safety of Kathy, Dominique, and Ashley, it's always in my mind. That's why I've been very reticent about having them in the public eye. I mean I'll have them with me sometimes, but I don't want them photographed or filmed. I'm continually surprised by where I'm recognized, and by whom, in Europe, in Africa. I was in a smoke shop with a friend in a small town up in Maine when an older white lady walked in and grinned and threw up her hand and said, "Al!" like she knew me. I couldn't believe it. It took me a while to adjust to that sort of kindness, and, I must admit, to the warmth of so many people, especially the whites.

You have to remember, I became well known as an antagonist of the mainstream, not through Warner Bros. marketing or something like that. I came out of battle not really paying attention to what was going on and suddenly everyone knew who I was. I was like, "Wow, what's all this?" I watched *In Living Color* by accident one night and they're doing riffs on me, I turn on Arsenio Hall and he's making Al Sharpton jokes, and it took me a little while to catch up. The other factor, I think, was that I had always been kind of famous my whole life, in my circle. From the time I was four, I was famous for a poor black person in Brooklyn. But now everybody, even little old ladies in Maine, knows who I am. I don't know that I will ever get completely accustomed to it.

I was sitting in Sylvia's restaurant in Harlem having breakfast with Alton Maddox on Tuesday August 20, 1991, when my assistant Jennifer Joseph called saying that there had been a racially based disturbance overnight in the Brooklyn neighborhood of Crown

Heights, and that the family involved—a little black boy had been killed by a Hasidic driver—wanted to talk to me. I told her that I didn't want to get involved, I didn't want to appear to be fanning the flames of conflict, until I heard directly from the family and they asked me to intervene. A few minutes later, a man named Carmel Cato called, and he said, "Reverend Sharpton, I'm the father of the young man killed and I would really like you to come out here. I believe there was some wrong here because the police roughed me up when I tried to get my son from under the car." Carmel Cato said he had complained to the mayor and the police commissioner, but received no satisfaction.

What had happened was that at about 8:20 on the night of August 19 the motorcade of the grand rebbe of the Lubavitcher, a Hasidic Jewish sect that had their world headquarters in Crown Heights, ran a red light, which they had permission from the police to do at all times—in fact, the motorcade had a police escort that evening—and one of the chase cars, driven by Yosef Lifsh, had to swerve off the street to avoid hitting a car that had entered the intersection. In a tragic accident, the out-of-control car hit two black children, seven-year-old Gavin Cato and his cousin Angela, killing the boy and seriously injuring the girl.

There are differing accounts of what happened next, but what is known for sure is that Lifsh was beaten by angry and distraught blacks at the scene and that he was taken away by a private Hasidic ambulance before the surviving child, who was seriously injured, received any medical attention. As word of these events spread through the community, there were several disturbances on the streets, and in one of these, a young Jewish rabbinical student, Yankel Rosenbaum, was stabbed to death by someone in a mob of blacks. That night was the beginning of what has come to be known as "Crown Heights." I will always be deeply sorry for what happened to Yankel Rosenbaum; it was the unfair and unfortunate murder of an innocent young man. And it was, for the black community, at best counterproductive, an unleashing of emotion that reduced that mob to the level of the killers in Howard Beach and Bensonhurst. We will not achieve justice behaving in the same exact ways as those we oppose.

After talking to Carmel Cato I headed directly to Crown Heights. When I got there, there were all kinds of people milling in the street, upset and angry, wanting to protest. The violence the night before had been more extensive than anyone had thought and the entire neighborhood was extraordinarily tense. I went inside the Cato family house, and I sat down with Gavin's father, his brother, and the father of the girl, Angela, and I remember them very clearly: they were dark, very intense and serious black men, and they said they wanted me to help. Something I've been accused of in the Crown Heights incident is helping to incite the violence of the first night, which is patently untrue, as I was unaware of what was happening as it unfolded.

I of course agreed to help, and having had experience in these sorts of tragedies, I started taking care of the particulars. Had anyone been to the morgue to identify Gavin? Has anyone been to see Angela? Have you made the funeral arrangements? Do you have a lawyer? The answer to these questions and all my others was no, so I decided that first of all we should go to the Kings County morgue and identify young Gavin. We can't even begin talking about a funeral until someone identified him, and it had been nearly twenty-four hours since he was killed. So we went, and also visited Angela.

On the way back to the Catos' house we were caught up in the second night's rioting. Gangs of young Jews and young blacks were skirmishing throughout the neighborhood, and the Jews are getting the better of it because the blacks were not expecting the attacks. A group of black nationalists led by attorney Colin Moore was marching, protesting, on one side of the street and a group of Hasids was yelling at them from the other when suddenly one of the Hasids comes flying across the street as fast as he could and whacks his fist as hard as he can against Moore's jaw, knocking him flat. All those hard-core militants took off like Jesse Owens—which I thought I'd never see—because they were completely caught off guard. Things then got out of control, people started stampeding, Peter Noel of *The Village Voice* got caught in it along with other reporters. The police came and started arresting people, but only blacks. No Jews. As far as I know, the police have not released the arrest statistics from those nights broken down by race, but that's what happened all over Crown Heights. I saw these things with my own eyes.

We eventually made it to the house, and we were sitting there trying to process what had just happened, and I got a call on my car phone that the cops have arrested two black reporters, Vynette Price and Chris Griffith, who is the older brother of Michael, the young man slain at Howard Beach. So I went out to the special precinct the cops have constructed at Prospect Park, where they were being held, to try and get them out. While I'm standing there trying to get Vynette and Chris released, I watch them bringing in vanload after vanload after vanload of black kids. Black kids as far as you can see. I'm thinking to myself, that's a mighty one-sided fight going on out there. But I finally got in to talk to the commanders and got Vynette and Chris out. That was the second night.

Crown Heights has always been a strange piece of the fabric of New York, populated as it is by a mixture of American and West Indian blacks (there is a difference) and a significant concentration of Hasidic Jews. The blacks have long accused the Hasidim of receiving special treatment from the police (the rebbe's motorcade a case in point), of cutting special property deals with the city—the city favoring the Hasidim for the purchase of lots and empty buildings—to increase their numbers, of blocking streets on the Sabbath, including streets that house non-Hasidim, and of harassing blacks into giving up property that fits into Hasidic designs.

The Hasidim are also felt to be particularly dismissive and contemptuous of blacks. They remain in the neighborhood in order to stay close to their world headquarters, which was built when Crown Heights was a largely Jewish community, and have built something of a Fort Apache in the black ghetto, which is a hot-and-cold irritant to their neighbors. The situation there is always tense but usually quiet.

The third day we went back and started making arrangements for Gavin's funeral. We had to bring family in from Guyana, and we had to raise money for that. Then I heard that some black kids were marching up the parkway, and we headed straight up there to see if we could calm them down, and as we arrived we saw they were about to post up in front of the Hasidic synagogue on the corner of King's and Eastern Parkway, and bricks started flying again on all sides. We immediately got out of there.

Mayor Dinkins had been booed by blacks the night before, and he had Deputy Mayor Bill Lynch call me and ask for my help in restoring order. I agreed to meet, but I also said they've got to start letting all those black kids out of jail. It quite simply wasn't fair. They were only arresting one side, and both sides were clearly involved. Then they said they couldn't look like they were "acquiescing." Acquiescing to what? I hadn't said anything at that point, things were moving too fast, but black folks aren't blind and they could see whose children were getting hauled off and whose weren't.

I agree to meet up with the mayor at Congressman Edolphus Towns's mother's wake at the Woodward Funeral Home on Troy and Fulton. We decided that Dinkins and I would meet at the funeral home and go from there to Restoration Plaza. Colin Moore, Alton Maddox, and two of the parents who had children in jail come along, and they suddenly lit into Dinkins—Uncle Tom this,

Uncle Tom that—and Dinkins got mad and went off on *them* and it took a while to get everybody calmed down. Milt Mollen, Norman Steisel, Bill Lynch, all deputy mayors, are in the room, along with a top police commander, when Zaire Africa, one of the parents at the meeting, made an extraordinarily moving plea for compassion regarding the children who had been jailed, but which fell on deaf ears. So I started yelling at them, telling them that they are letting the mayor take *their* whipping, because of the unequal situation, that's what's causing all the tension. And I believe that to this day. If some of the Jews involved had been arrested the second night, the whole thing could have been solved much more simply. As word got around the black community what was going on with the arrests, it was like pouring fuel on the fire.

I said, "You've got to release these kids. Nothing can happen until then." I had announced that we were going to have a march that Saturday down the Eastern Parkway, and the police were saying it couldn't be allowed, it would become violent. But I had never had a violent march and wasn't going to back down. At one point I left the room to go to the men's room, and while I was in there someone came up behind me and said, "That's it, Al, give 'em hell." It was Dave Dinkins. And I realized then that he was so tentative that he didn't want to offend even his own administration, the people he had appointed and could fire at will. He just didn't have that killer instinct. We returned to the room and couldn't resolve anything that night, but we met again the next day and were able to start getting kids released.

We buried Gavin that Saturday and marched three miles to the cemetery. Three thousand people participated, and though you could cut the tension in the air, it was the first nonviolent march of the week. A lot of the hard-core types were grumbling, "We want to burn down Crown Heights," but I said, "Y'all burned for three days and it didn't do nothing but get a bunch of young kids locked up, who we had to get out. Now I'm going to show you how to do it."

In the meantime, Charles Hynes, the Brooklyn district attorney, has convened a grand jury. The grand jury, along with the police, finds the driver, Yosef Lifsh, not guilty of any crime. Lifsh was released from custody and immediately left the courthouse for Kennedy Airport, where he flew to Israel. The problem with that is he left before the grand jury returned a verdict. How did he know he wasn't going to be indicted? There's something suspicious there. So we hit them with a civil suit. It's a wrongful death and he owed civil damages to the family. There were Angela's hospital bills, the cost of Gavin's funeral and burial.

When the suit was heard, the judge asked about the defendant. We said we thought he was in Israel. The judge then said we had to make an attempt to serve Lifsh and be able to prove that attempt before Lifsh could be held in default. "No problem," I said, "we're going to Israel." People thought I was bluffing, even when we made our reservations and paid for the tickets. But there we were, Maddox and me, flying El-Al to Tel Aviv on the weekend of Yom Kippur. We're on the official Israeli airline going over there to pursue and serve a Hasidic Jew and everybody on the plane knows it. The Jewish community views Crown Heights as an assault along the lines of Kristallnacht, and they're looking at us like we're monsters.

So we fly ten hours to Israel, not even talking, just sitting there. We land in Tel Aviv, go through customs, and when we come out, it seems like the entire Israeli press corps is there. Flashbulbs are going off like firecrackers, and then out of nowhere this man, long beard, comes up to me, holds a two-inch wad of hundred-dollar bills in my face, and says, "I'll pay you whatever you want to get out of our country."

Then a woman—and mind you, this is Yom Kippur, the high holy days, Jews from all over the world are flying in for the day of atonement to cleanse their sins—runs up to me and yells, "Go to hell, Sharpton, go to hell." And with my Brooklyn smart-mouth I say, "I am in hell." Of course, headlines in America the next day, on

Yom Kippur, bannered "SHARPTON SAYS ISRAEL IS HELL." It was like Howard Beach or Bensonhurst all over again, and that *was* hell to me.

Finally, we get out to the curb and try to get a cab. We had decided we were going to go to the American Embassy. We know we couldn't find Yosef Lifsh, he's somewhere out there in Israel, but the entire country is about to shut down for the holiday, and we need to see the consul and enlist his help. Our plan was to serve the embassy, which can, in legal matters, be his proxy, and then leave. But no cab would drive us. The Israelis just sat there, and when we'd say, "Taxi?" they would act like they didn't hear us. So we stepped out into the street, and we saw an Arab cabdriver and asked him if he would take us and he said yes. We rode into the city, and it occurred to us that we might not be able to get a cab back to the airport, we might not be able to get a hotel room. So we gave the driver a hundred-dollar bill and told him to wait. We had a very nice meeting at the embassy, we served them, and they said they would serve Lifsh if they could find him. They gave us a receipt, then we had coffee and headed back to the airport.

Everyone accused me of grandstanding by going to Israel, but it was very serious business. We were very carefully protecting the legal rights of the Cato family and building a case that is still pending. We were able to go to court, present the judge with airline tickets, which cost $8,000, and clippings, and prevent him from dismissing the case. We had made our best efforts to serve the defendant, and then some.

In 1993, in the middle of the mayoral race, Mario Cuomo, then governor of New York, issued a state government report on the events at Crown Heights. Cuomo had never seen the need to report definitively on Howard Beach or Bensonhurst, or anything else, but he put the entire resources of the state of New York into doing an extensive study of Crown Heights. And the conclusion of the report was that the police had been held back the first night, with the strong implication that Mayor Dinkins himself had held them back, and this sealed Dinkins's defeat at the hand of Rudolph Giuliani.

I denounced the report and demanded to meet with Cuomo. He refused to see either me or the Cato family and went to the length of holding a press conference to announce that he would not meet with us. This was classic Mario Cuomo, trying to have it on all sides, to be the great liberal hope of the modern Democrats, but not above a little race-baiting by posturing on Al Sharpton. Cuomo did agree to meet with the Black and Puerto Rican Caucus of the state legislature, and they met with the family and myself before going to see the governor. The report did conclude that the activists, including me, had nothing to do with inciting the violence. To this day there are extremists in the Jewish community who still insist that I did.

Something else about Cuomo's report that still bothers me is that despite the fact that Carmel Cato was an eyewitness to the crash and was brutalized by the police, who claim that he was the one who started the violence, he was never interviewed by the Criminal Justice Department. They interviewed me, who didn't get on the scene until the second day, for several hours, and they never interviewed the father. When the report came out and Carmel Cato protested to this omission, the investigators claimed that they had asked to see him and that he had refused. This was a lie.

So my conclusion has to be that Cuomo was playing games with Dinkins, trying to help Giuliani. And I think this ultimately did lead to Dinkins's defeat. The political irony of all this is that there are many who say that it was the killing of Yusuf Hawkins and the reaction to our marches that caused a lot of black anger and white guilt that helped elect David Dinkins, and the mirror image of that helped defeat him. Yankel Rosenbaum was the Yusuf Hawkins of 1993. A black martyr and a Jewish martyr. When Lemrick Nelson, the young black man accused of killing Rosenbaum, was acquitted, his family started acting like there had been some massive conspiracy, they accused us of intimidating the jury and the like, they questioned the entire criminal justice system. It hadn't, to their surprise, worked for them, as it often doesn't for most. They marched over the Brooklyn Bridge that night yelling, "Every Jew get a .22!"—something we've never done. We've *never* advocated violence. They marched to the federal building demanding a federal prosecution. I said if there was going to be a federal investigation aimed at redressing Lemrick Nelson, there was going to be a federal investigation reviewing the entire Crown Heights situation, including the nonindictment and flight of Yosef Lifsh.

In a postscript a couple of years later, after the 1992 election, I was sitting in C. Vernon Mason's office talking to my old enemy Curtis Sliwa's estranged wife, Lisa, and she says, "You know, Al, tomorrow Senator D'Amato, Robert Abrams, and the rest are going down to Washington with Norman Rosenbaum"—Yankel's older brother—"to deliver petitions, demand a meeting with Janet Reno and that she reopen the case." So I said, "Hmmm. Why don't we go? If they reopen, the Cato case is a part of it, we've got standing." So the next morning, we got up about three and drove down to Washington, and when I got there a huge press corps had already assembled. As I'm always saying, if you're an activist you have to know when to make your move and dramatize your cause. So we had a massive phalanx of media waiting, Norman Rosenbaum, D'Amato, and Abrams are gathered with about twenty rabbis and other Jewish leaders, and they were sounding off on how they need to have this case reopened, how justice was not done in the acquittal, and the rest.

The Justice Department guards—three black men—were standing at the door and saying they would receive the petitions but that they could not enter the building. Right in the middle of their press conference, I got out of my car and began walking toward the door. The black guards looked up and said, "Reverend Sharpton! How you doin'?" and let me in. Abrams, Rosenbaum, and D'Amato went ballistic. "You let *him* in and blocked *us*?" But the guards had no idea why I was there. I was just a citizen. So I got in the building, was able to meet with a Justice Department official and hand over my letter from the Cato family requesting that they not be excluded from any investigation.

Then I walked back out, all of the cameras on and taping, and the Rosenbaum party was apoplectic. They were screaming, a rabbi stood alongside me yelling, "I can't believe this, I can't believe this! We are left on the curb for the likes of Al Sharpton!" I said, "If you're here with D'Amato and don't have the access you need, maybe you should have voted for me. I can take you places he can't."

The Crown Heights incident has been like a stick of dynamite in the whole black-Jewish debate. There was a time when blacks and Jews were allies. The Civil Rights Movement was prominent, but since the *Bakke* case and the furor over affirmative action, there have been increasing rifts. I think that some Jews, like other whites, could deal better with blacks from a distance, when they weren't direct competitors. Now larger and larger numbers of blacks want the same things that Jews want—good jobs, decent housing, top schools—and the pie is getting smaller. Plus, I think that there is an extreme problem of paternalism toward blacks among some Jews and Jewish organizations. They sincerely want to, I think, fight for black causes, but in some instances they want to determine the cause, determine the strategy, and determine the leaders. That's not coalition, that's co-option.

If blacks and Jews are going to have real cooperation, and they should, there is much work to be done. As quiet as it's kept it's in the vital interest of both groups as outsiders in America. One way I think of it is, if the David Dukes of the world were to achieve their wishes and finish off the blacks, where would they turn next? I often think a lot of younger Jews don't understand this, they've gotten comfortable. They've assimilated and become part of the power structure, and they've benefited from the Civil Rights Movement, which loosened things up for everybody and which they were more prepared to take advantage of, but which they don't want to admit. A lot of the foot soldiers who kicked down the doors for Jews were black. They don't want to concede that they supported civil rights for more than just moral reasons, that they also gained from it, just like they can gain now if they come back home to their movement and support labor and jobs and health care and education for everyone, and stop thinking that the likes of Ronald Reagan and Pat Buchanan are their friends.

So blacks and Jews have pragmatic reasons to cooperate and put aside a lot of stylistic and linguistic arguments. Facts bear out that whenever a black official was elected with a significant portion of white votes, the majority of those whites were Jews. A disproportionate number of Jews were involved in struggles for black equality.

The natural ties that have bound us in the past must be reestablished. Jewish spokespersons must speak out more forcefully whenever black rights are trampled, just as blacks must protest every instance of anti-Semitism. Whether blacks and Jews on both sides realize it, our civil and human rights are intertwined. Those who paint swastikas on synagogues are inclined to be white supremasists as well. Gangs who get their kicks from beating up a black person in "their" neighborhood are likely to keep Jews out as well.

On foreign policy, why was Israel's illegal dealing with and support of apartheid in South Africa beyond comment? Conversely, black leaders must raise their voices against fascist regimes such as in Nigeria or Zaire.

And why should not a man who was responsible for the death of a seven-year-old child be handed over to face justice? We're not saying guilty or innocent, we're not saying he meant to do it. We're saying let the authorities sort it out, criminal and civil. Why hide him in Israel? Is Jewish life worth so much and black life so little? Isn't that the message sent to the black community? Isn't that a reason why teenagers might act out? Words against Jews from a lightweight and his eight or nine disturbed followers are more painful than the needless death of a child, and a refusal to *even pay insurance claims to a grieving family with large medical and funeral bills.* How does this look? Are blacks thought to be morons?

So if there's going to be real dialogue among blacks and Jews, we've got to be able to put more than what they refer to as black lunatics on the table, we've got to put real concerns on both sides. Otherwise, there can be no true, healing dialogue. Constantly throwing up whatever person is willing to be outrageous this week is, in reality, an excuse to avoid discussing anything substantive. The issue of one-sided accountability has to stop. Think of what Jackie Mason said about David Dinkins, "a fancy shvartzer [nigger] with a moustache." Can you imagine what would happen if Bill Cosby stood up onstage somewhere and used the equivalent language? When Michael Jackson, who says he was misheard, was accused of using the word "kike" on his new record, Jews demanded that Columbia Records be shut down and the records recalled, which they were.

Jesse Jackson is another example. Will he ever be forgiven for "Hymietown," which was dumb but much more a case of looseness than malignity? He has apologized up and down, he's gone to Europe and stood with Zionist forces against the Nazis, he's denounced, in public, black Americans who've played with anti-Semitism. And when he went to the synagogue on Park Avenue—presumably extremely wealthy, privileged, and cultivated people—he was booed and shouted down, he had to stop his speech twelve times before giving up, they called him names, screamed and hollered. In a synagogue. It was like an organized, planned attempt to humiliate a man of God in the house of God. Is something more going on here than "Hymietown"? I mean, he is not going to bow down and scrape, as I myself am not, nor is any other black leader worth the powder to blow him up. And what Jews have to understand is that if they *could* make us bow, then we would immediately lose all credibility in the black community. Do they think blacks will trust a leadership that can be made to submit?

There's another dimension to this as well. Unlike some other blacks who see Jews as landlords and shopowners, I do not stereotype them nor am I uncomfortable around Jews, because I went to school with them, I've always lived near them. One of my closest, dearest friends in high school, Shelly, was a Jewish girl, as I said, and a Jewish couple, the Greenbergs, were immensely good and kind to me when I was a little boy and going through all that trouble with my father. They were there for me.

When I was a kid, I had the great privilege of going with Jesse Jackson to meet Rabbi Abraham Heschel, one of the greatest Jewish clergymen of all time. He was a great mystic, and he marched arm in arm with Dr. King. Rabbi Heschel gave an autographed copy of all of his books to Jesse, and was extremely warm and cordial and empathetic with us. I was in the presence of a great human spirit, and that has stayed with me. But when I look at the Jewish leaders of the 1980s and 1990s, I don't see that caliber of person, that level of moral understanding. The Jewish leaders of our day won't condemn the blatant racism of an Ed Koch, they don't condemn the routine, daily race-baiting of local politicians and media people, the inequities before, during, and after the Crown Heights incident. Rabbi Heschel would have been in the forefront. So to the Jewish leaders who say they look at the blacks and don't see Martin Luther King, I say I look at the Jews and I don't see Abraham Heschel.

Until we have mutual respect, until we realize that not only do the skinheads want to kill both of us but that there are significant numbers of our fellow Americans who wouldn't particularly mind if they did, this fight between blacks and Jews will not be resolved. We could, and should, be each other's help, but only if there is honest, mutual respect. Until then, we'll continue to drag each other down.

So I knew that Jews were like everybody else, they weren't, as a group, exceptionally good or bad, there were some saints and there were some sinners. I'm a New Yorker, I know that there are subtle differences in experience and motive between, say, Jews and Italians and Irish. I grew up with that. And I spent a part of my childhood in Crown Heights, I knew the police favored the Hasidim even then. I didn't have to do a study. I knew, as Mr. Cuomo's million-dollar analysis didn't, that what happened there that week had to do with a lot more than, I'm sad to say, the deaths of Gavin Cato and Yankel Rosenbaum.

XIII.

After the stabbing I had wanted to become more visibly positive and proactive in my activities; the events in Crown Heights convinced me that the best way toward that goal was to politically empower the black community. We had to establish to the powers-that-were that we were a credible political force, and just as important, perhaps more so, we needed to create and accredit a feeling of power and achievement in our own community. No one really took the black demands and concerns seriously during Crown Heights, and I felt that much of it was simply because there was no fear of organized black retaliation. The black polity was taken for granted, even by David Dinkins.

In 1992 Bill Clinton was running for president.

Though many saw him as some kind of liberal savior, in my judgment he was seriously flawed—a member of an all-white segregated country club, a governor who was extremely cozy with big business like Tyson Foods, and a man who could calmly and cold-bloodedly order the execution of a retarded and lobotomized black man, Rickey Rector, to preserve his image as tough on crime in the presidential campaign. I myself was hoping that Jesse Jackson would run again and present a viable alternative on the Left. Jesse, for several reasons, including not polarizing the party in a year that the Democrats had a real chance to win, chose not to run.

Bill Clinton used that opportunity to play race politics by criticizing Sister Souljah at the Rainbow Coalition Conference. (The young woman said, later, that she was quoting someone else, and that the remarks were taken out of context.) This is not to say that black people who say some very injudicious things are above reproach; rather, Clinton accepted Jesse's invitation and hospitality at the conference, then embarrassed Jesse in Jesse's own house, so to speak, in order to distance himself from Jesse and the other blacks. It was the old southern race code of "I'm in charge of my niggers, things are in control around me." This is the same Bill Clinton that will sit up in a black church and sing spirituals, waving his hands and whooping with the congregation. I was outraged, and thought that the only way to deal with such maneuvering was to build a true political network, something that could make a Bill Clinton, a Mario Cuomo, a Daniel Patrick Moynihan, or an Ed Koch answer for his games, his trying to have it both ways.

As I thought it through, I realized that I might be able to do statewide in New York what Jackson did nationally in 1984 and 1988, which is enter Democratic primaries and put our black community issues and problems on the table, voice our feelings, state our concerns. If I wasn't in the campaign, then the Ferraros and the Abramses and the Holtzmans, the purported Democratic Party liberals, would not feel compelled to talk about social programs, educational inequities, or racism in the criminal justice system. Those concerns wouldn't even be broached. The entire campaign would be pitched to Manhattan liberals and upstate and suburban whites. My presence would force attention on these problems, and the black community would have to be acknowledged.

I also thought I would be able to mobilize grassroots activity and help get out new voters who could participate in electing new blood in some of the local races. With all the noise about U.S. president and Senate, it's easy to overlook congressional races, state senate, and state assembly. You've also got things like city councils and boards of education. Finally, there were no blacks in the U.S. Senate at that time (Carol Moseley-Braun won a Senate seat from Illinois that year), and there had never been a black elected statewide in New York at that time. (H. Carl McCall was elected comptroller two years later, and I can't help but think my campaign helped lay groundwork for that.)

So I had plenty of reasons to go for it. Immediately after I announced, the reaction of the press was that I was, literally, crazy. Who in the world would vote for Sharpton? I had to ignore the barbs and get busy; our first task was to get on the primary ballot. That wasn't going to be easy. John Marino, Mario Cuomo's handpicked state Democratic chairman, said that allowing me on the ballot would be like putting David Duke on the ballot. This was outrageously unfair, as I had never advocated violence against whites, had never attacked anyone on the basis of their ethnicity, and had never acted in any way that could remotely be called racist. Yes, I gave certain white folks hell, and I stood up to them without flinching when I thought they were wrong, but no one can accuse me of anything approaching the sort of behavior and language that was routine with Duke and the Klan. To Marino's surprise, he was attacked from all quarters of the black community, including David

Dinkins, who said, "I may disagree with Sharpton about a great many things, but he is a legitimate leader of our community, he's never been a racist, and should be allowed to run."

We pulled out all the stops to get me placed on the ballot. Since there was not an incumbent Democrat, the party had no real reason to block entrants into the primary. I had to, in effect, hold a primary to get into the primary, and I started touring the state, going city to town, asking the black leaders of Albany, Rochester, Utica, Buffalo, and all sorts of other places to support my candidacy and to pressure their local party officials to back ballot access on my behalf. What people in the white world didn't understand is that I had been traversing New York State for thirty years, first as a boy preacher, then as an adult minister and as an activist. These people, the millions of blacks in the state, knew who I was and trusted me, regardless of the media perceptions.

One of the problems with media interpretations of the black community, particularly those based on polling and on-the-spot interviews, is that most blacks do not tell the truth to strangers, especially if those strangers are white. Blacks will wonder, is this guy from the IRS or Immigration or something? Why does he want to know these things? Who the hell is this? They tell the questioner whatever it is they think he wants to hear. So: "Sharpton? He's a bum." Then they go in and listen to me preach at their church and throw ten or twenty dollars into the collection plate. Or they vote for me.

This misunderstanding led to my being allowed on the ballot. Cuomo and Marino said that, "in the interest of party unity," I would be allowed to run. At the state convention in Albany, Marino made it happen, twisting the necessary arms for me to be successfully nominated. I think the state party officials had polls where 1, 2, or 3 percent of blacks said they would support me, and concluded in their strategy sessions that I was no threat. I knew my base was stronger than that, but I think that Mario Cuomo decided that my

A lighter moment—Henry Kissinger and I were the toastmasters at Jackie Mason's bachelor party in 1991. *(Photo courtesy of Carl Redding)*

Looking sharp with Spike Lee, Denzel Washington, and Bobby Seale. I had a bit part in Spike's movie *Malcolm X.*

Picketing outside the Roosevelt Hotel, 1992. David Duke was speaking inside. (*Photo courtesy of Carl Redding*)

Cardinal O'Connor and I don't agree often, but here he offers congratulations on my return from Haiti, 1992. (*Photo courtesy of Carl Redding*)

Kathy and I with our beautiful daughters, Ashley and Dominique. (*Photo courtesy of Carl Redding*)

With Alton Maddox signing up voters during my 1992 Senate campaign. The man in the middle is Captain Yusef Shah, Malcolm X's captain of security. He is voting for the first time in his life. *(Photo courtesy of Carl Redding)*

Oil and water. Here I am with Al D'Amato and Bishop F. D. Washington. *(Photo courtesy of Bert Smith)*

And politics makes strange bedfellows. James Brown, his family, and I with Senator Strom Thurmond and the senator's Washington staff. *(Photo courtesy of Carl Redding)*

Upper hook on
Muhammad Ali, 1992.
*(Photo courtesy of Carl
Redding)*

With Jesse Jackson
and Al Gore, 1992.
*(Photo courtesy of Carl
Redding)*

Painting crack
houses as part of
our antidrug
campaign, 1993.
*(Photo courtesy of
Anthony Charles)*

It's now a tradition that we spend Christmas with Jesse and his family. Here Dominique, Ashley, and I are with Jesse and Jackie, Jr., 1993. *(Photo courtesy of Powell Photography)*

Jesse and I visited a former slave camp in Senegal. On the wall is a Jackson for President button, 1994. *(Photo courtesy of Kathy Sharpton)*

 for victory! In Soweto, South Africa, at the time of Nelson Mandela's election as president, 1994. *(Photo courtesy of Anthony Charles)*

Visiting a refugee camp in Rwanda, 1994. *(Photo courtesy of Carl Redding)*

Our baptism, Bethany Baptist Church, 1994. *(Photo courtesy of Al Jordan)*

After my thirty days spent in jail following the Day of Outrage, we had a party celebrating my release, 1993. Here's Kathy with David Dinkins. *(Photo courtesy of Al Jordan)*

During my campaign for Senate, 1994. *(Photo courtesy of Carl Redding)*

Addressing the crowd at a labor movement talk, 1994. *(Photo courtesy of Bill Moore)*

In response to Governor Pataki's proposed social service cuts in 1995, I led a protest march from Harlem to Albany. *(Photo courtesy of Carl Redding)*

Doing what I do best—preaching at Adam Clayton Powell's pulpit, 1995. *(Photo courtesy of Bill Moore)*

3 percent would come out of Elizabeth Holtzman's total—she had a pretty good reputation with blacks—and to a lesser extent, Robert Abrams's, which would benefit Cuomo's choice, Geraldine Ferraro. In a four-way race, the final fight could be 34 to 32 percent, so whatever I would siphon from the lunatic fringe would be beneficial to Ferraro, since her supporters could not be imagined to do anything but laugh at me. This was their plan, I think.

They opened the door. They never thought I would become a force they would have to reckon with. But how could they? I was a fool, a buffoon without a serious thought in my skull. They were so busy calling me fat and mocking my hair (something I mocked myself, another thing that no one noticed) that they never noticed that I had won a partial victory against Bernhard Goetz, clear-cut victories at Howard Beach and Bensonhurst, and even in the controversy of the Brawley affair, I hadn't backed down. I hadn't folded or run to save myself. But black people noticed, and they were with me, regardless of what they said on television or at the watercooler at work.

Cuomo, Marino, et al., also had no idea that I could handle a grueling campaign, the all-night drives and greasy dinners in strange places, but what else does an itinerant black preacher do? I had, in many ways, been campaigning since I was four. The powers-that-were also didn't think I could master the debates. They didn't do their homework. I was a debating champion and was on the team at Brooklyn College. I had been preparing my whole life for that primary. And when the party and the media figured that out, they got scared and it all started again, the negative press, the character assassination. I tried to counter it by telling jokes and being cheerful, saying things like I "had the right to throw my hair in the ring" and that my candidacy was notable not only because I was the first black candidate for a major party statewide but also because I was the first person in the nation to run against two people who had arrested me.

Of my opponents, I liked Geraldine Ferraro the most. She was candid and she seemed to respect me, even though she seemed a bit surprised at my grasp of the issues. As everyone knows, there is no love lost between me and Robert Abrams, and I'm not crazy about Elizabeth Holtzman either, who I think tried to have it both ways in the Bensonhurst case and what followed. Abrams and Holtzman perceived Ferraro as the front-runner, and they started beating up on her, dredging up all the old Mafia accusations and tax accusations, but I stayed out of it.

There were three reasons I refused to attack Ferraro. First of all, I took my chance to run for office too seriously to smear it with that kind of behavior. I was always thinking about and took to heart all the bloodshed and death that it took to get black folks the right to vote. I couldn't think of all those sacrifices and feel I could make a mockery of them by engaging in sleaze. Second, my agenda, to establish a political base and get the issues out there, would not have been served by mudslinging; it would have been lost. Third, I studied very closely how Jesse ran, and one of the things he did was stand above the fray.

Jesse told me a story about how when he ran the first time and was preparing for the first debates, he was petrified, and he called Dr. Samuel Proctor, who was the president of North Carolina A&T when Jesse was a student there, and who later became the successor of Adam Clayton Powell, Jr., as pastor of Abyssinian, for advice, and Dr. Proctor said, "Jesse, all you have to do is take the high ground, and raise the moral imperative, and you'll beat them every time." I took that advice and stayed above the fray and gained a lot of people's respect. I even showed up at one debate with a pail of mud to symbolize the silliness of what everyone was doing, and how I was going to remember why we were there and deal with the issues.

Only one black or Hispanic elected official supported me openly, Adam Clayton Powell IV, but I quietly started receiving help from various black elected officials as they started to feel the momentum moving in their base. Officially, I was off limits, but I had the ministers, like Rev. Franklin Richardson in Mount Vernon and Rev. Bennett Smith in Buffalo, preachers that I had marched and gone to jail with and preached for, and *they* had the people. I started preaching in those churches, as I had always done, but now I was stacking up five and six on a Sunday, every Sunday. And it didn't matter that the mainstream press was, as we say, "dogging" me. They could make fun all they wanted. I was preaching to five and ten thousand live bodies every week, and no other candidate was doing that. Congressman Floyd Flake—the pastor of a large and important black church—endorsed Geraldine Ferraro, but he had *me* preach at his church, and he got up that Sunday morning and raised a political offering for me, only the second time he had ever done that, the first being for Jesse. They pulled together several thousand dollars right there and gave it to the campaign.

I had IOUs all over black New York. I had the black radio stations, WLIB, WUFO, WDKX, I had the black newspapers, I had friends in Rochester, Buffalo, Albany, you name it. I knew that blacks trusted Donna Wilson, Dell Shields, Bill McCreary, Bob Law, Bob Slade, Ann Tripp, and Mtume more than they trusted the mainstream media. The strong stand of people like Bill Tatum, the publisher of the *Amsterdam News*, put progress ahead of business concerns and advertising by strongly covering and supporting me, enabling us to get a strong message out to the people. It was a guerrilla war that no one but me knew I was pulling together. The white press had never bothered to get to know me, and even further, they had never bothered to get to know and understand the independent black world, that infrastruture from the projects to the suburbs that protects and sustains our people. If they had bothered to learn about it, they might have seen me coming a long time ago.

In the mainstream community, I kept the high ground. I went to a Wall Street law firm, Milbank, Tweed, one of the most prestigious in the country, for a forum. It's a tradition of that firm and indicative of their place in the elite that they invite the candidates from the major campaigns to appear before the partners and associates, and those candidates come. When Ferraro went before Milbank, Tweed, fifteen or sixteen people came down to hear her, Abrams got about the same, and Holtzman less. The day I went, over two hundred people showed up, mostly out of curiosity, I'm sure. There was a young black lawyer there, Patricia Irvin, who rushed up to me after my talk and asked me to come to her office, where we talked. She said that she had only come to get a close look at me and that she had been sure I would embarrass her. My command of the issues so impressed her that she wanted to get to know me better, and eventually she became one of our most important fund-raisers. She was also a trustee of Princeton University and in that capacity introduced me to Cornel West. Pat also organized a forum before seven hundred black professionals for me at the Sheraton, where I was questioned by law professor Derrick Bell, Cornel, and Marcia Gillespie of *Ms.* magazine. That night led to a lot of my success with the black middle class, many of whom had been quite skeptical of me in the past. Pat Irvin was irreplaceable in that campaign, and the good things I achieved couldn't have been done without her.

I think the reason I did well with groups I wasn't expected to was that I was so well prepared and thought-out on the issues. People assumed that I was running only to spout off and aggrandize myself, but I viewed the campaign as serious business. I had substantively different positions than my opponents on the issues, and I was forthright about them. They were all talking what I would call Democratic Leadership Council/*New Republic*–type positions, which are essentially Republican and tailored to white suburbanites, while I was unabashedly talking about the unfashionable, among politicians, progressive, left-wing issues: full employment, housing, the inequities of the criminal justice system.

For example, in the area of criminal justice, I wanted to talk about the appointment of a permanent special prosecutor, someone who would be immune from political pressure and calculation, on cases involving police brutality and racial violence. Talking about this was important in my judgment, because I was running against three prosecutors, Abrams, the attorney general, Holtzman, the Brooklyn D.A., and Ferraro, a former assistant D.A. Now Rodney King had just happened, and I was coming off the Phillip Pannell case, and knew these things were much more common than was being reported. Large numbers of people, black and white, wanted to hear these issues discussed, and I was the only one willing to broach them. And neither Abrams nor Holtzman was appointing enough blacks into positions of authority in their offices. The absence of blacks in the criminal justice hierarchy was certainly one of the prime causes of racism, misunderstanding, and ill communication. You can't police a community without the presence of members of that community, from street cops to judges. Otherwise people won't have faith in the fairness and integrity of the decisions.

Related to all that was the issue of federal judges. The U.S. senator nominates the candidates for federal judge who are then chosen by the president. Alfonse D'Amato's record concerning blacks on this had been atrocious. What did the other candidates think about this? They didn't want to say. What does it mean when white Democrats are afraid to talk about racial justice?

Then there was the suspension and disbarment of Alton Maddox and C. Vernon Mason—though everything did not run its course until 1993. Why? Did they actually misbehave in ways other lawyers don't every single day, or did they merely prove too much of an irritant, perhaps even too successful, against the system? The accusations actually cited, financial and client mismanagement, are the sorts of things that are routinely excused or lightly punished by the bar overseers. Maddox was not even accused of financial or client mismanagement. As an attorney, what else was he supposed to do? What was his obligation to his clients? Since when does an attorney give up his client? I wanted to talk with those prosecutors about this. Mafia attorneys were never suspended, Alton Maddox was. Why?

My opponents believed that major corporations should be given tax breaks, which would then trickle down in terms of jobs and benefits for the community. It was warmed-over Reaganomics they were proposing, and these ideas had already been proven failures. All the cuts and breaks handed to Wall Street and the big companies were, in reality, corporate welfare. The trickle-down didn't happen. Unemployment was as high as it ever was. The corporations had no social commitments attached to these tax cuts—General Electric got a $400-million tax break in a year that they had a $4-billion net profit. So I was against the corporate welfare my opponents were praising. I believed that that money should be invested in expanding the job base. I advocated Jesse Jackson's platform of investing pension funds into infrastructure redevelopment, rebuilding bridges and tunnels and roadways all over the city of New York. We could provide hundreds of thousands of jobs. And these people would be taxpayers and spend that money back into the economy where it would work and expand further. People would be buying things, Wal-Mart would be building stores to accommodate them, and on and on. Those funds are just sitting there, waiting to be invested, and they belong to working people.

On international issues I wanted to talk about Haiti. I was against both President Bush's policy at that time of tacitly supporting the generals and candidate Clinton's advocacy of Guantánamo Bay as a clearinghouse. I went to Haiti in the middle of the campaign to dramatize the problems there. Haiti to me symbolized the problem of democracy in the Western Hemisphere, who is going to have it and why, what countries the United States will back up in their pursuit of democracy, and why. In Haiti you had a democratically elected president violently overthrown by generals who were essentially gangsters, traffickers in drugs, and callous exploiters of human suffering. I thought it was a valid topic because foreign policy is a large part of the Senate's business. If we had sent hundreds of thousands of people to the Persian Gulf the year before in the name of democracy, how could we have not backed a democratically elected president a few hours away?

We just got up every day that fall and did our best, just kept trying, kept hammering those issues, kept on going. In the middle of the campaign there were Senate hearings on the boxing industry, and a tape was released rehashing the old "Reverend Al and the Mob" accusations, and it didn't affect us. Didn't even register. We just kept going. I adopted one of Jesse Jackson's techniques when I was traveling, and that was to stay with people in their homes instead of hotels. I tried whenever I could to stay in the projects with poor people, as a way of expressing solidarity with them and learning firsthand about their concerns. I did that at least once a week. The night I arrived I'd meet with the tenants' association, then in the morning I'd go to the subway stop and shake hands and give out flyers. An added bonus was that the press would have to cover the projects, would have to go there and meet the residents. Just seeing some of those kids interact with reporters, seeing them believe that if I could do this, then maybe one of them could become a senator, was worth it in and of itself.

The campaign became like a crusade. We were at a project one night, the Tompkins Houses in Brooklyn, and Darryl Towns, the son of Congressman Edolphus Towns, was running for assembly in a Latino district where no one thought he had a chance. Darryl was supporting me, and when we went to the project for a tenant meeting, it was packed. Congressman Towns, who had endorsed Holtzman, showed up, just to see his son, and he was stunned by the number of people out supporting me. That night I went to sleep in an apartment, in a bedroom with twin beds.

At about two in the morning I woke up and got out of bed to go get something to drink and I looked over to the other bed to ask

Darryl if he wanted anything. It was Congressman Towns! There was so much excitement surrounding my campaign, he had decided to stay over and do television interviews with me the next morning. And on primary day, he handed out Sharpton towels and palm cards on the black side of his district, Holtzman stuff on the other. I was learning how politics was played.

We just kept battling like that, day by day, and as it got down to the wire, the press said the best I would do was 5 percent. The night of the election I sat in my office on Bedford Avenue, listening to the returns. There was a lot on my mind, all the places I had been, the people I had known. It felt like it was coming down to this one night. I had put my career on the line. If, after presenting and pleading my case all fall, I came back with less than a majority of the black vote, everyone would say that it proved I was a loudmouth and a bully, that I had no following, no constituency. I would be invalidated.

The calls started coming in from Albany and Rochester and Buffalo, the Hudson Valley, all over the state. It was increasingly clear that I was pulling well over two-thirds of the black vote, *statewide*. The press was stunned. They and I still didn't know I had won 15 percent of all votes cast. I headed down to the tennis club we had rented for the postelection party, and the place was in bedlam. I walked on the stage, and I remember that everybody was there. I saw Jitu Weisu, who was my Brooklyn coordinator, and it was like a circle closing, because he had come to Tilden High School when I was a student there and talked to us about activism. There were so many others there—Alton Maddox, Michael Hardy, Teresa Freeman Johnson, Norman "Granddad" Riede, Carl Redding, Anthony Charles, Sharon Smith, and Janet Baggot. But as I looked around the stage, the thing that made me happiest was seeing my mother; all I could think about was here was the woman who had scrubbed floors and sewn coats to give me a chance in life, and she had lived to see the day that the entire world had to admit that he was a legitimate force, someone to reckon with.

I kissed my mother onstage, then Kathy, and I held my daughters' hands, and I spoke to the crowd. I talked about the 16 percent of the vote I had received, and what it meant that we had finished in front of Elizabeth Holtzman. She was a proven vote-getter, someone who had been a congresswoman, a district attorney, and the city comptroller. She was no marginal candidate, and our grassroots campaign, which spent $63,000, had defeated her. And the nominee, Robert Abrams, who was said to dislike me more than anyone in the power structure, was put in a position where he was forced to deal with a man on equal terms whom he had called a liar and a fraud. If he had any hope of winning in November, that is. It reminded me of a scriptural passage, because all through this time since the stabbing I had been dealing with my spiritual life, the 23rd Psalm, which says that the Lord will preparest a table for you in the presence of thine enemies. Even Mario Cuomo, who had been so disdainful of me since the MTA battles and whose security men had tried to set me up in the FBI and drug scandals, said, "The real winner tonight is Al Sharpton."

What I will always remember from that campaign is how ordinary people organized, how they stepped forward and contributed whatever they had. I received 166,000 votes and spent less than $75,000, while my opponents were spending in the millions. We had no television, no professional staff, but we raised our money with little affairs, sitting around talking in people's living rooms. People would just call up and want to be involved in the campaign. I remember those nights spent in someone's apartment, how they would always cook something special for me, and then everybody in the building would come over. I remember how Jesse came in

toward the end to help, and his labor and women's group supporters
told him, "If you endorse Sharpton, you're dead." He campaigned
with me anyway, going through all the New York City boroughs,
and as he spoke for Congressmen Ed Towns and Floyd Flake he told
them, "Sharpton's got to be here with us." That really meant something to me. We had a little house in Brooklyn that we converted to
an office, and we were always short of money, but those little
people working out of that little building shook up New York State
politics.

If there's one single moment that was most meaningful for me, it
would have to be the night I came down to ABC studios and sat
across the table from Robert Abrams and Elizabeth Holtzman, satisfied and content in the knowledge that they never in their worst
nightmares thought that old loudmouth Al Sharpton, the buffoon
they had been carting back and forth across the city in their paddy
wagons all those years, would be the one staring back at them in a
live debate and standing between them and their dreams. In so
many ways they had been the ones (and the representatives of the
ones) standing between my community and *their* hopes, and for just
a moment, it is as if Abrams and Holtzman were on trial. I remember one of my few slips during the campaign, where I got a little
smart-alecky: Abrams and Holtzman were attacking Geraldine Ferraro on some old income tax business related to her husband, and I
interjected, "If anybody wants to see my tax returns, Bob Abrams
has 'em." It's not very Christ-like or charitable to admit I enjoyed
making them uncomfortable, but I did.

There are some stories, tender moments, that illustrate why it
was so important that I be in the race. A ninety-two-year-old
woman came up to me as I was touring the city on primary day, and
she took my arm and said, "Son, I'm sick and frail, but I got up early
this morning to pull your name. I never marched with you at Howard Beach, I never marched with you in Bensonhurst, I don't talk
back to white folk, but when I got in that voting booth and closed

the curtain and nobody could see what I was doing, I struck one blow for freedom, I knew I could get 'em someday." That is one of the things the power structure and the media didn't understand. This wasn't a march, people didn't have to expose themselves to danger, they didn't have to take off work or argue with their boss, they didn't have to be seen on television, they could quietly close that curtain and fight back, and that's what they did.

There was a man named Hassan Donald Washington down in Washington, D.C., and he had been a Harlem black nationalist leader since I was a little boy, and he became very close with me, sort of a guardian angel throughout the campaign. He got sick with about a month left before the election, and he refused to go home, he just kept working. And the night of the primary he worked until the polls closed, and then he went home and lay across his bed, really suffering, and when he heard how well we had done he cried like a baby. Three weeks later he died. But it was as if he didn't want to give up until we had made it. As a nationalist, he had been very suspicious of politics, but he thought what we had been able to do validated trying.

Captain Yusef Shah of the Nation of Islam came from Detroit with Malcolm X. He was Malcolm's running buddy, he's all through *The Autobiography of Malcolm X*. But when Malcolm left the Nation, Shah was the one who condemned him. He was the captain of the New York temple, he trained Louis Farrakhan, but when Wallace Deen Muhammad closed down the original Nation and folded it into orthodox Islam, Shah went with him. He was a pillar of that movement. Elijah Muhammad called him his favorite captain. He became a chauffeur for Don King, and he used to drive me home at night from King's office, telling me, "You don't need to be in promotion, you need to be out there preaching, you're a man of God." Even though I was a Christian and he was a Muslim, he was a very spiritual man and felt things. He, as much as anyone, preached me back into activism. We'd be sitting in the front of King's limousine, going over the Brooklyn Bridge at one or two o'clock in the morning, and he'd be saying, "God chose you, what are you doing?" I'd say, "But I'm making money here, Captain." And he'd say, "You wasn't made for money, you know your nature, go back where you belong."

When I ran for Senate, Captain Shah was close to dying, in his late sixties. The first time he ever registered to vote was in 1992, when he registered so that he could vote for me. He said, "Elijah Muhammad told us in *Message to the Black Man* that if we ever find a black man like Adam Powell, support him. I'm an old man, I've been a Muslim all my life and we turn our backs on the white man's politics, but I'm going to vote for the first time in my life so that I can vote for you." I started crying. I got him a voter registration form, and he had to mark an X because he couldn't read and write. Captain Shah died not too long after that, but the one time he voted, he voted for me, and he is a legend in the Nation of Islam. He wanted to support me in the process. Things like that are what I'll remember from 1992.

XIV.

After the primary I thought that we had the real beginnings of a political force in the state. And as white New York and the power brokers were trying to read-just to my surprising showing, my immediate goal was to concretize and make permanent the political operation. I formed a central committee made up of leaders from my campaign in the counties that have significant black populations throughout the state. We met every Saturday during the campaign, and we continued those meetings afterward because I wanted to make the gains that we'd initiated irreversible, and to make us ready for the next race. Even then I was toying with the idea of challenging Moynihan in 1994.

I started getting a whole new level of attention and respect from the media. *The New Yorker* did a thorough and complex profile on me, as did the *New York Times Magazine*. The *Times* piece, which was a cover, could even be said to be positive. I had arrived. Then I had Connie Chung from *Eye to Eye* and Mike Wallace from *60 Minutes* fighting over the right to do a profile. Chung was promising to be fair and positive, while Wallace wouldn't promise anything. But *60 Minutes* was the number one show in the country, and Mike Wallace had profiled Martin Luther King, Malcolm X, and Jesse Jackson, among hundreds of others. I wanted to see what he would do with Al Sharpton.

He traveled with me for three weeks. He filmed me speaking at Rikers Island, at a high school in East Orange, New Jersey, at my Saturday rallies. He interviewed a lot of different people. After I spoke in New Jersey, Wallace put sixteen kids on a panel and asked them about me, some of which ended up in the piece. He asked them, "Is Al Sharpton a true black leader?" Every one of them said absolutely. There were varying degrees of enthusiasm for me, but all of them were positive. I think he was stunned. And he saw people running up to me and getting autographs and introducing their kids and stuff.

One day while he was interviewing me he says I've got something I want to show you. It was a tape of me leading an Operation Breadbasket picket line at fourteen years old from the CBS archives. I talked about how I had grown up as an activist, and then we walked down 125th Street in Harlem and he filmed people shaking my hand and running up to me to talk, but what I was thinking about was how it was that CBS had that tape in the archives for Mike Wallace, why didn't they have it when Mike Taibbi was smearing me with Perry McKinnon and Samuel McCleese. Why didn't they tell the whole story then? Why did they act like I had just jumped out of a manhole? I had to conclude that, in 1988, they didn't want to find it.

At the tail end of the *60 Minutes* piece I'm seen in court having lost my appeal on the Howard Beach Day of Outrage, and being sentenced to forty-five days in jail. Mike Wallace was shocked. Before we went in he had said to me, "I'm sure they're going to suspend that. Nobody goes to jail in 1993 for nonviolent civil disobedience." I said, "Mike, this judge is going to put us in jail, right here in New York City." He didn't believe me and that's why he brought the camera crew.

When we got to court that morning there were cameras everywhere. Two thousand people were jamming the corridors. My codefendants, Timothy Mitchell and Charles Barron—everyone else had plea-bargained—and I walked in, and because Mitchell had a legitimate heart condition that we thought would get him excused, I turned to Barron and said, "Barron, we're going to jail." Barron said, "You think?" I said, "We're going."

The Reverend Charles Barron grew up in the black nationalist movement, and later was an active member of the Black Panther Party. Then he became a right-hand man to Rev. Herbert Daughtry, who also used mass action to protest injustice in New York City, the only other minister in New York to do so. I think this is why Barron understood so well what I was trying to do. We spent many hours in jail talking about leadership traditions, and this was the final piece in my emergence in the tradition of Powell, King, and Jackson.

Mason was our attorney. We sat down at the defendants' table and they called the case and told the defendants to rise. Mason stood and said, "Your honor, on behalf of the defendants," and the judge, his name was Albert Koch, says, "Excuse me, Mr. Mason, there's no argument here, you've stated all the arguments, you've lost the appeal, this is a surrender, turn the defendants over to the police." Everyone in the courtroom started screaming. I looked around, saw Kathy, and she broke down sobbing. I was going to be gone forty-five days—at least thirty, you had to serve two thirds of it. So I tried to gather myself and calm down, and with Charles Barron I walked toward the cops who were waiting. As I passed the judge I looked up and said, "God bless you, Your Honor," and I looked over at Mike Wallace, who was sitting there in disbelief.

We went out into a hallway behind the judge's chambers, and a white court officer—the captain—said to his subordinate, a black court officer, "All right, pat 'em down and cuff 'em." He wanted us frisked for weapons, which is standard procedure, and handcuffed for transport to Rikers. I turned and put my hands up against the wall, and the black court officer made a move to pat us down, then he said, all of a sudden, "I can't do it; I won't do it," and started crying. I looked at him and said, "Brother, it's okay. Just do it, it's your job. They will fire you." And he said, "I can't. You're doing this for us, and I just can't." I looked at the captain, the captain looked at the officer, and then said, "You know, I'm ordering you to do this." The officer, with tears running down his face, said, "I know, sir, but I can't." The captain looked at me again, then looked at the officer, and after a long moment, said, "Forget it, they're ministers anyway." He let it go.

So we got in the paddy wagon and they took us to Rikers Island. Then they decided we shouldn't stay there—apparently Dinkins was getting a lot of static that we had been sent to jail—and they moved us to the Brooklyn House of Detention. They put us on a tier all by ourselves, gave us a twenty-four-hour phone, and tried to get us to take work release, to only sleep in jail. Congressman Charlie Rangel even offered to have us work for him, he would supervise our activities. I said no, thank you. I work for Al Sharpton. And we stayed.

That was Saturday. The next day, Sunday, 60 Minutes aired Mike Wallace's profile of me. I watched it in jail, me and Charles Barron, in our private cells in the Brooklyn House of Detention. Something of a surreal experience, to put it mildly. We stayed there for ten days, fasting, and I grew a beard. Then Bill Lynch of the mayor's office comes down and says that if we are given work release to my office, and agree to be back by ten at night, with me as my own supervisor, will I take that? And Barron could be his own supervisor as well. We agreed to take it. Charles and I are probably the first prisoners in history who were released to supervise our own work release. We came back every night, and they were supposed to strip-search us, but they only did that the first couple of times. We'd spend the night, and the next morning at eight they'd let us out. During the time I was in, I was deeply touched by how activists led by Carol Taylor, Norman "Granddad" Riede, and Watchman Harris marched on the jail every day, even during a blizzard when there was no public transportation, and it seemed like everybody came and saw us, from Jesse on over.

In addition, I must say that I couldn't have done any of this without my longtime assistant, Chris Peoples, who kept everything going from the office in Brooklyn, and who I talked to each morning to find out what was happening and what needed to be done. Also, while we were in, Yuna Mulvac of the Liberation Bookstore in Harlem kept us well supplied with reading material, sending boxes of books.

The most difficult thing for me was when the warden, who was a minister and trying to be kind, bent the rules and let my daughters come visit me. Having to sit in that waiting room and explain to Dominique and Ashley that I wasn't in jail for doing anything wrong, but rather for my conscience, was probably the most difficult thing I ever did, because Ashley kept saying, "But if you didn't do anything wrong, why are you in jail?" And it showed me the sorts of things the old Civil Rights workers had to go through. How do you explain civil disobedience to a six-year-old? I did my best, and I'm sure Kathy did more when she got them home, but they just didn't understand. When I was on work release they could at least see me preach on Sundays and come see me at the office, and that was much better. Barron also had to endure the pain of his son, Juwanza, visiting him in jail. We talked a lot about that, and even cried.

The last day of my sentence, the other prisoners asked me to preach a sermon to the entire prison population, and they assembled all the men in the chapel, where I preached on the story of Lot's wife. That was a very meaningful day to me, and I'll always remember it, first because they asked me, and a preacher is always moved by a special request, and I was standing there before those men who'd had their problems and made their mistakes, and I told them about how if God delivers you from Sodom and Gomorrah, the only thing he asks of you is that you don't look back. Whatever it is that you've done in life, whether it's robbery, or drugs, whatever it was you did, you're going to get an opportunity to leave here one day, and you can't look back. Lot's wife lost everything because she couldn't leave her previous life; even though she had been delivered from the conflagration, she looked back. And that's when you get into trouble. It's the same counsel I gave to James Brown and Mike Tyson, and that was one of the few times I've been overcome during a sermon, because I realized while I was preaching that many of the men sitting there grew up in the same neighborhoods that I did, Bedford-Stuyvesant, Brownsville, and East New York, and by some blessing of God I took the right turn, while they, somehow, had taken the wrong one.

While I was in jail I met two or three guys that had gone to school with me. And I realized that my most predictable destiny in this country was to be in jail, or the graveyard fifty years too early, and that somehow, some way, with all of my problems, all my exposures to various pathologies, I was able to maneuver and survive. All of that came upon me, spiritually, mentally, and emotionally, that day in the Brooklyn House of Detention. I was never the same in terms of my compassion after being in jail, because I realized that a lot of those guys were bright little black boys with hopes and dreams running around in the sixties and seventies just like I had been. These were the boys and adolescents I had seen on the street, in the projects, in school. We were from the same place, only some of them had succumbed to certain things in their environment, and some of us others didn't. And I realized how much help I had received, from Bishop Washington and Rev. Banks and Mrs. Greenberg, from Bill Jones and Adam Powell and Jesse Jackson. With my drive and ambition, where might I have ended up without that kind of mentoring?

In the afterglow of the Senate race this was all very sobering, because with all the accolades and recognition, the newfound power and legitimacy, *The New Yorker* and the cover of the *New York Times Magazine*, I could still be put in jail for leading a protest against the violence at Howard Beach that no reasonable person could find objectionable, a protest firmly in the grain of American history and the American way. I was made to seem a criminal in the eyes of my children, and I had thirty days taken out of my life. Would this have happened to a white activist? I doubt it. ACT-UP went to St. Patrick's Cathedral, chained themselves to the pews during Mass and worse, and didn't get thirty days in jail. That was reserved for me.

But I'm absolutely prepared to go again. I've been arrested twenty times and jailed, for five days, five times. Aside from the arrest for fraud, they've all been civil rights cases. I never get a permit to march because I don't think I should have to, I think it's a human right to march. And every time someone asks me for a permit I say, "I got my permit on October 3, 1954, when they gave me my birth certificate. And I didn't apply for that one."

Something that most activists, black and white, don't understand is that you use going to jail to dramatize your plight. People pay attention, even with me they're wondering, why is Sharpton going to jail? You have to be able to bring fear and drama into your political causes or you'll go unnoticed. That's what Martin Luther

King was able to do, raise the level of theater so high that the whole world started asking Kennedy and Johnson, "What are you doing to black people in America?" I took that as a strong lesson, to create theater and drama of an intensity in New York City that people around the rest of the country would say, "I thought New York was a liberal place, why are they throwing those bricks? Why are black ministers going to jail? Why are black people jumping in front of subway trains? What's going on?"

In the summer of 1993, I was asked to come in and assist the Democrats in the mayoral race in New York City. Against the advice of most of my peers and comrades, I decided that I would do that, that I would support Dave Dinkins for reelection. Though Dinkins came from a different generation and had a different style from me, I thought that Rudolph Giuliani would be a disaster. So I campaigned throughout that summer, but we didn't get very far. I thought Dinkins was resisting his base, he was trying to woo whites and Hispanics, and when he finally, personally, made the move to energize his base it was too late. There was no effort at all in the black community until the last two weeks, and even then, with Jesse Jackson and me and others working the people for him all over the churches, he wasn't there himself.

On Election Day I got up very early, before dawn, and went to the Parkland Hotel to pick up Jesse, and at six in the morning we started up in Harlem and went to Queens and Brooklyn and the Bronx, ending up back in Brooklyn at nine when the polls closed. We'd been on a flatbed truck all day, trying to get people out to vote. We went back at about nine-thirty to the hotel, changed clothes, and headed over to the Dinkins headquarters at the Sheraton. When we got there, around ten, ten-fifteen, the ballroom was filled with media, and we went through and did several interviews. Then we went up to the twentieth floor, where there was a suite with about two hundred prominent political figures, but no Dave Dinkins, and were told to go see him in a private room on the fortieth floor.

When we got up there, I asked, "How does it look?" and everybody said, "It's gonna be close, it's gonna be close." Then Dinkins emerged from another room, looked at Bill Lynch, his longtime closest aide, and said, "Get Giuliani on the phone. It's over." So Lynch got in touch with Giuliani, and Dinkins took the call and conceded. Then he went out into the living room and told the people there what he had just done. People started crying, Hazel Dukes of the NAACP cried like she had just lost her closest relative. People were wiping their eyes, sobbing, and I looked around the room and the only one not crying was David Dinkins. And I thought that, as disappointed as he was, he was also relieved that the burden of governing the biggest city in the world was lifted from his shoulders.

We got ready to go back downstairs, and as we walked out Dave looked at me with sadness in his eyes and a little smile, and suddenly all those years of us fighting were gone and I was, for a moment, back to sitting in his office as a little boy who needed his help in starting my youth group. He said to me, "Don't worry, Al, Friday I'm going to Puerto Rico to play some golf and tennis and start the next phase of my life."

I realized standing there why I could never hate David Dinkins, because, in the end, he was just too much of a gentleman to fight the battles of New York City. He was and is too decent a human being to be mayor of New York, and that is to his eternal credit.

We went down to the ballroom, along with about three hundred other elected officials, and I stood right behind him as he conceded, and I thought about all he had tried to do, to heal racial polarization and all of that, and it became clear to me that the whites had quite simply voted against him. That was unfair, because he had met them more than halfway, he ignored blacks in order to placate and service whites. I didn't expect a lot of whites to vote for me because they don't understand me, but they had no excuse with David Dinkins, who went so far in trying to show respect as wearing a yarmulke in public. But Cuomo iced him by dropping the Crown Heights report in the middle of the campaign, roiling everything up again, and that was it. And it wasn't right, because Dinkins did protect the Jews in the disturbance. Do you know how horrific that could have been? The Jews are outnumbered there eight or nine to one. How could Dinkins have protected Yankel Rosenbaum? That was the *beginning* of the conflagration.

After the concession, some reporters gathered around me and Jesse, and Cuomo's top black aide walks over and says, "I'm sorry that Dave lost. And the governor's sorry"—the governor's sorry, he says, but the governor is nowhere to be seen during the concession even though he claimed to be supporting Dinkins. And I remembered that just two weeks before, Bill Clinton had come up from Washington and hosted a dinner for Dinkins, and Jesse Jackson brought me to the dinner, and while I was mingling and meeting people Clinton walked over and said, "How're you doing, Reverend Sharpton, you did a great job last year." And I said, "I'm fine, and I'm glad you came for Mayor Dinkins, but I don't approve of a lot of other things that you've done." And he said, with a smile, "I think you've let the country know that."

This is important because Bill Clinton, the president of the United States, can take an entire evening for David Dinkins, but Mario Cuomo, the leader of the New York Democrats, can't come out to support his own mayor, a longtime loyal Democratic soldier, a good man who has suffered at the hands of his own people in order to be fair to everyone. So then Cuomo's aide looks at Jesse and says, "Is there anything you'd like me to tell the governor?" And Jesse said, "No, thank you." But I said, "Yeah, you tell him to kiss my ———, that he betrayed David Dinkins, and that he is a low-down good-for-nothing son of a bitch . . ." I went off. And through my tirade I could feel Jesse tugging at my sleeve, and saying, "High ground, high ground, high ground." But it wasn't a high-ground moment for me—and I admit that there are times when it's hard for me to hold my temper—and I just turned abruptly and walked away.

I think Mario Cuomo laid the groundwork of his own defeat during that campaign. He's supposed to be this political genius, but apparently he can't count. He was going to need blacks the very next year—did he think we wouldn't notice what he did? It was just like Robert Abrams, who would have won in 1992 with black support. And truth be told, David Dinkins as well. Blacks may not have a loud public voice, but they're not blind. Cuomo turned his back on Dinkins for no good reason.

Who else could have kept Crown Heights as quiet as it was? If Richard M. Daley had been mayor, the violence would have been over in two hours, granted, but there would have been a whole lot of black people, and probably some whites, dead. So the real question is: is it better to have a mayor who is willing to kill black people to protect white property, or is it better to have a mayor who is patient and can save lives and still quiet things down? Dinkins quieted it down, and saved lives at the same time.

The Dinkins defeat was a Mario Cuomo setup from the beginning. There was the Crown Heights report, which had never been done before, and they put on the ballot initiative for Staten Island secession from the city, which brought out record numbers of whites on the island who had never voted before. And Dinkins didn't reach out to blacks. It is naive to think that the election was about security. Why would Rudolph Giuliani, who was federal prosecutor as the city was overrun by crack cocaine and vicious drug violence, make white people feel more secure? Dinkins won by two percent, and then he lost by two percent. It was not a mandate that brought him in, and it was not a mandate that took him out. And Mario Cuomo is the person most responsible.

XV.

In March 1995 I led a protest march from the Canaan Baptist Church in Harlem to the steps of the New York State capitol building in Albany to highlight the injustices of the proposed social service cuts in the state budget presented by the new governor, George Pataki. The state Medicare system was facing, for example, a $1.4-billion cut, which was going to be devastating to public hospitals. I wanted to draw attention to the fact that public hospitals already had an 80 percent higher infant mortality rate than private ones, and that after Pataki's cuts, city and federal matching funds would also be lost, home care for the elderly would be decimated, as well as much needed funding for the blind and handicapped. The governor was proposing to solve the budget crisis on the backs of those most in need, least able to fight back, and who were not members of the greedy constituencies most to blame for causing the problems in the first place.

The march, which was derided in some parts of the media, was a natural outgrowth of my 1994 campaign in the Democratic primary for senator against Daniel Patrick Moynihan. In that campaign, as in 1992, I enumerated the themes that I saw as essential for the city, state, and country in the coming years. I wanted to solidify the gains of 1992, and I wanted to encourage the coming together of a new coalition that I felt was forming as an alternative to the Cuomo-Koch-Moynihan Democrats.

Twenty-one elected Latino officials endorsed me, and I received half of the Latino vote, all of this against an incumbent Democrat who had massive power in handing out federal money, who was the sitting chairman of the Senate Finance Committee. It represents a maturing of the political process in minority communities, because it's one thing for white leaders to play Latinos and Asians off of blacks and each other by saying, "You're not like *them*," but it's something else to look at the data and note that mean income of minority families is 25 percent less than white families and all the rest. Blacks, in my opinion, have failed to reach out and get that message across to other minority groups. We're in this together, and the relationship doesn't have to be based on fellow feeling. Alliances aren't built on love, anyway; they're built on mutual self-interest.

So what I tried to do in '94 was begin conducting a real dialogue with the true leadership of other communities, not the ceremonial leaders and not the handpicked errand boys of the status quo powers. I want to work with the true leaders of each community, the people that can influence the debate and discussion of the issues in those communities, and get the message down into the grass roots. Jesse Jackson's insight with the Rainbow Coalition is exactly right, because if you could ever bring the disaffected groups of the country together—racial minorities, women, labor, gays and lesbians, the poor, the handicapped—that is the clear majority of the country and could bring about real change. But as long as they are separated and playing a zero-sum game off of each other, the ruling class is not threatened.

By 1994 I had reached, in my personal development, a place of deepening maturity and responsibility that had been building since the stabbing. I had to go from being the critic of society to actively trying to do something about it. I've spent enormous amounts of time analyzing, critiquing, and criticizing what didn't happen in the United States the past fifty years, but guess what—just because I've developed an eloquent and forthright *critique*, that doesn't mean anything changes. I haven't made anything happen. And someone younger will just come up behind me and say, "You're no better than those you slammed. You only pointed out what was wrong, you didn't actually *do* anything." I've learned that the analysis of a problem is not in and of itself the solution to that problem.

This has been the outcome of my decision to be proactive. I want to be more than articulate, I want to create change. I think each and every person has to make a choice between whether he or she wants to discuss history or make history. It's all right to be cynical—that means you're learning from history and experience—but that can't be all you are. A glib, cynical analysis will always get applause, but it doesn't get in the books. The biggest critic of Dr. King won't make the encyclopedias, because that's all he is, a critic of the man that was making the history. There's a place for study and analysis, but it should be a starting place, not a resting place. I'd rather be out there on the line, fighting to make something happen, than sitting in a room being clever and defeatist about why I'm doomed to fail.

The people I'm trying to help need more than analysis; they need answers. If I'm sitting up in an apartment in a project somewhere, I need real answers to real problems, not just a lot of discussion on *MacNeil/Lehrer*. A black mother whose husband has just walked out, who's trying to raise three kids and can't get a suitable job, and her kids can't get a summer job, that woman does not need a Brookings Institution critique of the NAACP and the failures of black leadership. She needs training programs and a job. That's my argument with many younger people. Why give up? Yes, mistakes have been made by your elders, some of them deliberately. People have sold out, people have suffered from failures of vision. So learn from those failures of commission and omission. Actively pursue doing what they have not done. If you see their mistakes, don't repeat them. I've had the option of saying, "NAACP ain't done nothing, the Urban League ain't done nothing, the churches ain't done nothing." Well, I've said all that, but when I got up and went to Howard Beach, something happened. Something none of us could have imagined. Three people went to jail for the racially motivated killing of a black man. If I had contented myself with being eloquent on the failures of my elders, those three boys would have gone on walking around free after killing Michael Griffith. And more black kids would have been killed. I knew then, and I know now, how corrupt and crooked official New York is, but I also knew they couldn't win forever. Let your cynicism fuel your activism, not just more cynicism.

The overarching lesson of 1994 is that we have got to figure out ways of opening up the political process, of getting those currently on the outside to participate, in a word, to vote. We've got to remind them that progress in America is never a gift, that it is earned, a reward for organizing and not giving up. And we have to remind them that there are always those who stand at the ready to rescind whatever progress is gained. In this country, voting has a direct correlation to getting what you want for your family and community, as evidenced by the fights over Social Security and Medicare. Or national health care. Those that opposed it felt they were already covered. I received more votes than I did in '92, both in absolute numbers and as a percentage of votes cast. In 1992 I received 166,000 votes out of 1.2 million cast; in 1994 I received 187,000 out of 700,000. With a 20 to 23 percent decline in the Democratic Party electorate over those two years, I was the only Democratic candidate in New York that received more votes in '94 than in '92. I also went against the downward trend in districts where the turnout was down 30 percent, yet I received more votes. Plus, black turnout was lower, but my percentages in those neighborhoods were way up. Another extremely positive factor was that I wasn't at the head of the ticket; there was the governor's primary and the attorney general's. I was in the third category on the ticket, and still went up, which stunned the political aficionados. Many of them had explained '92 by saying that I was at the top of the ticket. Ironically, conservative journalists like Fred Dicker of the *New York Post* were more willing to acknowledge our political strength than the so-called liberals.

We did all that with no debates, because Moynihan refused. Another explanation of '92 had been that I benefited from all the free television, which was true, but I was able to connect with people although I had no commercials and much less free publicity. And we only had about $100,000. What we did have, however, was the central committee that I had formed in 1992 and which had continued to meet every Saturday. And we had expanded, because we thought we were a believable political entity. In late 1993 we started targeting a potential race against Moynihan, planning what we might do and what that would take. Then, at about the same time, Reverend Jackson appointed me the coordinator of the National Ministers section of the Rainbow Coalition, and Rev. Wyatt Tee Walker, who had been the chief aide to Dr. King as well as a prominent member of the Harlem community, chairman. I began working very closely with Reverend Walker and ministers all over the country. I have always felt that Reverend Walker was one of the great unsung heroes of the Civil Rights Movement, and it was a great privilege for me to have been able to work so closely with him.

Through my capacity as the coordinator of the Rainbow Ministers I started meeting with labor leaders who had shunned me in the past, women's leaders, gay and lesbian leaders, all the people who wouldn't hear me in the past. A former Democratic district leader, Alan Roskoff, who is Jewish and openly gay, had fought for years to try and get whites to at least meet me and had been rebuffed. He now found himself being called and asked to bring me places.

In these discussions I began to realize that there was a lot of dissatisfaction with Moynihan in the state, that he was insensitive to the concerns of vast sections of the people. He was an institution, a pillar of the establishment, and he had never been challenged. Here was a man who had worked closely with Richard Nixon, who had made a national reputation talking about the breakdown of the black family. Wouldn't it be interesting, in this time of wrenching economic change and racial divisiveness, to put his record to a sort of referendum? The other factor was that Mario Cuomo was running for reelection as governor, and we needed to be in a statewide race in order to pressure him on the issues.

When I made my declaration speech at the New York State Democratic Convention in Buffalo in 1994, the main theme of the speech dealt with what I noted earlier: Daniel Patrick Moynihan was great at analysis, but where he failed was action. Moynihan said the black family would break down—well, plenty of people said that, including Kenneth Clark and Martin Luther King. Moynihan was aware that the black family was in trouble, but he never said, "Therefore, I will do so and so." We don't elect senators to be professors of analysis, we elect them to solve problems. So my speech stated that while Moynihan acknowledges that we have record umemployment, Sharpton says let's solve that by creating jobs out of pension fund money. When has Moynihan ever *solved* anything? He was the national expert on health care, but he couldn't get a bill. That's why he needed to be challenged.

Also, Moynihan felt that he didn't have to relate to the black community. He never even attended a black or Latino caucus dinner—professional respect, his fellow politicians—and he never appointed any black judges. When I announced that I was in the primary, he immediately nominated, for the first time, a black prosecutor to be the U.S. attorney for the Eastern District of New York, and he suddenly found several blacks qualified to be federal judges. He had never before done that, and he'd been in the Senate sixteen years.

I started my campaign at the corner of Franklin Avenue and Fulton Street in Brooklyn, under the falling-down Franklin Avenue El tracks, to illustrate how the infrastructure of urban areas had been allowed to deteriorate in the home state of the chairman of the Senate Finance Committee. Moynihan had all this juice in Washington, but public transportation was collapsing in Bedford-Stuyvesant. We stood out there in the rain with about five hundred people, and I talked about how I had ridden over that day on the same train on the same tracks as I had once ridden with my mother, and how far I had come while at the same time the city had fallen so far. Did Daniel Patrick Moynihan understand what was happening? Did he care?

As in 1992, the first problem for the campaign to solve was whether or not I would be able to get on the ballot. This time I was challenging an incumbent Democrat, and I wouldn't be automatically granted that status by the party. John Marino was no longer state chairman, replaced by someone who was adamantly opposed to me getting on the ballot. I thought it was my right and prerogative to run against the incumbent because I disagreed with his policies. In fact, I thought my views more authentically represented the traditional Democratic Party. I had the right to oppose that which I didn't agree with. Besides, the state party as it stood at that time was no friend of mine. The Democratic governor and the Democratic attorney general tried to put me in jail, and took the legal licenses of my friends and coworkers. Most of the abusive state action I fought, from Bernhard Goetz to Crown Heights, was initiated by Democrats. What was my loyalty to that structure?

What I'm advocating is that blacks play the political game like everybody else. "Love them that love you." If Mario Cuomo had been loyal to blacks with more than lip service, he would still be governor. If Robert Abrams had done the same, he would be a United States senator. Blacks grew disaffected with them and did not support them as enthusiastically or deeply as they could have. But this disaffection wasn't organized. It was more intuitive and emotional. Blacks have to mature politically and realize that sometimes our interests are going to be served by Democrats, sometimes by Republicans, sometimes by independents, and sometimes by none. As the old political saw goes, "No permanent friends, no permanent enemies, only permanent interests." That's how everybody else in the country plays the political game and how blacks are going to have to learn to play it.

After I announced, several elected black officials came to me and said that they were going to support me openly, but that they knew that I could not win the delegate votes at the state Democratic convention in Buffalo needed to get me a spot on the primary ballot. So we decided to ask to be heard, ask for time on the program, and not press for a vote, because the officials were sure they could go into the black community and the political clubs and get enough petition signatures to accomplish our goals. We contacted the state party, and they agreed to this plan.

In Buffalo we decided to have a rally in the black community, and I invited all the candidates for governor, senator—my opponent, Mr. Moynihan—and attorney general to come and address the rally. Rev. B. W. Smith had the biggest black church in Buffalo, Saint John the Baptist, and since he'd known me since I was a little boy and I'd preached for him often, he let us have his church. To our surprise, two days before the rally we received confirmation of one speaker, Mario Cuomo. No one in the press could believe that Mario Cuomo would speak at an Al Sharpton rally, but in fact, he was landing in Buffalo at five o'clock, and his first stop was going to be our event, which was his way of acknowledging that he needed my support.

When it came time for me to address the convention, there was concern that I was plotting to stage a demonstration on the floor as I spoke, because hundreds of people had come up from New York City, along with people from all over the state and the black elected officials. It was surreal, because in 1992 there had been only one black elected official who supported me, and in 1994 they were fighting over who was going to put me in nomination and who was going to second it.

I was told I had three minutes to make my speech, and I promptly took twenty-six. I was interrupted by several ovations, and what became interesting is that as I went on, even some of those Irish and Italian old-line upstate New York Democrats started clapping and cheering. Gail Collins of *Newsday* later wrote that it was by far the best speech of the convention, including that by Mario Cuomo, who spoke the next day.

That night we had the rally at Saint John the Baptist. Mario Cuomo pulled up to the church, we shook hands, then went upstairs to a private meeting with the clergy, during which we questioned him about everything from the budget—which we felt was unfair— to the criminal justice system and the Crown Heights report. Then we went back downstairs, into the packed sanctuary, and I introduced the guests. Cuomo stood up and said that he was honored to be there and such, and the press of course ran off with that to Moynihan and said, "What do you think of Cuomo saying that he's honored to be hanging around with Sharpton?" That caused a lot of friction between Cuomo and Moynihan. But Cuomo had no choice.

He had to appear to be reaching out to the black community. He saw the numbers from the Dinkins loss and knew that black apathy could cost him as well. But it was too little, too late.

After Buffalo I began touring the state getting my petitions in order, which I was happy to do, because it meant I would be appearing on the ballot on my own terms. But there were a lot of legal preparations because we were expecting to be challenged, and we had to raise a lot of money: you have to print petitions, open offices, which we had to do in Albany, Buffalo, Syracuse, the Bronx, Brooklyn, Manhattan, and Queens. But as the Latino and black officials endorsed the campaign, they started delivering their political clubs, which combined with my network to put us well past our requirements. Once we filed and Moynihan's people looked at the situation, he announced that he wasn't taking me to court after all. We needed fifteen thousand legal signatures, we had fifty thousand.

That summer, I became increasingly upset by what was going on in the central African country of Rwanda and in the refugee camps in Zaire. In August I decided to go over there and see what the African American community could do to help alleviate the suffering, and it was one of the most moving, and horrifying, experiences of my life. I have never, ever seen anything like what I saw on that trip.

There was one camp, called Goma, that had 300,000 refugees and only eight doctors. Walking through the camp, people would walk past you, look at you, then just keel over and die. I saw little kids die. I went to the orphans' camp, over 3,000 orphans, and they warned us very strictly not to touch the kids because of the risk of infection, but I just couldn't help it. I just kept picking up and holding them, I had to. They were the same age as my children, suffering so grievously, so unimaginably, from completely unnecessary tribal war.

I consider myself a Pan-Africanist in the Du Bois interpretation of that term, which means that I believe that there must be a commitment of people of color to the general empowerment and self-development of people of color around the world. We are caught in the same web of oppression because of skin color, suffering the same disadvantages and subjected to the same double standards. I don't see Pan-Africanism as positing an all-black world; that is unreal, especially given modern technology. It's impossible to be isolated from everyone else. But I believe that people of color, along with everyone else, can live and function in the world as productive citizens and go as far as they can go with their talents, and have a commitment against the historic double standard that afflicted their people.

That double standard plays out in different ways, but all are equally pernicious, in the United States, in the United Kingdom, in France and Germany, in Brazil, in Australia, and most tragically, in Africa. The macro-issues of American blacks are the same as those of Africans: self-determination, self-empowerment, the ability to define ourselves, the ability to set our own goals and achieve them on a level playing field. Our specific political environments are different and therefore will require different strategies that will manifest in different ways. We don't owe the global blacks anything as much as we owe ourselves; we owe it to ourselves to break the yoke of those that oppress us, which will help the others because it is the same yoke that oppresses them. The forces that exploit blacks in the United States, given the global economy, are the same ones that exploit Africa: the colonizers, the multinationals. So I'm not saying that we should fight for Africa because we're guilty or we owe them something, I'm saying that in order to get the monkey off our back we've got to get it off their back, because it's the same monkey.

Something that was deeply touching happened to me in Zaire, when I was asked to preach, with a French interpreter, at a church in Goma. There's a custom in Zaire that after church, even though they're very poor, the head minister has the visiting minister and any other clergymen present at the service to his house. The house we went to was the size of my living room, and it had a mud floor, but they had great dignity sitting around in a circle, serving tea out of an old battered pot. There was an old minister there who didn't speak a word of English, and he asked me through an interpreter, "Are you from America?" I said yes. Then he said, "I heard that long ago they took some Africans to America, and I always wondered what became of them." That shook me. It was a hard thing to think about because I thought, "Yes, they carried us off four hundred years ago, and what *did* become of us?" I couldn't really say.

I was at a loss for a couple of days until, as I was getting ready to leave, I went down to the lake to meet some Rwandan college students who were refugees. One of the students, about nineteen years old, looked me right in the eye and said, "You're from America?" I nodded. He said, "African Americans, the most educated and powerful Africans in the world. Why don't you act like it?" So I asked him what he would like for me to tell African Americans when I got back home, what could American blacks do for Africans? I expected him to say, "Send money, send medical supplies, send engineers," but what he said was, "Tell them the first thing they can do for us is tell the rest of the world the truth. If the truth is told around the world of how Europeans stole the resources of Africa and expropriated African labor to build these empires, the acknowledgment of the truth will begin the process of healing that is needed in Africa." That young man was right. Black Americans are the most stable Africans in the world, but we do not use our $400-billion consumer market wisely, for either ourselves or others, and we squander what could be enormous political power. If we took our $400 billion and consolidated it in economic institutions, undergirded black banks and businesses, there's so much we could do in our own self-contained world that could become a platform of freedom for blacks in America and around the world.

I remember a trip I took to Gorée Island in Senegal, where the slaves were actually shipped from during the Middle Passage. I think the absolutely most emotional experience of my life was going to that village in the slave quarters, looking in the little rooms where everyone was kept all crouched together, and looking through the door they call the Door of No Return—when you went through that door you were on your way to a slave ship and America, and you either died in the ocean or you made it to slavery and lived the rest of your life in chains.

From Gorée Island to mayor of New York, to chairman of the Joint Chiefs of Staff, to governor of Virginia, is a long, long trip, a trip that we black Americans don't tell our children enough about. If our children knew more about that journey, it would be more difficult for them to call their mothers, wives, sisters, and girlfriends "bitches," and it would be more difficult for them to stick needles in their arms and crack pipes in their mouths. It was a long, hard journey, but these American black kids don't know anything about it, what it cost, what it took. When we came out of that building, there were some African kids running around and playing, and inside of one of the houses there was a poster, "Jesse Jackson for President." As much as I had supported Jesse, and for as long, I had not understood until then what that means, that he ran for president of the United States, because those people there on Gorée can look out the Door of No Return and realize how far those slaves have come.

That is what black Americans have to recapture: a sense of destiny and a sense of mission toward what we have to achieve and accomplish. That's what we ignore right now. Every Irishman understands the rise of the Irish from Ireland to John F. Kennedy, every Jew understands the thousands of years of their history, they commemorate it each Passover. But every African American does not teach their children the story from Gorée Island through the Middle Passage to slavery to Reconstruction to Jim Crow to the Civil Rights Movement to today.

They need to know that Du Bois was right: the issue of the twentieth century is the color line, and it will be the issue of the twenty-first, along with the issue of rediscovery, reidentifying our mission, and recapturing our vision. Because other groups are not going to do anything for us anymore. In the new global economy, the powers-that-be do not have to deal with the variables they once had to deal with, they don't have to negotiate with labor, for example, they just move to a lower-wage country. Blacks are going to have to claim their own stake in the world, and we have to do it for ourselves.

Blacks have to begin to look at their history like this: if I walk over and hit you and knock you down, that's my sin, but if I come back the next day and you're still lying there, that's your sin. African Americans were not responsible for getting knocked down, but they are responsible for getting back up. And blacks have to face the fact that the people who knocked them down are probably not the ones who are going to help them get up. Blacks are going to have to come to that realization all over the world.

Too many young African Americans are preparing themselves in ways that won't be necessary to African Americans or Africans. They are not learning the tools and skills that will build anything, that will develop anything. Too many black students are studying what is essentially rhetoric—law, media, entertainment, music— when what we need are engineers and contractors. The last thing they need in Africa is a street-corner rhetorician. They don't need us to preach African culture, and neither do we. They need sewage systems and water systems and hospitals, they need a robust African American economy that can influence American policy. What they don't need is Americans trying to out-African them.

I went over the border into Rwanda one day, and every two miles these young Tutsi soldiers, fifteen, sixteen years old, stopped the car to see if we were Hutus. They stuck rifles in our faces and emptied the car. At the third checkpoint, two of the army guys jumped into the car and made us drive them to Kigali. The land is the most beautiful I've ever seen, steep mountains, narrow roads, and grain fields in the valleys, the most beautiful land I've seen. When we got to Kigali, it was deserted, shell-shocked. The U.S. Embassy was closed. U.S. armed forces had taken over the airport, so we went out there, and the commander of those troops let my party in and had me review the troops, because Charles Rangel and others had sent word ahead that I was to be treated as a dignitary. I deeply enjoyed reviewing the troops, as most of them were young black men from the United States, and they knew who I was, and it was meaningful to all of us to be in Africa trying to help out in such a terrible time.

When it came time to leave, the commander said, "Reverend, you need to spend the night with us and we'll send you back tomorrow in a military plane." I said, "What about the guys with me?" and he said, "I'm sorry, I don't have the resources to do that for them." I said I couldn't leave them. He said, "You don't understand, it's very dangerous for you to be out there after dark. There are snipers, you could get carjacked, robbed, anything could happen." I said, "We'll have to take our chances." He said, "If you must, at least let us dress up the van."

The American soldiers put U.S. flags all over the van so that people would see that we were Americans and wouldn't bother us. While we were driving back it did get pitch-dark, pitch-black, and everyone was terrified. It was one of the few times in my life when I was genuinely, with a feeling of powerlessness, scared. We're going up and down these narrow roads and I'm worried we're going to go over a cliff, then we had to deal with the checkpoints, and on top of that worry about who's out there planning to fire on our headlights.

But we made it back to Zaire, and I was able to bring film back to the United States. Three thousand people welcomed me home at the end of August, at the Concord Avenue Baptist Church in Brooklyn, and we showed the film of what was really going on in Rwanda and Zaire. I have always considered it a hypocrisy for American blacks to constantly talk about "the motherland" while millions died in famines, disease outbreaks, and tribal wars. The suffering isn't African enough for us, we want to wear African clothes, we want to talk Swahili, but when Africa needs us, the Afrocentric believers among us don't seem to be able to deal with that. The situation in Rwanda got to me so deeply that I decided I couldn't continue that hypocrisy. We were able later to air-freight tons of supplies over there, sponsor doctors, and raise money for other organizations, just a drop in the bucket of need, but a small start.

I had been to Africa once before, in March of the same year, as part of the delegation of ministers who served as election observers in the first South African elections. Our delegation was sanctioned by the council of churches in South Africa and was led by Rev. Wyatt Tee Walker, who had been active for a long time against apartheid. I had met Nelson Mandela a few years before—this is a complicated story—when he came to New York and the United Nations to announce the end of sanctions. Mandela had come to New York before that, when he got out of jail, but I was excluded from those ceremonies because David Dinkins was angry with me over various things, and I was on trial for fraud. The press tried to make it look like Mandela had snubbed me as unworthy of being in his presence.

On the U.N. trip, however, Jesse Jackson brought me to a private meeting of black leaders as his guest, and after the meeting, he walked me over to Mandela, and Mandela smiled and said, "Ah yes, Reverend Sharpton." We had a picture taken of us all holding hands. Then we went over to the U.N., and I sat with Jesse and Dave Dinkins as Mandela addressed the General Assembly, and I sat next to Mandela at the press conference he held afterward. Pictures of that appeared in *Jet* and many other national periodicals.

The first Sunday we were in South Africa for the elections, white supremacists bombed the African National Congress headquarters in downtown Johannesburg. The airport was also bombed, in the last gasp of the white right wing. But it didn't affect anything. I remember there was a church right across the street from the ANC bombing, and even though their building was damaged they didn't stop their service. These people intended to have their elections.

We got up early the first morning of the elections, and at 5:30 we went out to Soweto and saw people lined up for five or six miles, three, four, five thousand people lined up to vote for the first time. We went in, helped get the polls ready, and I saw old, crippled women coming in to vote, they'd been waiting all their lives for this. And I thought about all the blacks in America who had this right handed to them but are too lazy and ungrateful to get up and go to the polls, while here were women who lived in shanties but had got up and walked for miles and stood all day in the hot sun for the chance to vote. I talked to a lot of them, and they didn't necessarily expect that it would immediately make things better for them, but that it might make things better for their children. I remember thinking, this is what it must have felt like to be in Selma, and I was honored to be there and be involved with the actual making of history, the democratic empowerment of black people.

The last night we were there, I had dinner with Jesse and Danny Glover, then I got on a plane and prepared to come back. Jesse had been appointed by President Clinton as the head of the official American delegation and had come over on *Air Force Two*, with heavy guard because he had received Afrikaner death threats, but we had spent a lot of time together and considered the trip a success. Dan Rather and David Dinkins happened to be on the same returning plane as I was, and we talked much of the trip. When we stopped to refuel, we looked out on the tarmac and there was a huge plane that said "The President of the United States" on the side.

Rather says, "Is Clinton going over there?" I said, "No, that's Jesse."
We had a huge laugh, and Rather looked at me and said, "Both of
you have come a long way."

When I landed at Kennedy Airport, my assistant Carl Redding
was waiting for me at the gate with a woman who was distraught.
She was the sister of Ernest Sayon, who had been killed by the
police in Staten Island the night before. He was unarmed and had
been choked to death. There had been some violence the night
before, and the family wanted me to come out to Staten Island. At
three o'clock that afternoon, with no sleep, I found myself leading a
march in Staten Island. From one of the highest points of my career
and a world-historical triumph for blacks to "Here we go again." It
reminded me of what Frederick Douglass said, Life is a struggle and
the struggle is your life. You can never sit back and think it's over.
Every day for twenty-six years, since I was fourteen years old, I've
been on the front line of the movement, and I haven't had time until
now to even pause and reflect, because I have to get up every day
ready for war, and I go to bed every night thanking God that I made
it one more day. I try to have a long-term vision, but I have to
discipline that into daily action, because you don't know what the
day will bring.

You have to try and have some eternal principles, because that
will last longer than whatever's on your schedule. My life since the
stabbing has been from shantytowns in South Africa to street
marches in Staten Island, from the governor's mansion in Albany to
the refugee camps in Zaire. I've been walking around Hollywood
and Las Vegas with Wesley Snipes and James Brown and Don King,
and I've been at the White House with Bill Clinton and Nelson
Mandela and Jesse Jackson. I went from the White House lawn to a
rally in Brownsville, Brooklyn. To others it may look like too many
pieces, like I'm stretched too thin, but to me it's all for the same
thing, the same cause. In many ways I think God let me grow up
under the diverse tutelage of people like James Brown and Don

King and Jesse Jackson to prepare me for now, for what I've been doing since the stabbing.

The 1994 election was, of course, a watershed in the history of the country, the Republicans seizing legislative control of the federal government and making inroads all over the nation. In New York State, with the defeat of Mario Cuomo, it represented the end of an era.

I was able to get a larger number of votes from fewer voters, one of the few candidates to maintain or increase their 1992 returns, and that was my real success. Given the 30 percent decrease in voter turnout, I should have done much less, and that was a real achievement against someone of the stature of Daniel Patrick Moynihan. I received a much higher percentage of the black vote than in '92, 87 percent as against 66 percent, even running against an incumbent who spent $4 million in mailings and television in the primary versus my $100,000.

The real dilemma for us in the 1994 election season was the gubernatorial race. We had talked about forming an independent party called the Freedom Party but were not successful. Our idea was that the Liberal Party was no longer liberal, having endorsed Rudolph Giuliani in both '89 and '93, and actively helping him in the campaigns. The Freedom Party didn't work in '93, but it's an idea whose time has come. We need third and fourth parties around the state to keep the dialogue fresh and the major parties honest.

Reverend Jackson came in and endorsed Cuomo's reelection. I refused to endorse Cuomo, because I felt that even though Cuomo was good on the death penalty and some other things, he had just done too much, from stabbing David Dinkins in the back to his handling of Brawley and Howard Beach, for me to in good conscience support him. Cuomo had some of the black leaders ask me to support him, and I told them to tell him to call me and I'll discuss it with him. They reported back to me that Cuomo said he won't call *you*, but he will take a call *from* you.

Wait a minute, I said to myself. Who wants whose support? Why play ego games if he needs me? I was not about to call him, because I want him to respect me and listen to what I have to say. I want to talk to Cuomo about Alton Maddox's license, about a special prosecutor on police brutality, and let's talk in detail about the budget. Those are some of the things I would have to get some answers on to entertain endorsing him. But I was open to it, if he had called. He asked Jesse to talk to me. Jesse said, "Do you want to be responsible for the election of George Pataki?" I said you do what you want, I'm not going to endorse him unless he calls me and deals with these issues. And I didn't. A lot of analysts said that my not supporting Cuomo was a large factor in him not getting the black vote he needed. After he won, Pataki invited me and twelve other ministers to breakfast in the governor's mansion in Albany on Martin Luther King's birthday. I had never been invited to the mansion by Cuomo or Hugh Carey, but Pataki invited us in, so to speak, the first month he was there.

About a month later, George Pataki announced his first budget, and from my point of view it was a disaster. The Pataki administration was planning to cut Medicaid, cut home care for the elderly, raise tuition by $3,000 for State and City University of New York students. There were many other cuts I simply couldn't agree with. I decided that we needed to rally the state against the budget and that, as always, we had to dramatize our opposition. We decided to walk the 170 miles from New York City to Albany, and to have rallies in cities along the way. Thus, the March to Albany was born.

The first day we walked seventeen miles to Mount Vernon and had a rally at Rev. W. Franklin Richardson's church with over one thousand people. Betty Shabazz, Malcolm X's widow, was there and spoke, and it was a tremendous experience. The next day we start walking from Mount Vernon to Yonkers, and then to White Plains, and then to Spring Valley. What surprised—and cheered—me more than anything else as we walked was that in some places as many whites as blacks came out to the rallies, whites were driving by in their cars honking their horns and saying, "Go get 'em, Al!" This included places where I used to be heckled and harassed unmerci-fully like Yonkers, where when I led an open-housing march years ago the police and a large number of citizens literally tried to run me out of town. In small villages upstate white people would bring us coffee and rolls. It showed me that if you hang tough and raise the true issues, even those who misunderstood or opposed you will come around and stand for what is right.

We arrived in Albany, and on that day five thousand people and Jesse Jackson joined the core marchers, myself and twelve others. One of the ways the media tried to belittle our efforts was to claim that the number of marchers proved that no one cared. The truth was, who would have performed the logistical management that would have been required to march with five thousand almost two hundred miles? Feeding them, housing them, providing sanitation facilities? That is something of a scale that only the armed forces could pull off. We knew there would be a core group, with supple-mentation at the beginning and at the end.

At the end of the march we stood in the rain at the capitol, read our concerns, made speeches, and met again with Governor Pataki. My feeling about Pataki is that, like a lot of these conservatives, he's an ideologue, he's a true believer, and he's sure that he's right. He's not Machiavellian like Cuomo, which makes him more inflexible and therefore more dangerous. In our meeting, he argued the points, and I must say seriously, with me and Reverend Jackson and the others—those that marched all the way I brought into the meeting, along with Hazel Dukes of the NAACP and other black leaders—and we made our feelings known. I think that what we are entering is a battle for the soul of this country, between the Gingriches, the Patakis, the Giulianis, and the Helmses on one side and those of us on the other who believe with Lincoln and Roosevelt and JFK that the government exists to serve the people and not just police them.

There is much talk in the country these days as to how everything has shifted to the suburbs and the people who have money and how everyone else is essentially irrelevant. But isn't that what they said in the fifties, and blacks won great gains? Dr. King changed the terrain of the battle. The way the forces of progress can beat Newt Gingrich and his ilk is by taking the battle and the power to make the decisions out of the suburbs and registering people in the cities, in the rural poverty centers, by taking away the power of the suburbs to decide, and making those people have to bargain like everyone else instead of dictating. We've had very small voter participation the last twenty years, and basically what is happening is that the privileged are voting themselves what they want, and even this is not uniform. There are plenty of people in the suburbs who see what is happening with the economy and want something done. They voted for Bill Clinton, didn't they? So I say to all progressives, there is absolutely no reason that the suburbs and that limited selfish Republican viewpoint have to have the vote or the veto on everything.

We do have to work on educating the suburbs to the realities of the new society, but we shouldn't concede. We have the numbers in the cities, it's a matter of organization. If the same number of blacks had voted in '93 that did in '89, David Dinkins would still be mayor, and would be enumerating an entirely different set of priorities. Again, the reason the suburbs are defining everything is that no one is organizing and energizing the inner city. I'm not willing to write off the housing projects and ghettos and barrios. When, like the Democrats of the eighties and nineties, you're afraid to talk to the people you need to organize, you are bound to lose. And, I must say, I don't think this is all about race. Race is a part of this battle, a large part, but it is in actuality a weapon used by the right wing to divide and conquer economically, and I think the more it's exposed, the less effective it will be. I think many whites in the suburbs are going to see that they're going to get chewed up in this new world order as well. I think a lot of them see it already. As Ralph Ellison wrote, "Who knows, but that on a lower frequency, I speak for you?"

When I first heard about the Million Man March, planned for October 1995 on The Mall in Washington, D.C., I had, I must confess, some reservations. I wasn't sure about the notion of "atonement" that had been connected to the event—what about all those black men who had dedicated their lives to doing the right thing, and didn't such an orientation risk blaming black men for what had been done to them by the wider society? I wanted there to be a positive dimension, aspects of affirmation and celebration.

I wasn't bothered, however, that the march had been called by Louis Farrakhan. I've worked with many groups over the years that would have been outside the parameters of my sponsors at Washington Temple—gays, feminists, Marxists, why not Farrakhan? He saw the need and the possibilities, and he should get credit for that. He had the nerve. In 1969, there was a huge antiwar march, but no one remembers who called it. No one remembers who called the women's marches of the 1970s, the gay march of 1993. Why is it that when the gays march it's about gay rights, but when the blacks march it's about who called the march? I think it's a double standard, and it detracts and distracts from the issues. The media analyzes and argues about Farrakhan rather than looking at why so many young blacks are incarcerated.

But it was a great day, for black men, and for America. Black men are often castigated or ridiculed or dismissed, and there were one million of us together in honor and fellowship. Looking out over all those men assembled together peacefully and joyously, I

couldn't help being profoundly moved, and as I was being introduced before I spoke I couldn't help thinking about my brother
Kenny, and how there was a need for some forms of atonement in
our community. Had Kenny chosen the street life, and had he
landed in prison, because of the emotional pain and estrangement
he felt after he learned of the circumstances of his birth? That was
still running through my mind as I talked about living up to obliga-
tions, family renewal and unity, and being open to what we as black
men needed to do to prepare ourselves, our children, and our communities for the future.

There are some things I'd like to say to young people in particular, in the hope that they might benefit from some of my
experience. First of all, whoever you are, learn your roots, find out
who your people are, where they came from, what it took for them
to arrive at the place you find yourself. Whether that place be a
housing project or Scarsdale, the only way you are going to progress is to build on what came before. If you are African American,
you need to know the struggle, exactly what it cost, and what
remains to be done. If you are Irish, for example, you need to know
something about the famine and the great hardships that led to
emigration. The same for Jews, Italians, Slavs, and other European
groups. There are many different stories on this continent, and
knowing your own, the truth of it, not the myth, can help you
empathize with and understand others. The same for members of
more recent groups—learn the country's history and tapestry before
declaring on present events—and it goes also for that great WASP
grouping that is often thought of as not having an ethnicity. Everybody didn't come over on the *Mayflower*, and of those that did, not
all were Miles Standish.

You can better develop your fruit if you know where your roots
are. When you understand where you came from, wherever and

whatever that might be, when you see how those people sacrificed and struggled to get to the present day, then you will realize that you have the ability and capacity to become whatever it is that you truly commit and discipline yourself to becoming. Most people don't get anywhere in life because they are not heading anywhere. You should set your sights on a destination, then always leave room in the journey to be of service to others, to humanity, because the measure of one's character at the end of one's life is what one was able to do for others and oneself. I always say that the hardest things for a preacher is to preach the funeral of those who never did anything in life for anybody else because there's nothing to say over them at the service. If all they accomplished in life was to buy a big house, a nice car, get a fancy degree, who cares when they die? It won't matter to anyone but them.

Live so that when you go, people can say there was a meaning to your life, that you were committed to more than personal aggrandizement. Also be sensitive to the historic context you live in—what are you doing in, about, the time you live in? My biggest fear is that God will say to me, you lived in the latter part of the twentieth century, the first part of the twenty-first, you can't be judged by how well you can recite what Moses did in his time or David in his or Jeremiah in his. You've ultimately got to stand on what you did in the time in which you lived. In my time, drug abuse was high, unemployment was high, the right wing was on the rise— Al, what did you do in *that* time?

Don't put symbolism over substance. Some might think that odd coming from me, but I stand on my record of real accomplishments. What I'm referring to is the human tendency to want to look more progressive than we are, to look hip and fashionable, to be silent about our true beliefs in order to fit in. We substitute style for depth, so we appear militant, appear radical, but we are really not doing all that much to change society.

Have dreams. Don't let anyone tell you that's corny. Have

dreams, and remember dreams are democratic, you can dream in a jail cell, in a hospital bed, in a shack in a shanty, in the projects or in a mansion. And if you focus on your dreams, believe in them, and work to make them real, they will come true. It happened for me.

Choose heroes, the right heroes. Choose people that have the posture and qualities that you would want to have, and don't be afraid to emulate them. Often through emulation of the right people we can learn skills and habits that we might otherwise be afraid to attempt. And those of you coming out of single-parent homes, look for alternative role models, and be very careful whom you choose. And be careful to let them know that you have chosen them, so they can help you become what you want to be.

We're about to close a century that has made tremendous progress technologically and scientifically, but has not made a lot of progress in human relations to one another. We have the information highway, the Internet, but we've also got the Ebola virus and AIDS, we've got tribal wars in Rwanda and Bosnia, we still have racism in the United States and elsewhere, and we still have corporate greed. One percent of the population controls an inordinate amount of wealth. We've got to solve the problem of human relations, that it is more important to try and live in a just and equitable way here on earth than to be able to live on the moon. It's the challenge of the new generation to try and bring us closer to that. Anger, rage, and cynicism are not enough. Those in power don't care how angry we are, they don't care how much rage we've got, they don't care how cynical we've allowed ourselves to become. They care about us having the ability to organize under the laws of the Constitution and changing the power equation. So in our rage and our anger there must be sound, thought-out strategy, and a commitment and discipline to it. Otherwise, our anger and rage are merely entertainment for those who know we'll do nothing about it.

Don't take yourself too seriously, know that the best you can do is make a contribution, that all of us are just walking through here for a minute and can only make a contribution. The world won't stop when we go, as it didn't stop when we came. Make the best contribution that you can, then hope somebody remembers you as long as they can and tells someone else about you along the way. Don't get caught up in your ego, but don't be afraid to take chances. It's going to be a gamble, but the more you put on the line, the more that you can win. If you go at life halfhearted, you only win half the pot. If you put it all on the line, you can win it all—don't be afraid of risk, because the more risk, the more reward. The more faith you show, the more God will answer your faith.

I honestly believe that right is stronger than might. I heard Samuel Proctor say that he never thought he'd live to see the destruction of the Berlin Wall. He never thought he'd see the Soviet Union, an empire rivaled only by the United States, crumble from the inside. The Soviets had military all over the world, had consulates and embassies, but they fell from the inside, from their own mistakes. Sam Proctor never thought he'd see a frail black man, with no armies, no consulates, no billions, nothing but the righteousness of his cause, walk out of the Robben Island prison one sunlit morning and preside over the dismantlement of the most viciously racist regime on earth. Nelson Mandela showed that the meek could be raised from prisoner to president, because the rightness of your cause will vindicate you.

Do what's right, and you will win. If you don't know what to do, do what's right. Out of all the slickness, all the maneuvering, all the manipulation, I've found the only thing that wins is being right. If you have those kinds of values and morals, you'll go far, and you'll be at peace when you get there. If you get there the wrong way, which is possible, you won't be there long, because you will be your own worst enemy, you will have laid the seeds of your own defeat. And the Bible says, "What profits a man to gain the world and lose his soul?" Losing your soul means that even if you get there and you're not you, you didn't, in fact, get there. Some fabrication of you got there, and you won't be there long.

For young African Americans in particular, but in a way speaking for everybody, you've got to reconnect to the roots of the struggle. We can't be more decadent than those we wish to challenge. You can't beat Pharaoh by matching his tricks; he will destroy you and laugh. You beat Pharaoh by matching tricks with miracles, and miracles are the fruit of righteousness. And sometimes, even if you can't defeat Pharaoh, there's a victory in telling him the truth. Even when I knew I couldn't win, I told the truth, and that was a victory in itself. If you can't win, keep lifting your voice until you can win. It will come around.

I've been thinking a lot lately about black leadership, where it's been and where it's going. There have always been divisions and debates in direction: Booker T. Washington and W. E. B. Du Bois; Marcus Garvey and A. Philip Randolph; Martin Luther King and Malcolm X; Jesse Jackson and Louis Farrakhan. I have never necessarily believed that they've conflicted, which is not the same thing as saying that they're equals in stature or represent the same goals. They represent different strains of thought at the same time, and had vastly different numbers of followers and influence.

They're often right about different parts of the problem. For example, Booker T. Washington and W. E. B. Du Bois are often portrayed in opposition, but they're really paired. Booker T.'s vision—get a job, be industrious, accumulate property—is essential and true, but once you've done those things, it still doesn't solve the problem that you're disenfranchised. You've laid a foundation, which enough blacks have not done, but it's not enough. I enjoy and learn from both Washington and Du Bois because I agree that we should be industrious, I agree that we should be employed, but I also believe we should have our enfranchised rights. One does not eliminate the other. You need both. The difference between them was that Washington understood the political landscape at that time, not necessarily better than Du Bois, but he came to terms with it in a way that Du Bois didn't or refused to, and realized that he could get more done at that time, given that body politic, advocating those positions. Du Bois knew he couldn't get as much done, but he refused to accept that he had to take less than any other person because the political environment was hostile.

This applies to today. We have various leaders saying various things, but what it all boils down to for me is that we need a generation of sacrifice. I think we had a generation of social sacrifice in the fifties and sixties, but we need another one, maybe more than one, and this time it has to be about personal and economic sacrifice. The parents of people my age and younger accepted that there were going to be certain limitations to their lives, and they decided that they were going to work beyond, around, and through those limitations to achieve some specific goals for their kids. So somebody's father said, I work in an auto plant and I'll never get to Harvard, but I will make sure my daughter does, and I'm going to pay that tuition and all the other bills. My mother said, I couldn't vote until I was a middle-aged woman, but I want to make sure, by sewing people's clothes and cleaning their houses, that my son can be in a place where he can run for the U.S. Senate. My generation has not made those kinds of definitive commitments to those following, we have not said we're going to accept some deprivation to ensure that our children go further. We have accepted a generation of decadence and no goals, and have not planned for our children, and therefore our children have no direction, no plans of their own. The previous generation had some idea of where they wanted to see us go and prepared us for that.

We have to tell the next generation that the issues are economic. We must build black economic infrastructure and independent leaders who can stand up and call for that. Too many of our leaders are still, as was Booker T. Washington, sponsored by white business interests. We've gone from preachers to politicians, and we need businessmen, so that we don't have to be at the financial mercy of others. One of my dreams and goals is to reopen a black commercial bank, so that black families have somewhere to go and be welcome to borrow money to mortgage houses, cars, or whatever. To finance their dreams. We've got to recycle that $400 billion that blacks generate through our community. Unfortunately, history teaches us that there is nothing permanent in economic clout for blacks in assimilation. I can imagine black banking linkages, black communications systems, black grocery stores—not racist, mind you, anyone who wanted to do business or be employed there would be welcome—owned by blacks and providing the economic bulwarks of the black community.

It seems to me that most white people do their business in their community, and that is seen as normal. As I said in the movie *Malcolm X*, I never went in a Jewish community and saw a Marcus Garvey delicatessen, I never went in an Italian neighborhood and saw a W. E. B. Du Bois restaurant selling Martin Luther King linguine. The only community you go in and see everything controlled by outsiders is the black community. *Everybody in the normal course of business tries to do business with his or her own.* We must learn to do the same. We need mass leadership to articulate this message to the masses. It's not racist, it's the American way. Otherwise we're just consumers, never producers, never owners, never players in the new economy.

I am as sure of this as the next direction for black people as I was of getting out of that car and walking into that pizzeria in Howard Beach. I want the freedom of my people, in matters large and small, and this is the next frontier. I don't feel vindicated in my beliefs thus far, in the sense of vindication meaning triumph, because I feel I'm on a higher mission. It's hard to understand me without dealing with my religious beliefs. I think this is why the media have missed what

I have been trying to do these years, that before all else I was a devout Pentecostal Christian. And I always viewed the storms of my life as tests that would be rewarded. I always felt, in the middle of the trial, in the worst of Brawley, through the attacks of Mike Taibbi, Robert Abrams, and the FBI, that if I could just hold on, God would reward me. I guess in many ways I never got much past Bishop Washington and Washington Temple in my thinking. I think I really believed those sermons that I preached. So better than vindication, I've felt fulfilled, and I'm ready to go on to the next phase.

It has never mattered to me, pro or con, what other people thought. What mattered to me more was what I was doing and how God would give me a reward. I've worried about spiritual fulfillment and pursued that. Where vindication applies, in my opinion, is with those who believed in me, who worked with me even though they were harassed and ridiculed. I'm talking about my wife, my mother, Alton Maddox, C. Vernon Mason, and Jesse Jackson, who I know fought his friends many times on why he had faith in me. Those people were vindicated, I was just fulfilled.

In March 1994 my sister Cheryl got married, and I flew to Atlanta to do the ceremony. My father was there. It was the first time I'd seen him in many, many years. He had another family—his new wife and kids were there with him—and my mother was there. Tina was there, too. It was the first time we were all together in the same place in twenty-nine years. Many days sitting on airplanes, many long nights sitting in hotel rooms by myself, I had thought about the various ways I was going to curse out my father if I ever saw him again. But when I did see him, I didn't do anything but smile, because it didn't really matter anymore. I won. I had made something out of myself and my life. It would have degraded my personal victory to attack him. I didn't have to be bitter. The victory is in being able to absorb the pain and keep going.

In late 1995, I again encountered my need to continue to grow and be faithful to the standards that I was trying to set for myself. A record-store merchant on 125th Street who I had known for twenty years was being evicted by a black church landlord and a white lessee. The record-store owner came to me and various groups and we supported him because of his long standing in the community and our concern for small black entrepreneurs being forced out of Harlem when they had no place else to trade.

Outside Freddy's Clothing Store people had been picketing, and I visited once to support the picketers and to talk to all sides. On December 8, 1995, according to police, a lone gunman went into the lessee's shop. He shot several people and started a fire that killed seven innocent employees and himself.

Immediately Mayor Giuliani accused the picketers in general, and me in particular—calling me the "outside agitator"—for creating the climate that led to this massacre. At once I dealt with the absurdity of such claims. But after a few days, tapes of some statements made by me calling the lessee a white interloper, and then some more offensive and hateful statements made by others when I was not present, at my Saturday morning rally, were released by a right-wing media watch group to further the mayor's reckless charges.

Though I clearly knew that the mayor was attempting to criminalize protests and damage my political standing, I also realized my responsibility to be vigilant about words that I say, or words that are said under my sponsorship. The Bible says you must refrain from the appearance of evil. And even though I knew my comments were not said in hate, I also knew that if we lose our strongest weapon—a strong moral position—we open ourselves to attack when our words lead to misunderstanding. We must remain ethical and disciplined and keep our eyes on the prize.

I was not guilty of inciting violence, but I was guilty of not upholding the standards in my speech and the use of my organization by those who had misspoken. I guess part of maturity is being able to admit first to yourself when you are wrong, and then to the public at large. But we must not compromise on black business support.

I'll never forget a night I was sitting down and having a leisurely talk with Reverend Jackson, and he told me something that has stayed with me. He said, "Good leaders are famous, energizing types of people, inspirational to all kinds of people. But great leaders are those who can learn to suffer and take pain, and still give out positive auras and inspirational hope while never betraying the pain that they experienced. That's what made Dr. King great, what made Nelson Mandela great." The pain is part of the price you pay if you're going to lead, and if you're not willing to pay that price, you ought not to lead. The more I hear leaders complaining about how they've suffered, what they went through, the more I know they're not prepared to lead. What I've experienced, I now see, is par for the course. What were my opponents supposed to do, not fight back? If I start feeling sorry for myself, well, maybe I shouldn't have been in that fight.

It's like a guy in a boxing match. He fights ten rounds, then in the tenth round, with one minute left in the fight, he knocks his opponent out and everybody runs into the ring and celebrates and the commentator says, "Champ, you did it!" What is the new champ supposed to say, "Yes, but in the third round he was really hitting me hard, it hurt, and then in the fifth he kneed me in the groin and nobody saw—" He won the fight, and that is what you have to go through to win. The guys that complain are the guys that don't win. The victors take the body blows as the price of winning. That's why I was never really bitter, because I somehow knew that was the price I would have to pay, and, as a Christian, I knew that if you could endure the crucifixion, you can celebrate the resurrection. We all want Easter Sunday, but we don't want to suffer through Good Friday. There is no Easter without Good Friday. If you can't take the crown of thorns, you can't be crowned.

I've always said the basis of my personality is my spiritual life. I would never have thought about attempting these things if I had not had that kind of spiritual belief. The most effective leaders of African Americans have traditionally been people with a spiritual basis in life. Rev. Nat Turner, Harriet Tubman, Martin Luther King, Malcolm X, Adam Clayton Powell, Jesse Jackson. You have to be marching to a different drum to be able to do this. If you're marching to the beat of the people you're fighting, then they've already defeated you.

One of the reasons the powers-that-be couldn't deal with me, from Koch to Cuomo to Abrams, is that they didn't understand my rhythm. We were on different wavelengths. They were on AM, I was on FM. So they couldn't jam my signal. Whatever they threw at me, criminal, buffoon, informant, it didn't work because I wasn't there, I had never been there. It didn't bother me. I just kept going. I imagine that many nights they sat around scratching their heads wondering, "What is it with this guy?" But they didn't understand, they couldn't hurt my feelings because that's not where my feelings were. All along I was really just a boy preacher from Bedford-Stuyvesant doing what I felt the Lord was calling me to do. So I couldn't be embarrassed, because I wasn't out there looking for acceptance. The rejection of most of society didn't hurt me, because acceptance wasn't my goal.

I didn't want to be one of the boys in the club. I don't want to be in Pharaoh's army or in Pharaoh's court. And that's the difference. I was only interested in justice, and that's still all I'm interested in. I want the country to work for *everybody*, I want every little kid to have a chance to become whatever he or she can imagine, I want to help get my people out from under the grip of Pharaoh—the blind and arrogant indifference to their lives and hopes by individuals and institutions in the country of their births that has maimed, for no reason, so many for so long.

INDEX